EUROPEAN UNION COMMON
FOREIGN POLICY

Also by Martin Holland

AN INTRODUCTION TO THE EUROPEAN COMMUNITY
  IN THE 1980s
CANDIDATES FOR EUROPE: The British Experience
ELECTORAL BEHAVIOUR IN NEW ZEALAND (*editor*)
THE EUROPEAN COMMUNITY AND SOUTH AFRICA:
  European Political Cooperation under Strain
EUROPEAN COMMUNITY INTEGRATION
EUROPEAN INTEGRATION: From Community to Union
  (2nd edn)
THE FOURTH LABOUR GOVERNMENT: Radical Politics in
  New Zealand (*co-editor*)
THE FOURTH LABOUR GOVERNMENT: Politics and Policy
  in New Zealand (2nd edn) (*co-editor*)
THE FUTURE OF EUROPEAN POLITICAL COOPERATION:
  Essays on Theory and Practice (*editor*)

European Union Common Foreign Policy

From EPC to CFSP Joint Action and South Africa

Martin Holland

Senior Lecturer in Politics
University of Canterbury, New Zealand
and Alexander von Humboldt Fellow
Arnold Bergstraesser Institut, Freiburg, Germany

Foreword by Sir Leon Brittan

Published by
PALGRAVE
Houndmills, Basingstoke, Hampshire RG21 6XS and
175 Fifth Avenue, New York, N. Y. 10010
Companies and representatives throughout the world

PALGRAVE is the new global academic imprint of
St. Martin's Press LLC Scholarly and Reference Division and
Palgrave Publishers Ltd (formerly Macmillan Press Ltd).

ISBN 0–333–61768–1

This book is printed on paper suitable for recycling and
made from fully managed and sustained forest sources.

A catalogue record for this book is available
from the British Library.

Transferred to digital printing 2001

Printed and bound in Great Britain by
Antony Rowe Ltd, Chippenham, Wiltshire

For my parents

Contents

List of Tables and Figures

Tables

Figures

Foreword

The European Union's common foreign and security policy (CFSP) came into being in 1993, following the ratification of the Maastricht Treaty. CFSP is still at a nascent stage, it is largely inter-governmental with joint actions still jointly prepared by all the Member States and the European Commission. However, it is, I believe, a growing field of action for the European Union. This is not just due to the overlap of the political and the economic in international relations, the fact that markets are globalizing and the world is becoming more interdependent but also because in many foreign policy areas all Member States of the European Union do tend to have common views on the major foreign and security issues of our time. There is also the resource element – does it make any sense for the European Union to have twelve independent foreign and security policies with every country in the world?

The policy of our Member States regarding South Africa was already the subject of close coordination as early as 1977. The European Community's policy towards South Africa in those days was focused on the question of how to increase pressure on the apartheid regime to force democratic reform and the respect of human rights while providing enough incentives for this to happen. The simple fact that the majority of EU Member States agreed on the need to impose sanctions implied that close coordination of policy towards South Africa was necessary.

In all modesty it is right to say that the European Union has played an important and positive role in the political process that culminated in May 1994 in the installation of the government of National Unity under the leadership of President Nelson Mandela. But our commitment has not ended. The wave of optimism following the successful political transition cannot hide the fact that South Africa is faced with massive economic challenges. Alongside the consolidation of the new democratic structures, it is necessary to improve quickly the living conditions of many millions of underprivileged South Africans, who suffered great discrimination under apartheid. Healing the wounds of apartheid will in the first place mean creating jobs which are

badly needed and providing decent living conditions for those
that have been deprived. It also means ensuring the supply of
electricity, fresh water, sanitation and health to everyone. The
European Union is by far the largest donor of development
assistance to South Africa and has helped towards providing these
essential services. It will go on doing so. Europe's commitment to
making the new South Africa successful is firm and resolute.
Already, barely months after the new government has taken
office, the European Union has granted the benefit of its
Generalized System of Preferences to the new South African
Government of National Unity and I signed the first Cooperation
Agreement with the new government, on 10 October 1994, setting
out the framework for our future relations. This Agreement
emphasizes the respect of human rights, maximizing our
cooperation efforts in all fields of activity and beginning work
on our long-term relationship, which will include the development of our trading relationship. With this Agreement in place,
which is a political signal of European solidarity with the new
democratic South African Government, the European lending
institutions such as our European Investment Bank can begin
their work. We are also committed to instituting a political
dialogue at the earliest opportunity to cover all political issues of
mutual interest – including regional development and cooperation.

South Africa's reconstruction to some extent resembles the
great challenges faced by the founding fathers of the European
Union. There is a need to build new institutions to restore and
consolidate democracy and human rights and bring together all
segments of the population. The European Union recognizes the
importance to the whole of Africa and the Southern Africa region
of ensuring lasting political, economic and social success in South
Africa. The Union will continue supporting South Africa to
achieve these goals, through trade, development and financial
lending policies. We are politically committed to its success.

But the European Union cannot do everything. South Africa
itself has to modernize, dismantle its seige economy, liberalize its
trade, privatize industry and support enterprise to attract the vital
inward investment it needs.

The work of Dr Martin Holland helps to explore the importance of CFSP in relation to South Africa, a subject that has, to
date been under-researched. This book will be important reading

for students of EU–South African relations, but also for all those people who search for practical examples of the EU's emerging Common Foreign and Security Policy, and its relationship with other areas of Community action.

Sir Leon Brittan, QC
European Commissioner for External Economic Affairs

Acknowledgements

I would like to acknowledge the support provided by the following institutions. First, the University of Canterbury who were generous in their leave provisions enabling me to spend 1993 in Europe conducting research for this manuscript. Second, to the University of the Western Cape whose invitation to teach enabled me to carry out fieldwork in South Africa. Third, and most importantly, my thanks go to the Arnold Bergstraesser Institut who provided an academic environment and infrastructure during my stay in Germany. The research undertaken at the ABI in Freiburg that has lead to this publication was funded through an Alexander von Humboldt Fellowship.

I would also like to extend my thanks to the numerous conference participants who shared their views and insights with me during 1993. In particular, I am grateful to the participants at the European University Institute conference on CFSP (Florence, July 1993); the Wilton Park conference on southern Africa (Steyning, November 1993); and the Centre for European Policy Studies Working Group on CFSP and South Africa (December 1993–January 1994). The success of this research was dependent on the cooperation of many individuals in the Commission bureaucracy and member state diplomatic services. I owe a particular debt to Ove Juul Jorgensen (Commission DGI); Leonardo Schiavo and Steffan Stenberg (Commission DGIA); Erwan Fouere (Commission Head of Delegation to South Africa); Barbara Simons (MEP); and Peter Hansen and Geoffrey Adams of the Danish and British missions to South Africa respectively. I was also privileged in April 1994 to be invited by the Commission to be a member of the European Union Election Observer Unit to South Africa and was able to add a practical perspective to this otherwise academic study.

Working away from the security of a normal institutional environment is of course stimulating, but it can also prove a solitary experience. For that reason am I especially grateful for the academic support and encouragement I have received while writing this manuscript from Heribert Weiland, the Secretary General of the ABI, and from Professor Jack Spence, Director of

Studies at Chatham House. Lastly let me express my thanks to my various and varied "freunde und freundinnen" in Freiburg and farther afield whose good humour, friendship and encouragement have helped to motivate me during this past year. Conducting the research for this book involved extensive travel during 1993–94: to Brussels on numerous occasions, to South Africa, as well as to conferences and working groups in England, Germany, Italy, The Netherlands and Switzerland. Malcolm Bradbury's observation from *Dr. Criminale* about "the new phenomenon: the intellectual as frequent flyer, more airmiles than Dan Quayle" became an increasingly perceptive – and worrying – commentary.

While acknowledging the important contribution made by all of the above and others too numerous to mention, I remain exclusively responsible for both the merits and defects of this examination of Europe's transformed relations with South Africa.

ABI, Freiburg   MARTIN HOLLAND

List of Abbreviations

ACP	African, Caribbean and Pacific states
ANC	African National Congress
ASEAN	Association of South-East Asian Nations
AWEPAA	Association of West European Parliamentarians Against Apartheid
CFSP	Common Foreign and Security Policy
CMA	Common Monetary Area
CODESA	Convention for a Democratic South Africa
COREPER	Committee of Permanent Representatives
COREU	EPC Telex network linking member states and Commission
DGI	Directorate General I (External Economic Relations)
DGIA	Directorate General IA (External Political Relations)
DGVIII	Directorate General VIII (Development)
EC	European Community
ECOMSA	European Community Observer Mission to South Africa
ECSC	European Coal and Steel Community
ECU	European Currency Unit
EDF	European Development Fund
EFTA	European Free Trade Association
EPC	European Political Cooperation
EU	European Union
EUNELSA	European Union Election Unit in South Africa
GATT	General Agreement on Tariffs and Trade
GDP	Gross Domestic Product
GSP	Generalized System of Preferences
HDL	Higher Datum Level
IEC	Independent Electoral Commission
IFP	Inkatha Freedom Party
LDC	Least Developed Countries
MEP	Member of the European Parliament
MFN	Most Favoured Nation

NAFTA	North American Free Trade Association
NATO	North Atlantic Treaty Organization
NGO	Non-Governmental Organization
OECD	Organization for Economic Cooperation and Development
PAC	Pan African Congress
PTA	Preferential Trade Area for Eastern and Southern Africa
POCO	Political Committee (EPC/CFSP)
RSA	Republic of South Africa
SACU	Southern African Customs Union
SADC	Southern African Development Community
SADCC	Southern African Development and Coordination Conference
SADF	South African Defence Force
SEA	Single European Act
SLL	Supplemented Living Level
TEC	Transitional Executive Council
TEU	Treaty on European Union
UN	United Nations
UNHRC	United Nations Human Rights Commission

Introduction

The CFSP will be developed gradually and pragmatically according to the importance of the interests common to all Member States; the European Council asks the Council, as a matter of priority, to define the conditions and procedures for joint action to be undertaken in the following areas: . . . South Africa. (Presidency Conclusions, 29 October 1993, p. 3)

The elevation of the topic of South Africa from what had been formerly the subject of European Political Cooperation (EPC) by the European Community (EC) to a position as one of the first five "joint actions" of the European Union (EU) under the provisions of Maastricht Treaty on European Union, illustrates both the importance of the European-South African relationship and confirms that this case-study constitutes a significant "test" of the Common Foreign and Security Policy (CFSP) procedure. While the case-study is detailed in its analysis of South Africa as a foreign policy issue, more general insights into the transition from EPC to CFSP, their similarities and their differences, are drawn.

Before embarking on the following examination of policy towards South Africa, a distinction between the language of EPC and that of CFSP is required. EPC, which existed from 1970–93, was a Community activity: the collective policies adopted under this framework were enacted by the European Community. In contrast, CFSP is an activity governed by the European Union, a body established by the Treaty on European Union. Consequently, Europe's foreign policy actions after 1 November 1993 are the competence of the Union, those before this date the responsibility of the Community. The introduction of this constitutional and procedural innovation caused international confusion diplomatically, in the media, and more parochially for academics trying to follow specific foreign policy case-studies that straddled the transition date. Thus policy towards South Africa prior to November 1993 is referred to in this book as an EPC activity of the EC; activity after this date as the CFSP (and where appropriate, a joint action) of the European Union. However, even this neat dichotomy is, on occasions, found wanting, as discussion and analysis can cut across the EPC and CFSP periods. Foreign policy towards South Africa did not metamorphose over night, but adapted incrementally. With this linguistic rider in mind, the remainder of this introductory chapter presents a brief overview of the book's argument and summarizes the key themes that are subsequently developed.

It is no longer sustainable to question whether the European Community was, or the new European Union is, capable of exercising foreign policy. In the early years of the Community's developing pattern of external relations, such a criticism was certainly possible and perhaps valid. After the creation in 1970 of European Political Cooperation, the foreign policy of the EC appeared sporadic, conservative and largely symbolic in effect. Since the late 1980s, while the Community demonstrated an increasing willingness to involve itself in international political affairs, its record of foreign policy successes is strikingly modest: the impotence of Community policy when confronted by military aggression was highlighted by the Gulf War and conflict in the former Yugoslavia. It is both ironic and significant that both these international crises took place during the Maastricht interregnum: the Gulf War was set against a background of negotiating the terms of the Treaty (1991), whereas the Yugoslavian civil war straddled both the negotiation and the ratification process of the Treaty on European Union signed at Maastricht (1991–3). Given this paternity, the common prognosis on the viability of the foreign policy initiatives introduced in the new Treaty stressed, understandably, caution bordering on the pessimistic. The promised Common Foreign and Security Policy was for many at best an unhelpful chimera, at worst an unattainable objective that would facilitate Community disharmony rather than promote integration.

Criticism of both the Community's and the Union's unique brand of foreign policy cooperation is not without foundation. Yet, as this study helps to illustrate, it is important not to assign unrealistic expectations and objectives to the process; there are constraints on all international actors, including the dominant global power, the USA. Furthermore, selective amnesia seems to colour our memory of past Community foreign policy successes, perhaps because these are less demonstrative than failure, or are achieved as much by quiet diplomacy as by overt action. The foreign policy case-study examined here presents the best possible example to evaluate the relative success of past Community, and latterly Union, action.

Why is a study of European relations with South and southern Africa appropriate? First, policy towards South Africa is the EC's oldest foreign policy issue; the first EPC declaration was issued on the topic as early as 1976. Second, the policy has employed a wide range of the foreign policy tools available to the Community. Third, it offers a rare opportunity for analysis to focus on policy transition, in this case from punitive sanctions to cooperative measures and development assistance. Fourth, and related, the topic of South African policy provides a comparative context; while it originated under the EPC rubric, it also represents an example of "joint action" under the CFSP provisions. The continuity as well as differences between EPC and CFSP constitutes an important sub-theme running throughout the following chapters. Lastly, the topic's intrinsic importance always made it a potentially divisive issue within the Twelve; consequently, as such it represents a good test of foreign policy success and the *communautaire* spirit of cooperation – both EPC and CFSP. Thus the principal focus of this analysis is on the process of foreign policy building within Europe's institutions, rather than on the South African question *per se*. Existing literature on EPC, with few notable exceptions, can be criticized for having a surfeit of theoretical and descriptive content, but a poverty of illustrative case-studies. This book is an addition to this small but crucial body of literature (see, for example, Holland 1988a, 1993; Ifestos, 1987; Pijpers, 1984; Tomkys, 1987).

Past work on Community-South African relations focused primarily on the difficulties of achieving an EC consensus on sanctions and criticized the weak foreign policy instruments chosen to enact collective policy. It is now possible to look beyond the issue of sanctions and explore the degree to which EPC/CFSP has matured into a more flexible common approach that is able to promote foreign policy initiatives rather than be purely reactive in nature. The emphasis is on policy analysis and positive develop-ments in a regional context rather than the previous negative focus of the implementation of punitive sanctions. As appears inevitable, there is never a right time to write about the "status" of European foreign policy; nor for that matter, a right time to comment on South Africa. Political events in both these spheres move unpredictably and often with a speed that can embarrass the most carefully considered academic analysis. Consequently, this book is primarily concerned with understanding the policy environment (political, institutional and bureaucratic) that shapes Europe's foreign policy actions, rather than with crystal-ball gazing, although the implications of alternative policy positions are explored.

In Chapter 1 some of the theoretical questions relating to the foreign policy making process are considered in order to provide a broad analytical canvass against which to interpret the details of Community and Union policy. However, the appropriate theoretical approach remains a contentious issue. How should we understand this process within the Community? Are the models and assumptions typical of national foreign policy making valid in the supranational context of Europe? Both general and Community specific approaches are examined. For the purposes of this analysis an assumption is made that the Community's foreign policy reflects the multiple actors present in the decision-making process, a feature unique in many respects to the Community. Consequently, the various actors involved in the process have to be understood within their own theoretical context: looking for a single rationale behind EPC or CFSP is appealing, but ultimately flawed. For example, the influences over the Community's post-apartheid policy come from, at least: the various national governments and their own domestic environments; the European Parliament in the form of plenary debates, resolutions and Committee Reports; the presidency of the Council and of the European Council; and, crucially, the Commission. Within the Community's bureaucracy competition over policy domains is prevalent in foreign affairs; South Africa provides a typical example. Initially, two Directorates-General (DGs) were directly involved: DGI (External Relations) and DGVIII (Development), each with its own agenda. The intro-duction in May 1993 of a new Directorate-General (DGIA) specifically for foreign policy did nothing to simplify this situation. As has been noted in studies elsewhere, Community foreign policy is often better understood from an intra-Community perspective than in terms of the external policy situation. Europe's South African policy was influenced by internal bureaucratic issues and the process of integration as well as the desire to find the best policy initiative to replace sanctions and isolation.

From this basic theoretical survey an overview of the past two decades or more of EPC is presented to locate this particular study of foreign policy coordination in context. The implications derived from the Maastricht Treaty for the Union's foreign affairs are examined, and how these might translate specifically for South Africa. The difference between a consensus-based EPC and the "common" foreign policy under the CFSP is more than just of semantic interest. The margin for national interpretation and, occasionally, prevarication is considerably reduced under the new procedures. By the conclusion of the opening chapter the constraints and limitations placed upon European foreign policy, as well as the opportunities and abilities, should be self-evident, and it is with these riders in mind that the remaining chapters address the specific case-study of policy towards South and southern Africa.

Chapter 2 provides an historical introduction by examining the Community's earlier relations with South Africa, in particular the years 1985–1989 and the question of Community sanctions against apartheid. The first half of Chapter 3 continues this historical assessment by detailing the policy reformulations that began in February 1990 with the release of Nelson Mandela and culminated in April 1994 with the first multiparty non-racial democratic election held in South Africa. The second half of the chapter provides a detailed introduction to the implications for policy making and institutional relations of the decision to designate South Africa as a CFSP joint action. Chapter 4 explores the actors and the institutional aspects of the 1990s policy developments, and the political and bureaucratic processes of policy transition within the Community are investigated. In addition to a reassessment of the major actors involved, the roles of the European Community Observer Mission (ECOMSA), the Programme Coordination Office and Commission Delegation (all resident in South Africa) are analyzed, as is the behaviour of the member state embassies. The accusation that there is often a gap between the foreign policy cooperation and cohesion as manifest in Brussels and its practical application in third countries is addressed.

Chapter 5 examines these specific post-1990 policy developments in greater detail. Particular attention is given to the adaptation of the positive measures into a development programme. Again, a comparative context is crucial as the Community-Union approach to South Africa cannot remain *sui generis*, but has to follow the parameters that have been established for all European-developing country agreements. The emerging role of the Union as an international mediator and election monitor is also considered. All these developments are indicative of Europe's desire to behave and be respected as a full and leading international actor, a question that has remained contentious ever since the signing of the Treaty of Rome in 1957.

The next two chapters extend the scope to consider southern Africa as a region and, in that context, the appropriate type of relationship that should develop between the EU and South Africa. The Community is constitutionally bound to encourage comparable regional groupings to emerge and, wherever possible, establish group to group dialogues and agreements rather than create a whole series of bilateral relations between third countries and the EC. Therefore the question of South Africa's membership of the Southern Africa Development Community (SADC) and the implications concerning the EU's relationship to this body are germane. Of similar sensitivity is the related issue of membership of the Lomé agreement for South Africa. What is the appropriate framework for organizing future EU-South African relations: through the existing Lomé framework despite South Africa's comparative economic well-being *vis-à-vis* the ACP states (African, Caribbean and Pacific); or via an independent bilateral agreement with Brussels? These regional questions – South African membership of Lomé and of SADC – further complicate the central issue of establishing a new foreign policy towards southern Africa in the post-apartheid era.

The final chapter places the South African case into a broader perspective by asking what general lessons can be drawn for the conduct of EPC and the new CFSP? Behind the unique peculiarities of the South African case many of the broad themes and common problems associated with collective Community, as well as Union joint action, are apparent. The comparative "success" of the policy in the region at least suggests that the case-study has the potential to be instructive and heuristic. It also raises the important and legitimate issue of whether, and if so to what extent, CFSP is different to EPC. Without being prescriptive, the concluding remarks identify those topics where either a policy vacuum exists, or where the policy decisions of the early 1990s were, at best, short-term expedients that will require more developed policy proposals. Again, a mark of the Community's foreign policy maturity is its ability to influence international affairs rather than merely respond to them, an objective first set out for EPC in the 1980 London Report. Some fifteen years later, this criterion above all others is the greatest challenge to the idea and exercise of a common foreign policy for the European Union.

The book concludes with a postscript concerning the practical implementation of the election observation role of the joint action. The perspective is from that of a practitioner and recommendations are suggested whereby future EU observation roles can be improved.

1 The Foreign Policy Making Process

European foreign policy is not a contemporary innovation; since its creation in the 1950s the Community has exhibited an external role. Indeed, the architect of the Community, Jean Monnet, explicitly included political union and a single foreign policy in his original idea of a federated EC. Yet the question of foreign policy making has often remained shrouded by contention and confusion. As a leading commentator and practitioner has argued, EPC was a "closed" system, not open to normal EC scrutiny because in origin EPC "was a private club, operated by diplomats for diplomats, and some of that same ambiance has persisted to this day" (Nuttall, 1992, p. 11). The legitimacy of EC foreign policy making has not been challenged, but its scope and application have regularly been in dispute. In part, the 1957 Treaty of Rome offers an explanation: at one level its priorities emphasized economic integration and intra-European interests; however, this apparent inward economic exclusivity of the Treaty was a superficial veneer which belied a more comprehensive global role for the nascent Community. Thus the Treaty provided for a clear international political role, albeit largely expressed through economic mechanisms: Article 113 (Common Trade Policy), Article 132 (association with overseas territories), Article 238 (association agreements with third countries), Article 228 (the power to conclude international treaties), and more generally, the legitimacy to receive and establish its own independent diplomatic missions (Wessels, 1992, p. 163). The basis for external relations was explicit and legitimate; consequently the latter developments of European Political Cooperation and a Common Foreign and Security Policy have their foundations, if not their explicit competences, clearly in the founding Treaty.

What, then, is understood by the term Community or Union foreign policy? Normally, what is meant is the procedure known as European Political Cooperation which existed from 1969–1993; after this it was superseded by the Union's Common Foreign and Security Policy. While there are important differences between

1

EPC and CFSP which are discussed below, they share common attributes that help to delineate European foreign policy. Thus European foreign policy is not simply the aggregation of twelve national foreign policies: rather, it is a distinct process that combines certain national foreign policy attributes with features and capabilities unique to the EC/EU. This distinction from nation-state foreign policy making is crucial to understanding Community/Union behaviour. There are limitations placed upon the sphere of action that are not, generally, imposed upon individual nation-states. Once this characteristic is appreciated, the nature of European foreign policy becomes less opaque. Whether discussing the Gulf war, sanctions against Serbia or policy towards South Africa, the trap to be avoided is to expect the EC/EU to behave like a nation-state: it is a foreign policy actor, but one that operates within its own specific constraints.

The relationship between foreign policy and the EC's own internal dynamic is fundamental and, in part, explains the conflicting interpretations of EPC. How the Community's international relations are comprehended is dependent on the wider federal-intergovernmental debate which is at the heart of Europe's overall political, economic and social development. Consequently, foreign policy making can only be understood in the context of the general and pervasive process of European integration. EPC or CFSP is as determined by this process as is the Single Market or Monetary Union. Foreign policy does not stand in splendid isolation; like other policies it is a manifestation of the internal cohesion and development of the Community into a Union. As such, the exercise of collective foreign policy

> is central to the intergovernmental–federal debate on European Union. To the one extreme the creation of a common European foreign policy is equated with a federal Community: to the other, the Community appears tantamount to a purely inter-governmental association while the conduct of external foreign relations remains a national concern. (Holland, 1993, p. 117)

This linkage is of central importance to the case-study of South Africa analyzed in the following chapters.

Given this uniqueness, what, if any, typical international relations theories are useful in establishing the conceptual framework for interpreting Community and Union foreign policy? Indeed, is it even appropriate to impose such nation-state frameworks on a supranational actor? An academic consensus on these questions has been largely absent; too often, theoretical questions have been ignored in EPC analyses, with studies being largely atheoretical or claiming individual uniqueness as a rationale. Where theory does exist, it has been eclectic in its intellectual origins: diversity, however, is not necessarily a strength. To summarize these attempts at theorizing, while approaches from the field of International Relations are predominant both Comparative Politics and Public Policy theories have been adopted with some success. Beginning with the Traditional, or Realist, school of international studies, Pijpers (1991) has forcefully argued that the basic assumptions and concepts involved in this approach are fundamental to any meaningful understanding of EPC. Thus, the pre-eminence of security; the concept of the balance of power; the marginal impact of domestic politics; the role of the state as an international actor; and the anarchical nature of international society are regarded as the dominant criteria that shaped EPC. Although devised in a Cold War context, the collapse of the Soviet empire and the ensuing disequilibrium within the international community during the 1990s, suggests that this supposedly old-fashioned theory deserves reconsideration. Whatever the internal dynamics within the EC and its member states the *realpolitik* of international affairs circumscribes behaviour and it is in this sense that the Realist approach may provide a fundamental over-arching framework for considering Community foreign policy. Although such a macro-approach suffers from an excessive degree of generality, specifically focused middle range or micro-theories that dismiss its underlying perspective do so at their peril. Although not sufficient in themselves, Realist assumptions need to be incorporated in any composite theory dedicated to conceptualizing European foreign policy making.

A second approach offered by George (1991) argues from a similar position. He, too, suggests that it is misconceived to categorize and segmentize different forms of Community activity and then to study these in isolation; above all else, the Community operates on the basis of policy linkages; consequently, an exclusive focus on the political aspects of foreign policy produces a distorted interpretation. What is emphasized is the dependent relationship between foreign policy and the broader actions of the EC/EU as a global economic as well as political actor that is in direct competition with the other rival economic cores, the USA (or

NAFTA) and Japan. This world systems approach is distinct from the Realist's concern with security and belligerency; however, both approaches accept as their essence the inherent conflict and competition (political and economic) in which Europe finds itself located internationally. A practical consequences of this is the rejection of the artificial policy demarcation that has been generated both in Brussels and in academic analyses, for example the so-called exclusive competences of EPC, of Lomé, or of other forms of external relations. Mirroring the call for a broad theoretical framework, a world systems approach necessitates a comprehensive understanding of the interconnected nature of Community activity. Foreign policy does not operate in a vacuum; nor is it insulated from the consequences of decisions taken in other policy domains, both internally and *vis-à-vis* third countries, in particular the USA and Japan. This theoretical position is appealing as it intuitively reflects the practical operation of Community policy making and bargaining. To recall the language of the earlier neofunctionalist writers, the process is one of policy spillover central to the logic of integration theory. South Africa provides a suitable case for examining the relevance of such decisional spillover and the interconnected nature of policy making. As the subsequent chapters demonstrate, there is no simple answer to the definition of boundaries of Europe's policy making towards South Africa, or of the internal and external influences that such a policy is subjected to.

A third general approach has been expounded by Allen and Smith (1991). Their argument is, perhaps, the broadest as it adopts an almost unstructured interpretation of Community foreign policy. They regard the concentration on EPC as too constraining and prefer to view foreign policy in terms of Western Europe's "presence" (defined as economic, military and political authority) in the international system. Thus EPC is not valued for its actual content or procedural developments but for its pervasive, if discrete, impact upon behaviour of Western Europe as an international actor. Consequently, EPC or CFSP are not a sufficient focus for understanding behaviour; they constitute individual elements – albeit important ones – in Europe's more complex involvement in international society. While probably too encompassing in its implications, this approach is useful once again for defining a general framework within which to study EPC/CFSP. Nor is it, necessarily, incompatible with the macro-approaches of either George or Pijpers. However, as a tool for a specific foreign policy case-study its level of generality is unhelpful; as a reminder that foreign policy is more than the sum of EPC/CFSP it is instructive and complementary.

Turning to middle-range theories that are directly applicable to case-study analysis, the dominant approach here is undoubtedly the domestic politics model. There are various hybrids in existence: however, the basic assumption of the approach is common to all. It contends that the individual domestic political contexts of each member state has a determining impact upon Community foreign policy outcomes. This approach has been used with success in European studies, particularly with respect to sanctions and South Africa (Holland, 1987; 1988a), but also in a more general theoretical way by Bulmer. He asked the critical question determining Community foreign policy action: namely, "why a member state sees the EC as the most appropriate level of action on some issues, whilst on other issues, the nation-state or other international organizations are seen as the most appropriate?" (1983, p. 356). The tendency has been for the Community to be seen increasingly as the appropriate, but not exclusive, forum for foreign policy action and coordination. However, this does not in any way make redundant the assumption that different domestic environments impose limitations on common action, which in the past have then been employed as an "alibi for inaction" by recalcitrant states (Wallace, 1983a, p. 100). What can be added to this generally accepted statement is that the expectations developed over a period of collective policy making can also act to institutionalize and encourage common action: the domestic environments remain crucial, but in this case they constitute a positive reinforcing element rather than a negative impediment to common action. Whatever the outcome, the domestic politics perspective remains particularly useful for interpreting the apparent inconsistencies and modest achievements of a number of past attempts to produce a collective and unified policy stance across a range of international events. Within the general framework assumptions outlined above, the domestic politics approach plays a central role in the subsequent examination of the EC's, and latterly EU's, South and southern African policy.

Lastly, the question of implementation of foreign policy actions has been directly applied to the European Community. The analysis of Allen and Byrne (1985) is confined to examining EPC prior to the Single European Act, let alone the creation of CFSP under the Maastricht Treaty. However, despite this historical limitation, a number of general assumptions remain theoretically insightful. First, they expose the false dichotomy posited by traditional studies of foreign policy in which domestic policy is somehow distinguished and isolated from foreign policy. As noted already, the Treaty of Rome demonstrates *par excellence*, this categorization is empirically meaningless; domestic and foreign policy spheres are interdependent and intertwined. Second, the unique identity of the Community and Union sets it aside both from nation states and other international organizations and leads to a level of complexity that exceeds either. Third, and most usefully for this study, they draw attention to the resource aspect of implementation. Successful foreign policy implementation is dependent on adequate financial, staffing and political resources, conditions which are of direct relevance to the CFSP joint action on South Africa (see Chapter 8 for further commentary). Finally, the analysis emphasizes the complexities involved in the implementation of European foreign policy:

> implementation at the European level faces many problems that we also find at the national level – ambiguous goals, imperfect procedures and instruments, bureaucratic resistance and inadequate control mechanisms. In addition to these, however, the context of multilateral decision-making introduces new complications – the interplay between national and European interests, the lack of a clear central authority, doubts about the competence and commitment of partners and working within a relatively inflexible ideological framework. (Ibid., 1985, p. 141)

The chapter now turns to examine these actors who are collectively responsible for additional "complications".

THE ACTORS

With these general theoretical considerations in mind, it should not be surprising to learn that the question of who constitutes Europe's foreign policy actors is not as straightforward as often presumed. As Wessels has remarked, the "simple question of 'who makes decisions' is difficult to answer" (1992, p. 165). Whereas the institutions and personnel involved in national foreign policy making is comparatively coherent and condensed, the Community experience demonstrates the dispersed nature of foreign policy making. The task is further complicated by the fact that "EPC operates by talking incessantly" with over one hundred meetings occurring at all levels per annum (Nuttall, 1992, p. 12). The major actors that can be identified are discussed in an introductory manner in this section: the Council of Ministers; the presidency; the European Council; the Commission (and its internal divisions); the European Parliament; and a range of minor and external third party actors such as the Political Committee, Working Groups, the EPC Secretariat, lobby groups, diplomatic missions and the context of international society.

THE COUNCIL OF MINISTERS

The Council of Foreign Ministers represents the political decision-making centre of foreign policy. It is through this forum that policy options are considered, disagreements addressed (and usually resolved) and foreign policy statements and initiatives issued. The Council does not have exclusive authority in this sphere – the presidency and European Council can usurp its position – however its participation and consensual agreement is a requirement before any international action can be undertaken whatsoever.

There is both a regular schedule as well as provisions for emergency meetings; in addition there is an extensive and continuous structure of diplomatic contacts that facilitate the coordination and consultation process central to foreign policy. Consequently, even in times of international crisis the EC does not usually respond through unconsidered spontaneous reactions; wherever possible policy positions are established in a traditional bureaucratic manner, through planning and advice. Of course, foreign policy is more prone to sporadic and unforeseen crises than most other areas of policy making. However, in general the Community's various decision-making complexities and processes are more notable for their similarities than their differences.

A second similarity that the Council of Foreign Ministers shares with other EC Councils is its volatility in membership. Each Minister sits by virtue of their domestic portfolio and individual authority is derived from their respective national political environments, not the Community. This familiar national–supranational balance has significant consequences: the political balance and personnel of the Council is under constant possibility of change. Member states, not infrequently, replace their Foreign Ministers either by choice or by circumstance. For example, in the first month of the 1993 Danish presidency, Foreign Minister Uffe Ellemann-Jensen was replaced by Niels Helveg Pedersen in Denmark after the resignation of the former Prime Minister Poul Schlueter, and his replacement by Poul Nyrup Rasmussen. Member state electoral cycles further complicate matters; the tendency for voters to use elections to defeat current governments is well-known. In the Community context electoral defeat for an incumbent administration has more than domestic implications as the political balance and informal personal working relationships developed between the twelve Foreign Ministers are disrupted.

These nationally enforced changes can influence the prospects for foreign policy coordination – detrimentally or favourably. Two events in 1993 illustrate this significance: the removal of the French Socialist government of the late Pierre Bérégovoy by the Gaullist Edouard Balludur administration which appointed Alain Juppé to the post of Foreign Minister; and, the removal of senior Italian Ministers on corruption charges and the selection of a new government led by Carol Azeglio Ciampi and Foreign Minister, Beniamino Andreatta. While all of the Twelve are deemed to be equals in Community foreign policy making, clearly the larger member states have an informal authority: changes in government in two of these within one month of each other complicates, to say the least, efficient and effective European foreign policy making. These unique characteristics of foreign policy making should not be ignored; much of the Community's seeming inability to establish effective past foreign policy initiatives stems from this nationally imposed complexity. It is a constraint that individual nation–state international actors are not subject to.

THE PRESIDENCY

Despite concerted attempts to reform the system of six-monthly presidencies, this mechanism for distributing the Community's titular leadership remained unimpaired by the Maastricht Treaty.

Consequently, at present each country holds the presidency for six months once every six years. The only incremental change agreed to at Maastricht was that the alphabetical order would be partially inverted. Thus as the new cycle began in 1993, Denmark (Dänmark) assumed the presidency for the first half of the year and Belgium for the second half; in 1994 the order is Greece (Ellas) and then Germany (Deutchland), and for 1995 France followed by Spain (España). A subsequent decision taken at the European Council meeting of December 1993 established a new half-yearly rotational order which anticipated an enlarged Union. Alphabetical order was jettisoned in favour of the principle that guaranteed that one of the larger member states would always be part of the Union's troika. Thus the expected order beginning on 1 January 1996 will be: Italy, Ireland, The Netherlands, Luxembourg, the UK, Austria, Norway, Germany, Finland, Portugal, France, Sweden, Belgium, Spain, Denmark and Greece.

The role of the presidency has evolved significantly. While constrained by the principle of consensus-building, increasingly individual presidencies can colour foreign policy priorities. However, a presidency that tries to run too far ahead of the Twelve and impose its leadership invariably finds that its authority is undermined by the collective resistance of the member states. Perhaps the most substantial example of this danger was provided in 1991 under the Dutch presidency who issued an explicitly federal working document as the basis for discussions on the Maastricht Treaty. Confronted with substantial opposition, the Dutch presidency was faced with the ignominy of having to withdraw its proposal and reinstitute the more balanced version drafted by the previous Luxembourg presidency. Thus the power to set the EC agenda is limited by finding a consensus around which a proposal can be built. This general rule extends to EC foreign policy priorities as well: no matter how opposed or enthusiastic a presidency may be over a specific foreign policy objective, it cannot exclude or promote that objective without the acquiescence of the member states. Past policy in the case of South Africa illustrates this reality: in 1986 the UK's opposition to the imposition of sanctions against South Africa could not prevent the Twelve insisting on sanctions being introduced under the auspices of the British presidency (Holland, 1988a, *passim*). However, different member states can give different levels of priority to non-crisis topics in foreign policy. In 1993 both the Danish and Belgian presidencies placed South Africa high on their list of priorities, as the subsequent chapters illustrate.

A less glamorous but essential responsibility of the presidency is the efficient organization of business. In foreign affairs this means establishing the Council's schedule and those of the various working groups, and structuring liaisons with the Commission and member state embassies and Commission Delegations in third countries. The presidency involves a management task, and although it assumes leadership in providing position papers and agendas, this is not an exclusive function; other member states who wish to contribute can intervene (Nuttall, 1992, p. 18). However, it remains the case that successful presidencies are often judged more by their administrative competence than for the introduction of any foreign policy initiative.

THE EUROPEAN COUNCIL

The role of the presidency is extended to organizing the business and agenda of the European Council and its leadership is under similar constraints. The constitutional incorporation of the European Council under both the Single European Act and the Treaty on European Union merely formalized what had become normal but informal practice and procedure since its creation in 1975. The *raison d'être* behind the European Council was to provide leadership. In contrast to the role of the Council of Ministers it was not intended to be a forum where policy technicalities were discussed or majority voting took place. Rather it is a body that operates along informal lines to establish a common European perspective at the elite level. It deals in grand principles and ideas, not the specifics of policy implementation; or at least this is the conventional wisdom of outsiders. One analyst with direct experience is more cynical: while Nuttall acknowledges that the European Council is meant to be the political apex of EPC, he suggests that it rarely acts as such and cites the failed attempt to resolve the South African issue at the 1986 Hague summit as evidence. Clearly, a distinction needs to be made between theory and practice and analysis should not be too uncritical of the problems within the European Council system. Yet, there has been a progressive acceptance of its leadership role culminating in its elevation under Maastricht to provide the

Union with "the necessary impetus for its development and shall define the general political guidelines thereof" (Article D, Treaty on European Union, 1993).

As the meeting of the Heads of State and of Government and the President of the Commission, the European Council represents the apex in the decision-making pyramid for foreign affairs; as the Maastricht Treaty states, it defines "the principles of and general guidelines for the common foreign and security policy" (Article J.8). However, its elite stature makes it both an effective and also ineffective forum for determining foreign policy. The European Council can be used to great effect by the presidency to generate the political will to address a foreign policy question and can have a direct repercussion on the momentum at the Council of Ministers level and below. It acts as an important catalyst for policy action. As noted above, in contrast it is poorly suited to examining the detailed complexities of a particular foreign policy issue and rarely, therefore, does it decide upon more than a general policy framework. The nature and duration of the European Council meetings dictate this characteristic. Although primarily designed as occasions where Europe's global role can be examined, business is not confined to foreign affairs but can cover the full range of both internal and external policy. In this the Prime Ministers and the French President are assisted by their respective Foreign Ministers whereas the President of the Commission has the support of a fellow Commissioner. The Maastricht provisions confirmed that the European Council normally meets "at least twice a year". South Africa has been a regular topic at European Council meetings, particularly in the mid-1980s and more recently at the inaugural CFSP meeting in late 1993.

THE COMMISSION

In the early days of political cooperation foreign affairs was regarded as an exclusive political domain; the distinction between economic competences covered by the Treaty of Rome and those intergovernmental political decisions that operated outside it was maintained, despite the fraudulence of the dichotomy and its increasing unworkability. Consequently, the Commission was confined to economic activity and excluded from the discussion of foreign policy. Nuttall has argued that the Commission's natural instinct was not so much as to involve itself in the extra-Treaty activity of EPC, but conversely "to ward off encroachment on its powers within the Community system" (1993, p. 1). Thus, both the Commission and the member states went to great pains to protect (if for conflicting reasons) the boundaries of Community competences from EPC contamination.

The politico-bureaucratic nature of the Commission has always given the EC its unique policy making context. It is the Community's civil service, but also has the exclusive right of policy initiative under the Treaty of Rome, a traditional source of political authority. The nationally appointed Commissioners have formerly all been leading politicians in their own right and, in terms of foreign policy, often continue to act as such. Fitting this institution and these individuals into the EPC structure was the necessary and logical extension of the Community's attempt to increase its global image; however, the practical arrangements took over a decade to mature. Some national governments were suspicious of Commission involvement and sought to protect their political prerogative. However, the logical inevitability of at least Commission partnership in EPC prevailed. By the early 1980s "the Commission began to take on a substantial *de facto* role in EPC, as Member States found themselves increasingly obliged to turn to EC instruments in order to implement EPC policies": this was clearly demonstrated in policy towards South Africa where "the Commission played an indispensable part, whether proposing sanctions or implementing positive measures through the Community budget" (Nuttall, 1993, p. 2).

The Single European Act symbolizes the acceptance of the Commission as an equal and legitimate partner in foreign policy making. It became "fully associated with the proceedings of Political Cooperation" (Article 30.3b); and the SEA also required closer interaction between the Council of Foreign Ministers and the Commission who were now to "meet at least four times a year within the framework of European Political Cooperation" (Article 30.3a). Both these requirements and the general position of the Commission was reinforced in the Treaty on European Union and there was one new development introduced at Maastricht. In deference to national political sensitivities, the Commission's normal Community exclusive right of initiative was not extended to foreign policy; the member states and the Commission now "share" this authority. When the Union meets to discuss CFSP it does so as the Thirteen and no longer as the Twelve, although where decisions are adopted by majority vote the Commission is not included. In a general sense, there has been a normalization of foreign policy since the mid-1980s with the policy making process now more closely reflecting the EU's internal procedures for economic and other sectors covered by Community competences. The external events of 1989 onwards also facilitated this maturity: for example, the international community invited the Commission to coordinate western aid to Central and Eastern Europe; it was instrumental in the unification process in Germany; and, the Commission assumed responsibility for negotiating agreements with former communist states on future relations with the EC. The Commission had become in every sense an equal foreign policy partner: the question was whether it was threatening to become more than equal. If such ambitions were held by Delors, these were shattered by the after-effects of the Danish "No" referendum result. Arguably, one of the causes of this result was the perception that the Commission was attempting to extend its authority in significant ways including in the execution of foreign policy. After May 1992 there was a noticeable moderation and modesty in the Commission's external role – at least until the reversal of the referendum decision in June 1993.

To facilitate an effective contribution to foreign policy the Commission, or at least the President of the Commission, requires a specialized and independent source of information. This was not possible much before the 1980s. Other Directorates-General were only consulted on an *ad hoc* basis where necessary. Over time a specialized EPC unit developed in the Secretariat General which began "to collect and exploit information from various sources, especially the Commission's Delegations, in a first move towards setting up an autonomous input capacity" (Nuttall, 1993, p. 2). After the SEA, a full time Political Director for EPC was appointed in the Secretariat General with a dedicated Directorate which included, for example, the European Correspondent's service, cypher communications, and a planning unit which, collectively, considerably enhanced the Commission's information autonomy. It was only post-Maastricht that the Secretariat General lost responsibility for EPC within the Commission to a newly created Directorate dedicated to the functioning of CFSP (see Chapter 3 for details).

THE EUROPEAN PARLIAMENT

The democratic deficit in the Community's parliamentary structure extends to the consideration of foreign policy. In the original treaties, the European Parliament, or Assembly as it was then known, had few general competences and no involvement in foreign affairs, other than through the mechanism of debate which had no formal relationship to decision-making. This lack of legal capacity did not inhibit the elected Parliament after 1979 from issuing declarations and opinions across a wide range of foreign policy issues, including European relations with South Africa's apartheid regime. The SEA was, in part, a response to this growing parliamentary involvement. Limited but specific powers were bestowed on the Parliament. Significantly, the European Parliament was given the right to ratify new treaties and association agreements concluded with third countries. This implied veto offers the Parliament a potentially important leverage in extending both its formal and informal involvement in foreign policy. The procedural links between the Council and Parliament were also improved: the Parliament was to be "closely associated" with the workings of the Council; the presidency was required to inform the assembly regularly on EPC matters and to "ensure that the views of the European Parliament are duly taken into consideration" (Article 30.4).

At Maastricht, parliamentary hopes for a greater say in foreign policy were largely disappointed: there was no significant direct increase in the formal powers established by the SEA, although in an indirect manner Parliament's position was given a greater potential. Parliament has to be "kept regularly informed" about policy developments; the presidency is required to "consult the European Parliament on the main aspects and basic choices of the common foreign and security policy" and, once again, ensure that Parliament's views "are duly taken into consideration". In addition, the Parliament can question the Council presidency, make recommendations and holds an annual debate "on progress in implementing the common foreign and security policy" (Article J.7). The opportunity to give the Parliament a substantive formal role in creating foreign policy was denied: yet the Parliament's power to provoke, to comment and criticize is not insignificant. Its debates and specific policy reports do contribute, albeit in a legally non-binding manner, to the Community's

general foreign policy development. Further, Parliament forcefully indicated that it took its right to consultation seriously with
respect to CFSP joint action (see Chapter 4).

SUBSIDIARY ACTORS

The minor actors in the foreign policy making process can play
important subsidiary roles. The most important of these in terms
of policy initiation are the Political Committee and the various
Working Groups. The Political Committee has been described as
"the hub of Political Co-operation, preparing Ministers' decisions,
directing the work of the Working Groups . . . and frequently
taking decisions on its own responsibility" (Nuttall, 1992, p. 16).
It is composed of the Political Directors of each of the Twelve
Foreign Ministries and a representative of the Commission and
meets at least monthly: consequently, the working arrangements
are "friendly, almost casual", unlike the more formal atmosphere
of COREPER, the member state ambassadors who compose the
Committee of Permanent Representatives. Because the Political
Committee have "the authority to engage in bargaining and to
strike a deal", they often "play a decisive part in EPC" (ibid.,
p. 16).

The bulk of the detailed EPC work is performed by the various
Working Groups (which are organized either geographically or
by subject). Their main function is "to exchange information, and
on the basis of that shared information to arrive at common
analyses" (ibid., p. 17). Working Groups are responsible for
making recommendations to the Political Committee level; they
cannot take any decisions independently. Working procedures are
again comparatively informal. The presidency compiles an "oral
report" (which does not require consensus but is rarely amended)
on the proceedings of each Working Group, and the chair of each
Group is usually present at the Political Committee level when
their area is the topic for discussion. A third bureaucratic actor
that impacted upon Political Cooperation was the EPC
Secretariat created by the SEA. Its influence, however, was
considerably constrained; it replaced the role of the Group of
Correspondents rather than challenged the authority of either the
Political Committee or Working Groups. The Secretariat's main

functions were to service all EPC meetings; provide draft replies to European Parliament questions relating to foreign policy; and, importantly, to act as EPC's memory. It did not exercise a right of, or the capacity for, policy initiation, disappointing many hopes and expectations at the time of its creation in 1987. This was because of both member state opposition to an independent Community "Foreign Office" and bureaucratic competition from existing institutions for foreign policy influence. The Secretariat was reliant on the good grace of the member states to provide it with information. Consequently a "lack of a consistent and homogeneous source of information has been one of the main obstacles in the way of the Secretariat's undertaking the regular analysis of events which would be the foundation for any role of initiative" (Nuttall, 1992, p. 21). The Secretariat was, therefore, a minor actor in EPC. It remains to be seen whether the enlarged CFSP Secretariat within the Council Secretariat (which was created by Maastricht and replaced the EPC Secretariat) will play a more intrusive role.

More than 140 countries have diplomatic relations with the Community (Wessels, 1992, p. 168); therefore by necessity, the Community Delegations and the member state embassies in third countries are also important actors in the policy implementation process. There is an important distinction to be made between these two groups: the Delegations are staffed and responsible to the Commission, whereas the member state embassies represent the individual national governments as well as act collectively to safeguard European foreign policy interests. Delegations have spread internationally throughout the 1980s and the Commission now has direct representation in 110 countries. The tasks of each Delegation are tailored to local circumstances, but in general they are responsible for the efficient conduct of relations between the EU and a third country; for informing the Commission of relevant political and economic developments; and, maintaining contacts with Ministers, parties, government departments, interests groups and the media. They provide the Commission with an independent source of third country information and evaluation, an increasingly important role given the Commission's expanded foreign policy involvement. Third countries too, see Delegation representation as beneficial, providing direct access to Commission policy making. Consequently, there is a greater demand for Delegations to be established than can currently be met by funds. However, the political decision was taken in 1992 to establish a Commission Delegation in South Africa once free elections had taken place. This Delegation (established in early 1994) assumed the tasks previously performed by the semi-official Programme Coordination Office based in Johannesburg (see Chapter 4 for further details).

In contrast, the individual member state embassies have a dual task; they represent national as well as Union interests. While national bilateral foreign policies obviously still exist and national foreign policy remains in tact, the embassies of the Twelve also act in a coordinated and collective manner in line with CFSP positions. Thus both in Brussels and in third country locations there is shared diplomatic information and, increasingly, common diplomatic activity. The country holding the presidency is responsible for coordinating these ambassadorial links. Again, depending on the nature of the third country, links may be formal and intensive or more loosely structured: however, in all third country locations the member state embassies do coordinate their foreign policies and duties. In those cases where the country holding the presidency is not represented in certain third countries, the responsibilities are transferred to another member state embassy which then act on behalf of the presidency. In South Africa this has historically been of some importance as three states did not have direct diplomatic representation during the 1980s – Denmark, Ireland and Luxembourg.

The SEA and Maastricht confirmed the importance of both Delegations and member state embassies. Article J.6 of the Treaty on European Union provides the new legal basis for what had become informal practice in the 1980s:

> The diplomatic and consular missions of the Member States and the Commission Delegations in third countries and international conferences, and their representations to international organizations, shall co-operate in ensuring that the common positions and common measures adopted by the Council are complied with and implemented.

> They shall set up co-operation by exchanging information, carrying out joint assessments and contributing to the implementation of the provisions referred to in Article 8c of the Treaty establishing the European Community. (Treaty on European Union, 1993)

The roles of both Delegations and embassies are not confined to simply projecting European policy in third countries. They also contribute to the foreign policy making process by providing detailed reports and local interpretations of political and economic events. As such embassies and Delegations are crucial to the background research and advice which shapes and influences the political decisions ultimately taken by Brussels. Their policy contribution is not tangential or minimal; any substantive analysis of Community and Union foreign policy needs to acknowledge the importance of this diplomatic characteristic.

More disparate and peripheral actors that affect foreign policy include third countries themselves, both in their home locations and in Brussels. The lobbying process between third countries and the various Community institutions is in many cases sophisticated and formalized. While imprecise in its effect, third countries clearly see the enterprise as worthwhile: hence the explosion in the number of third countries establishing missions or embassies in the Community capitals, especially Brussels. The South African case again illustrates the emphasis given to this relationship by third countries. Other forms of pressure groups typical of national foreign policy making are also relevant to collective foreign policy. Consequently, the national policy making styles also become part of the explanation of Community foreign policy.

In a general sense, EPC or CFSP has not developed in isolation but reflects, responds and reacts to domestic policy environments, Europe's own policy level of integration, and ultimately to the global international environment. The ability of any international actor to formulate and implement a foreign policy is constrained by a range of external factors. The former Cold War, the balance of power, or the contemporary political vacuum and potential instability of central and eastern Europe, all to varying degrees influence foreign policy possibilities. The Union is not immune to this limitation; in fact it is often more susceptible to it. Commenting on the post-Soviet opportunities that face the Community Duchêne has observed, "[E]verything depends on how the transition to a new system is secured. At this point, the Community issue becomes subsumed, as in fact it always has been, in the fate of the international order around it" (1990, p. 21). Community history bears witness to this view: its very origins were shaped by the priorities of international relations in the 1950s.

Thus, in addition to the existing self-imposed constraints of consensus policy making, the Community's expression and execution of foreign policy operates within the international environment, and is limited by it. Attempting to make sense of these disparate influences is complex, but essential to a comprehensive understanding of EPC and CFSP.

COMMUNITY FOREIGN POLICY: THE FIRST 25 YEARS

As the introduction to this chapter argued, the 1957 Treaty of Rome laid the legal foundations for the Community's external relations. Foreign policy in an explicitly political sense was grafted onto the Community in 1969 at a meeting of the Heads of State and Government in The Hague. The then Six, anticipating enlargement to include the UK, Denmark and Ireland, took the initiative to transform the Community from a purely economic common market into a political and economic international actor. However, it is important to realize that from 1969 through to the SEA of 1986, Community foreign policy operated in tandem with the Treaty of Rome, providing EPC with its extra-Treaty characteristic. The procedure was informal and without legal redress: over the subsequent decades this evolved through practice, shared experiences and some successes, into the formal treaty activity described in the Maastricht Treaty (Holland, 1993, p. 118).

With hindsight, the aspirations and ambitions of the Six meeting in The Hague were premature, perhaps foolishly so. The final declaration that launched European Political Cooperation called for "a united Europe capable of assuming its responsibilities in the world . . . of making a contribution commensurate with its tradition and mission" (The Hague, 1969, p. 11). With expectations set so unrealistically high it was not surprising that the first decade of EPC led more to disillusionment than jubilation. The procedures for coordinating EPC were addressed in the Luxembourg Report of the following year. However, EPC gave the appearance of nothing more than an expectation of behaviour: it was imprecise, fluid, and for its critics, elusive and probably illusory. As a leading EPC commentator has suggested, "it promised everything and nothing. There was no commitment to agree, but simply to 'consult on all important questions of foreign policy' " (Wallace, 1983b, p. 377). Defining the objectives of EPC, the Luxembourg Report concluded these were:

[T]o ensure greater mutual understanding with respect to major issues of international politics, by exchanging information and consulting regularly; to increase their solidarity by working for a harmonization of views, concertation of attitudes and joint action when it appears feasible and desirable. (1970, p. 11)

The practical implementation of these goals was to be realized through a formal schedule for ministerial meetings to discuss foreign policy topics. These meetings were independent and separate from the Community meetings because of their extra-Treaty character. Modest bureaucratic support was supplied in the form of a Political Committee and *ad hoc* working groups. EPC was explicitly an intergovernmental process and as such both the European Parliament and the Commission were marginalized. However, despite these inauspicious and modest beginnings, finally a framework had been created within which foreign policy could be considered, albeit technically outside the legal provisions of the Treaty of Rome. The first steps towards a common foreign policy that had full treaty status had been taken.

Over the next decade three reports were issued to improve collective action and EPC procedure: the Copenhagen Report (1973), the Tindemans Report (1976) and the London Report (1981). The first of these introduced procedural modifications rather than advocated any radical policy departures: EPC was still an intergovernmental exercise and the boundaries between it and normal EC business were to be maintained. At Copenhagen the then Nine agreed to share information about international affairs; to achieve this a Telex network, known by its French acronym COREU, was established between member state Foreign Ministries. Similarly, greater cooperation between member state embassies in third countries was introduced; bureaucratic support for EPC was increased with the creation of Correspondents Groups; and ministerial meetings were intensified. In sum, the Report provided the foundations on which foreign policy coordination could prosper. The contribution was principally procedural in emphasis, but a necessary initial step. The expectations were expressed by the Report's statement that

"Europe is becoming a real force in international relations", and in the stated objectives of Political Cooperation. Thus:

> Governments will consult each other on all important foreign policy questions and will work out priorities, observing the following criteria:
> (i)   the purpose of the consultation is to seek common policies on practical problems;
> (ii) the subjects dealt with must concern European interests whether in Europe itself or elsewhere where the adoption of a common position is necessary or desirable.
> On these questions each state undertakes as a general rule not to take up final positions without prior consultation with its partners within the framework of the political cooperation machinery. (Copenhagen Report, 1973, pp. 17–18)

The next procedural innovation occurred in 1981 with the issuing of the London Report. In the intervening years the EC's foreign policy performance had been disappointing; its response to a series of crises that developed towards the end of the decade – the Soviet invasion of Afghanistan, Iran, Poland – was lethargic and ineffectual. EPC's existing pragmatism had proved inadequate and the objective of the London Report was to remedy this situation so that "the Community should seek increasingly to shape events and not merely to react to them" (1981, p. 14). However, the chosen mechanism for addressing these short-comings was to codify and extend EPC procedures; in doing so it avoided confronting the fundamental reason behind the apparent failure, the extra-Treaty nature of collective foreign policy. EPC remained an intergovernmental exercise distinct from the legal authority of the Treaty of Rome. EPC and EC activities continued to be separate and the persistent but spurious dichotomy between political and economic affairs was maintained. The *communautarization* of EPC – its incorporation within the Treaty – was not advocated. In contrast to this myopia, the procedural reforms reflected much of what had already become informal practice between the Twelve. The important role played by the European Council (which was established in 1973) in conducting foreign policy was recognized; the coordinating role of the presidency enhanced; the Troika arrangement (whereby the current, preceding and succeeding presidencies operate collectively) was extended; and a 48-hour emergency meeting procedure was introduced. The EPC mechanism was fine-tuned, but its content and application remained suspect.

Although never implemented, the 1976 Tindemans Report is important for the light that it sheds on the conservative nature of EPC in these formative years. Tindemans proposed a radical, federal approach to foreign policy. The voluntary gentlemen's agreement approach was to be swept away and replaced by an obligation to comply with and act on common decisions which were underpined by the full force of Community law. Majority voting in foreign policy was to be the norm. This bold plan did not quite match the political realities of the mid-1970s, or even of the 1990s. The innovations of the Maastricht Treaty are less ambitious than those proposed by Tindemans more than fifteen years earlier.

The Single European Act of 1986 was the most significant EPC development prior to its replacement by CFSP in the Maastricht Treaty. Its preamble calls for the Community to be given "the necessary means of action" with the goal of "speaking ever increasingly with one voice and to act with consistency and solidarity". Crucially, EPC activity was brought within a treaty framework and it was integrated with EC business, finally removing the legal though impractical dichotomy that had existed since the 1969 Hague conference. At first glance the provisions of the SEA seem modest; however, their interpretation had a considerable and cumulative effect of member state behaviour and on the ambitions and expectations for a common foreign policy.

Title III of the SEA laid out the new and separate legal foundation for EPC. Although it conferred a treaty basis, this was not identical to that for the Community in general; the decision-making process for foreign policy was to remain consensual, with majority voting confined to certain aspects of the Single Market and other EC economic policy sectors. Other reforms were more innovative. First, the role of the Commission as an equal partner in EPC was acknowledged: the Commission and Council of Foreign Ministers "meet at least four times a year within the framework of European Political Cooperation" and the Commission is "fully associated with the proceedings of Political Cooperation" (Article 30.3a-b). In contrast, as noted previously, Parliament's involvement was limited to being "closely ciated". Second, EPC was given its own Secretariat and the functions and interlocking roles of Political Directors, Correspondents Groups and working groups were codified. Admittedly this was a limited bureaucratic reform, but the concession to an institutional infrastructure shifted EPC away from intergovernmental informality towards a system of regularized and structured policy making. Third, the seeds for extending EPC to cover security questions were sown: EPC was given the task "to coordinate (their) positions more closely on the political and economic aspects of security" (Article 30.6a).

Despite these progressive indications, EPC remained constrained by the principle of consensus. Member states were urged not to block the emergence of consensus positions, but this was to be achieved through voluntary restraint not obligation. The condition advocated by Tindemans of an obligatory foreign policy derived from majority decisions and binding on all member states was rejected in favour of an improved form of intergovernmental agreement. Typically, the optimism of SEA's rhetoric stood in stark contrast to the practical reality of EPC action: member states

> . . . shall endeavour jointly to formulate and implement a European foreign policy;
> . . . shall ensure that common principles and objectives are gradually developed and defined;
> . . . shall endeavour to avoid any action or position which impairs their effectiveness as a cohesive force in international relations;
> . . . shall, as far as possible, refrain from impeding the formation of a consensus and the joint action which this could produce. (Article 30.1–3)

Criticism of EPC, both from those who bemoaned the implied loss of national foreign policy sovereignty and those who were frustrated by the limited nature of the Community's collective action, is common. However, as imperfect as EPC may have been, and despite the obvious and often cited shortcomings, the foreign policy behaviour of member states undoubtedly changed and EPC had developed into a systematized procedure prior to the ratification of the Treaty on European Union in 1993. In summary, the intergovernmental foundations and mechanisms of EPC were clearly defined; the role and function of the presidency representing EPC was established; the bureaucratic structures were operational; the Parliament was conferred with adjunct status; and the Commission became the thirteenth participant in EPC decision-making which continued to be governed by consensus (Holland, 1993, p. 122).

A COMMON FOREIGN POLICY AND MAASTRICHT

With the ratification of the Treaty on European Union EPC was relegated to the annals of history and replaced by the more *communautaire* sounding Common Foreign and Security Policy. Indeed, the Community itself was replaced by the Union when dealing with foreign policy. Titles, however, are often misleading. In theory, the implications for CFSP go far beyond the limited notion of EPC. However, the early expectations of the Intergovernmental Conference (IGC) that began the Maastricht process in December 1990 were soon to prove too ambitious. The debate about the future Union foreign policy replacing EPC did not get beyond the essential characteristics (and hence limitations) of the existing form of policy coordination. A variety of radical innovations were proposed, such as expounding a general set of principles to determine foreign policy action, and the *communautarization* of decision-making by acting according to majority votes. Ultimately, an intergovernmental approach remained in ascendency. The provisions agreed to in the Treaty on European Union are remarkable more for their similarity to, than their differences from, EPC. The chosen name, Common Foreign and Security Policy, suggested Euro-optimism rather than harsh reality. The reforms, although not insignificant in many respects, continued to rely on intergovernmental solutions and voluntary consensus.

The central question of consensus policy making proved difficult to resolve. The final compromise solution allowed for majority voting only under well defined and limited circumstances. It was agreed that the existing consensus rule would remain intact for defining those topics to be included in the Union's CFSP: once this had been unanimously accepted, majority voting could be used for the implementation of specific policy proposals. Thus, Article J.3 of the Treaty stipulates:

1. The Council shall decide, on the basis of general guidelines from the European Council, that a matter should be the subject of joint action.

Whenever the Council decides on the principle of joint action, it shall lay down the specific scope, the Union's general and specific objectives in carrying out such action, if necessary its duration, and the means, procedures and conditions for its implementation.

2. The Council shall, when adopting the joint action and at any stage during its development, define those matters on which decisions are to be taken by a qualified majority.

This concession is potentially important despite the series of qualifications and escape clauses. A more effective use of instruments may be facilitated without imposing a collective decision on a member state without prior unanimous approval. Past relations with South Africa illustrates this point well. While a decision to accept South Africa as a topic for a common policy would be made unanimously, the actual execution of that policy, the implementation of sanctions for example, could be decided by a qualified majority vote (of 54 votes of at least eight member states).

But perhaps the overriding success of the Treaty that compensates for a whole range of more disappointing features is the new notion of a joint, or common action that has binding force once agreed and commits member states to specific positions and courses of action. A joint action has the force of Title V; while no sanctions for non-compliance are provided for, the incorporation of joint action within the legal framework of Maastricht provides it with increased moral and political authority. In that sense CFSP constitutes a significant advance beyond the traditional EPC of the past by intensifying and institutionalizing cooperation.

However, for other aspects of the new procedure the rhetorical ambitions of the Treaty promised more than was delivered. The opening article of section J that deals exclusively with foreign policy states that the purpose of the Treaty is to "define and implement a common foreign and security policy . . . covering all areas of foreign and security policy". The objectives of such a common policy were:

to safeguard the security of the Union and its Member States in all ways;

to preserve peace and strengthen international security, in accordance with the principles of the United Nations Charter as well as the principles of the Helsinki Final Act and the objectives of the Paris Charter;
to promote international cooperation;
to develop and consolidate democracy and the rule of law, and respect for human rights and fundamental freedoms. (Article J.2)

These were to be achieved through the "systematic cooperation" and implementing "joint action in the areas in which the Member States have important interests in common" (Article J.3). Repeating existing EPC protocol, in achieving a common policy member states are requested to "refrain from any action which is contrary to the interests of the Union or likely to impair its effectiveness as a cohesive force in international relations" (Article J.1.4). Again, reminiscent of the SEA's language, the new CFSP provisions called on member states to consult on any topic of general interest "in order to ensure that their combined influence is exerted as effectively as possible by means of concerted and convergent action" (Article J.2.1); required national foreign policies to conform to common positions (Article J.2.2); and instructed states to co-ordinate their actions and to promote common positions in international organizations (Article J.2.3). Other aspects of the CFSP text simply clarified or modestly enhanced the existing SEA codification of EPC. Article J.5 confirms the responsibilities of the presidency and the "fully associated" status of the Commission; Article J.6 reformulates the content of the equivalent SEA articles calling for closer diplomatic cooperation and consultation between member state embassies and EC Delegations in third countries and international organizations; Article J.8 modified that existing 48 hour emergency procedure; and, Article J.7 preserves Parliament's right to be "kept regularly informed" and consulted with its views "duly taken into consideration".

The enlarged status of the Commission as the thirteenth partner in the Union's CFSP may well prove to be the most significant reform. The implications go far beyond the seemingly bland words of Article J.5 or the shared right of initiative under Article J.8.3. In October 1993 the Commission issued internal guidelines on how it viewed its participation in this new procedure which came into force on 1 November 1993. The Commission saw its involvement as an extension of its authority, but also appreciated the need to simplify the complexity of the Union's foreign policy making. As the following chapters illustrate, the South African case as one of the first "joint actions" under the CFSP provisions underlined the potential contradictions and lack of coherence between the various actors in the policy making process. In response to this issue the Commission drafted "an internal code of conduct to guarantee the effectiveness and coherence of its contribution to the foreign and security policy of the Union in particular by rationalizing its decision-making process" (Secretariat General, 1993, p. 4). Because CFSP had created new and unique institutional processes, the Commission was in the exclusive position of being able to ensure the consistency between what were "Community" structures, and what had now become after Maastricht "Union" concerns. As the Commission document confirmed:

> it is important to make the best possible use in the new structure of the combined effects of the instruments provided by the second pillar and the economic, commercial and development instruments already available to the European Community. The Commission, for its part, will seek to ensure that these two functions are complementary and that its contribution lends added value. (Secretariat General, 1993, p. 4)

The Maastricht CFSP articles were the result of intergovernmental bargaining and compromise. In places the text is intentionally, if frustratingly vague; existing practice is complicated unnecessarily; or, occasionally, it is silent on key issues. While the expectations for a fully *communautarized* foreign policy were disappointed, foreign policy coordination was advanced procedurally. Foreign policy remained primarily intergovernmental, but it was an improved intergovernmentalism that facilitated the possibility of more effective coordination and collective action. On balance, the progress made since the launching of EPC some quarter of a century previously has been considerable despite not yet matching the requirements of a fully integrated common foreign policy. As the final section of the chapter concludes the limitations imposed upon Community foreign policy remain considerable.

THE DILEMMAS AND LIMITATIONS OF A COMMON FOREIGN POLICY

Before examining the intricacies of relations with South Africa the limitations imposed upon Europe's foreign policy action need to be exposed. Indeed, the greatest limitation is that of expectations. Community and Union action is constrained formally, as outlined above, or informally through what is politically possible. Criticisms of foreign policy too often seem to set expectations of action at an unrealistic level, showing a disregard or misunderstanding of Europe's capacity. When examining the history of EPC–CFSP the most important question that has to be asked is what could the EC realistically be expected to have done? This is not in any way meant to denigrate the achievements of past policy, simply to remove the unrealistic facade imposed upon foreign policy by its critics.

First, the most obvious limitation appears to be that of consensus decision-making. Designing a policy that can accommodate what are often disparate views and conflicting national interests within the Twelve is not without its costs. Compromise positions can often appear similar to ineffectual lowest common denominator concessions. Of course, there are examples that can easily be found over the past 25 years that suggest this phenomenon is prevalent; yet progressively, EPC positions became clear, appropriate and in line with the positions adopted by other major actors in the international community. Furthermore, it remains to be proven that so-called compromise policy positions are less desirable than radical options. Perhaps finding the consensus is a more appropriate and 'better' foreign policy as it can produce policy consistency and stability over time. Extreme policy positions are always more vulnerable to policy reversals and challenges. The centre ground for CFSP could well prove the wisest choice. In this sense consensus-based foreign policy while a constraint, is possibly advantageous in the longer term and any move towards majority decisions potentially destabilizing.

A second often argued inhibition is the limited range of policy instruments available for exercising Community and Union foreign policy. Possessing a capacity to act is a prerequisite for an effective foreign policy. The tools available to the Community are quite varied, but do not typically reflect the full range of instruments associated with nation states, in particular the resort to military conflict. Aside from this important exception, however, EPC had, and CFSP has redress to significant mechanisms to secure foreign policy goals. Instruments employed by the Community include, amongst others, demarchés (collective diplomatic statements made on behalf of the Twelve); positive and/or humanitarian aid; association or preferential trade agreements; and the severance of diplomatic relations. The most public instrument, however, is the imposition of sanctions. Under the Treaty of Rome the EC has the legal authority to implement selective or complete economic sanctions against a third country. For example, Article 113 (common commercial policy) was used to invoke sanctions against Iran and the USSR in the early 1980s; Article 224 was employed as the legal basis for adopting sanctions against Argentina over the Falklands War; and in 1980 Article 223 was used to impose an arms embargo against Iran (Holland, 1991, p. 184). With sufficient political will, legal sanctions can be imposed as effectively as any other international actor. Indeed, given the Community's position as the world's largest trader, arguably it has even greater power to make its sanctions effective if it so wishes.

The difficulty for Europe is less in agreeing to sanctions (although this can be problematic) or in selecting a Treaty basis; rather it is the effectiveness of those sanctions in achieving their stated foreign policy goals that is questionable. First, the type of Community decision invoked is influential. Sanctions that are imposed by an EC regulation are the most comprehensive and foolproof as they require a uniform application of the decision across the member states. Typically, however, sanctions adopted by the Community have been in the form of directives which can facilitate varying national interpretations in their application. As the Treaty of Rome explains, regulations are directly binding in every respect as well as being directly effective, whereas directives are only binding in the ends to be achieved and not in the means. Past sanctions against South Africa are a classic example of this tendency (see Chapter 2). Second, the application of the selected sanctions and the comprehensiveness in scope are also crucial. Again, the Community has often balanced its imposition of sanctions with a transition period of weeks or months, thereby facilitating a rush of exports of targeted goods prior to the sanctions deadline. Further, it was more common for the Community to adopt symbolic sanctions rather than impose a comprehensive embargo against a target state. The effectiveness of such symbolic action remains debatable.

Given these reservations, what is the rationale behind their adoption by the Community? There can be varied explanations: typically, however, they were the result of EPC consensus and compromise. Sanctions can draw together divergent Community opinion and in that sense they have an important integrative function. Learning to act collectively in foreign policy has repercussions for other forms of policy making. Of almost equal importance was Europe's desire to be seen to be acting concretely. Quiet diplomacy may be more constructive, but faced with a sceptical European population in the past the Community often found itself needing to demonstrate that it had a foreign policy, that it could act substantively and that its rhetoric was matched by practice.

A third limitation on the execution of foreign policy relates to constitutional provisions in selected member states. This consideration is of particular concern to the development of CFSP. Ireland's constitutional neutrality has caused problems in the ratification of both the SEA and Maastricht, whereas the geographical limitation imposed on the deployment of German troops remains an unresolved quandary for future Union foreign policy outside the NATO zone. New member states may also complicate EU action. Sweden operated a policy of neutrality during the Cold War and Austria has explicit constitutional provisions protecting its neutrality. Obviously, the meaning and implications of neutrality in the post-Soviet European theatre require revision. Nonetheless, these and possibly other constitutional issues pose a potential limitation on the exercise of EU foreign policy.

A less tangible fourth restriction is the reactive nature of foreign policy. As noted already, early EPC declarations called for Community policy that was proactive and would contribute to shaping international affairs, rather than just react to crises on an *ad hoc* basis. It has only been comparatively recently that this expectation has begun to look like something more than wishful thinking. Despite the series of failed initiatives during the ex-Yugoslavian conflict, Europe strove to implement peace-plans and marshall the warring factions towards a solution. The attempt was essentially proactive. Lastly, returning to some of the themes considered in the theoretical preface to this chapter, the international environment is itself a limitation on European foreign policy. This however, is not a unique restriction, but common to all international actors. The EU can only move as fast as international opinion allows, or act in a manner that meets with the approval of other significant actors.

To balance this litany of restrictions, a number of factors underline both the significance and the importance of EU foreign policy. First, the success and longevity of CFSP is central to global stability and security. With the certainty of the Cold War gone, a collective European response is needed to occupy the security void that has been created by the breakup of the Soviet empire. Second, the progress towards European integration cannot be separated into political and economic components. The process is interrelated and mutually dependent. A failure to secure a CFSP will cause disequilibrium within the integration process and have detrimental effects on other areas of European cooperation. Thus for an intra-Union rationale, foreign policy cohesion is essential. Third, the CFSP should not be seen as a *fait accompli* prohibiting the legitimate exercise of national bilateral foreign relations. The common policy is not a single policy. The Treaty provides sufficient clauses whereby member states can opt out of a common approach where justification exists. Consequently, CFSP and sovereignty need not be mutually exclusive. Indeed, the opposite can forcefully be argued. Rather than ceding foreign policy sovereignty by engaging in CFSP, the counter proposition is that national sovereignty is actually enhanced, indeed maintained, though this process of cooperation among the Twelve. Sovereignty, if it has any meaning at all in the contemporary world, implies that ability to control one's own destiny. Individual European states, be they France, Germany or Luxembourg, do not possess that capacity in any real sense. Only collectively through the European Union can those individual sovereignties be exercised. Consequently, the CFSP is not the antithesis of national sovereignty, but rather its saviour and compatriot.

This chapter has provided a theoretical, historical and policy context for the remainder of the book. The question of Community relations with South and southern Africa involves all of the issues, opportunities and constraints identified so far. It also suggests a number that are unique to the case-study. Above all, however, it illustrates the fusion of Europe's economic and political character in the expression of foreign policy, be that in the emerging post-apartheid policy, or in the past policy of sanctions. It is on a summary of pre-1990 EC policy that the next chapter now focuses.

2 Diplomacy, Codes and Sanctions: 1977–1989

In the 1970s the EC was faced with the challenging and perhaps perplexing task of designing the scope and content of its foreign policy. Confronted with a *tabula rasa*, understandably, this process was initially reactive: where possible, political cooperation provided a collective response to international events as each situation demanded. This intrinsically *ad hoc* procedure was admittedly unsatisfactory, but it reflected the insecure nature of EPC in its formative days. Consequently, the EC did not approach the question of South or southern Africa with a clearly delineated set of policy objectives. No such policy existed in practice or in abeyance awaiting implementation. Rather, the policy was reactive in origin and borne out of an international incident, the Soweto uprisings of 1976 and the repressive South African Government response. In this sense, policy in southern Africa has followed the traditional path of incrementalism typical of the majority of early Community foreign policy actions.

In contrast, the European Community's earliest formal relations with Africa were not within the political framework of EPC, but were specifically trade related. In 1963 the first of two Yaoundé agreements were signed. This provided 18 former Belgian and French territories with preferential trade relations with the then Six. At that time the countries of southern Africa remained peripheral to Community interests: Angola and Mozambique were regarded as autonomous Portuguese foreign policy issues, Rhodesia (Zimbabwe) exclusively a British concern and despite shared historical and cultural links, for reasons of trade and investment South Africa was considered part of the British rather than the Dutch foreign policy sphere. As a result, for the period up until the early 1970s southern Africa was an area where the EC "tacitly agreed to follow national priorities rather than develop a common European strategy" (van Prag, 1982, p. 134).

With the first enlargement of the EC in 1973 and the setting up of the Lomé Convention to embrace British post-colonial and

33

Commonwealth global responsibilities there slowly emerged a recognition that bilateral approaches to southern Africa were no longer sufficient. However, these were rudimentary days in political cooperation and the new Community was still wary of committing itself to more than cautious statements. The EC's muted responses to both Angolan and Mozambique independence were typical of this initial hesitation. However, as an emerging international actor the Community could not avoid reacting to the developments in South Africa. The first EPC statement on South Africa was issued in 1976 in which the then Belgian presidency called for the "condemnation of the policy of apartheid in South Africa" (Foreign Ministers, 1976). This statement, while of historical importance in the development of EPC did not end the preferences for bilateral positions on South Africa; a collective Community perspective took longer to gestate.

THE POLITICAL OBJECTIVE: THE ABOLITION OF APARTHEID

The enduring nature of the South African question has made this the Community's oldest foreign policy issue. From 1977 onwards, the EC operated dual collective foreign policy objectives: the instigation of democratic reform leading to the abolition of apartheid in South Africa; and support for the economic independence of the Southern African Development Coordination Conference (SADCC) states (the then so-called "frontline states") from South Africa. While both policies were enacted in tandem within the framework of EPC, understandably, the priority was initially on how to secure the abolition of apartheid, with regional development a taking second place (see Holland, 1987, 1988a). Only with the eventual removal of apartheid legislation, enfranchisement and the transition to democratic rule in 1994 was this first objective realized. This chapter examines the policies adopted between 1977–89 to achieve this political objective.

In contrast with the low profile consensual procedure that characterized the EC's economic regional objective, the political objective of ending disenfranchisement and racial discrimination in South Africa was acted out publicly and often acrimoniously. While the Community agreed on both the need for, and the appropriate form of, regional assistance, how to address the political objective exposed the potential flaws and limitations of EPC. The consensus on the goal of abolishing apartheid did not extend to how that was to be achieved and this has remained a divisive factor throughout the history of relations with South Africa. It should come as no surprise, then, to learn that rhetoric generally outshone action until at least the mid–1980s. For example, in 1985 the year prior to the adoption of the first Community sanctions, an EPC declaration was issued declaring the objective of the Community's South African foreign policy was "the complete abolition of apartheid as a whole and not just of certain components of the system. There can be no such thing as a good and a bad apartheid" (Foreign Ministers, 1985a). Good intentions aside, the capacity and appropriateness of the selected mechanisms chosen to realize this objective was a matter of considerable dispute. EPC continuity disguised these internal Community political tensions. To understand the dynamics of this process, it is helpful to distinguish between three distinct policy periods in the evolution of EPC and apartheid: that of policy consensus (1974–84); conflict (1985–86); and of policy compromise (1987–1989)(Holland, 1993, p. 132). The characteristics of each of these is summarized below.

Policy Consensus

As already noted, Community policy towards southern Africa in general was absent until the accession of the UK in 1973. In fact no Working Group existed on Africa as late as 1974; it was not defined as an EPC area. However, by 1977 "African affairs were taking up a large part of the time of Political Directors and Ministers" (Nuttall, 1992, p. 127). Nonetheless, the comparatively immature structure of EPC meant that action *vis-à-vis* South Africa which went beyond declarations was initially difficult to agree upon. As Nuttall has observed, "for the first time the Nine found themselves facing the problem of sanctions, and in disarray" (ibid., p. 132). Throughout 1976 policy development proved impossible. Consequently, "[F]aced with this difficult problem, the Nine decided not to discuss it. It has always been both a strength and a weakness of Political Co-operation that its agenda can be infinitely adjusted to avoid controversial topics" (ibid., p. 132). This inertia was broken in

June 1977 when the Africa Working Group finally issued a report, although even at this stage differences remained. The issue was resolved at the 12 July 1977 Council meeting with the adoption of the Code of Conduct and an instruction to the Working Group to examine possible additional measures.

In keeping with EPC's early incrementalism, this initial position adopted towards South Africa was largely framed by British influence and the UK's existing bilateral approach. As Barber has convincingly established, Britain's approach was cautious and hesitant with an absence of "clear-cut policies based on stands of principle" (1983, p. 96): this encouraged the development of a Community policy characterized by neglect rather than involvement. Yet within this general *laissez faire* approach there existed a paradox. Since 1974 the British had operated a policy of intervention into the domestic employment practices of UK firms with subsidiaries operating in South Africa (known as the Code of Practice). The Community inherited this policy contradiction almost without revision, and the 1977 EC Code of Conduct resembled the original British initiative in both spirit and substance. The Community could boast a defined and focused policy, although this did not dissuade its critics that the Code was a placebo to deflect criticism from the continued economic relations with Pretoria. It is difficult to deny that, at least in part, the EC policy was designed to anticipate and forestall anticipated international and European protests over links with South Africa in the wake of the Soweto riots (Holland, 1988a, p. 32; Barber, 1983, p. 94). As the Code noted, "it is in interests of companies themselves that they should maintain the best employment practices in South Africa and be seen to do so". Political and moral arguments were in harmony with economic self-interest.

The Code of Conduct was the totality of the collective policy towards South Africa until 1984, after which time it became just one element in a more comprehensive approach. However, not only was it the original EPC policy, it also persisted into the transitional post-apartheid phase of policy making, albeit it in a revised form. The Code was also developed exclusively within the EPC framework; the Commission and the Parliament were not involved, a decision that provoked considerable complaint. This EPC facade concealed fundamental divisions within the Community during the 1970s that "prevented more than routine condemnation of the apartheid system" (van Prag, 1982, p. 145). There were concerted pressures for more strident action, particularly from the leading anti-apartheid trio of Denmark, Ireland and The Netherlands, who lobbied for a mandatory Code. The EC's version was voluntary in application, yet the Code's modest requirements had already stretched the limits of political cooperation. Certainly, within the context of 1977, the Code was a unique and revolutionary step for the fledgling nature and capacity of EPC. It was the first time the Community had taken joint action beyond its immediate environment of Europe and the Mediterranean (Nuttall, 1992, p. 135). In that sense alone, the agreement to adopt a Community policy towards South Africa was an EPC success; the policy was indicative, even if hesitantly so, of the possibility of consensual collective action. A collective foreign policy had been introduced and an instrument to give it effect created.

The Community's Code of Conduct for EC firms operating in South Africa established guidelines for employment practices designed to counter discrimination within the apartheid labour system. The Code's provisions were uniformly applicable, within the voluntary constraint alluded to already, to all EC firms. From 1977 until 1984, the Code covered six specific employment practices: the forum for black representation; migrant labour; rates of pay; wage structures and promotion; fringe benefits; and desegregation in the workplace (Holland, 1989, *passim*). EC firms were encouraged to recognize and negotiate through the emerging system of black trade unions and to work simultaneously to phase out the use of migrant labour. Minimum wage levels that were at least 50 per cent above "the minimum level needed to satisfy the basic needs of an employee and his family" were advocated, and the principles of equal pay for equal work, job advancement and fringe benefits for black employees were promoted (Department of Trade, 1977). The Code did not impose any legal obligations; EC firms were only requested to report annually on the progress made in applying these provisions. The reports were then submitted to the respective national governments who were responsible for compiling summary national reports: subsequently, the presidency of the EC Council was to issue a composite annual EC report. The Code remained an exclusive EPC domain, and excluded Commission participation.

As the Community's first and only foreign policy instrument during this period, the Code was an opaque, peripheral and blunt tool for attaining the stated objective of removing apartheid *in toto*. More critical assessments reject the Code as an instrument for change and regarded it as having deflected attention from the case for total economic isolation and the imposition of effective sanctions. The Code's impact was, it was argued, marginal and its rationale a spurious justification for continued involvement and profit by European companies. Were such criticisms valid? The 1986 Sixth Summary Report which covered the last year under which the original provisions of the Code were examined, provided the following conclusions. The report was based on the responses of 234 European firms (predominantly British (135) and German (58) and covered a total of 121,155 black workers. It was acknowledged that the Code was far from universally applied, but still suggested that "generally good progress was made in line with the Code's aims" (Presidency, 1986, p. 8). Black unions were in existence in a majority of EC firms and legal agreements or informal dealings with unions often existed in parallel with other consultative structures such as liaison committees. The use of migrant labour remained widespread, particularly in British companies which alone employed 11,000 migrant workers. The minimum levels of pay recommended by the Code were not uniformly met: for example twenty four German companies could not achieve this requirement (involving 4,729 workers); for British companies the record was better with 92.8 per cent of firms paying at the suggested Higher Datum Level (HDL), but this still left 7,752 black workers below this independently calculated living standard. Interestingly, the EC report rationalized this performance in terms of the South African recession: companies in breach of the agreement argued that payment of wages at the Community's HDL rate was not commercially viable (*passim*). The bulk of EC firms accepted the principle of equal pay for equal work; the application of this principle in practice was less comprehensive. Rather than setting a universal rate for a particular job, factors such as gender, marital status and family size effected remuneration so that the same work resulted in differential rates of pay, a practice that would not be condoned in Europe. Advancement into middle management positions remained modest. Desegregation in the workplace was achieved in all Belgian, Danish, Dutch and French firms; eleven German and eighteen British companies failed to meet this basic requirement.

The Code was never intended to constitute the totality of Community policy; but progress during the early years proved impossible despite the view that the Code was "seen by some Member States as only the first step towards a much firmer policy, culminating in the imposition of sanctions" (Nuttall, 1992, p. 152). The record of the Code from 1977 to 1984 was conflicting: at one level it was a common uniform measure; and yet as the evidence demonstrates, there were serious discrepancies in application between member states resulting in a superficial uniformity. More problematic was the expectation that the Code was both an appropriate and effective execution of EPC. Yet the Code, together with the occasional diplomatic démarche represented the sum of EPC activity and reflected the political reality of the period. A more intrusive or detailed level of cooperation originating from Brussels was not possible prior to 1985, despite some member states advocating more rigorous and comprehensive EPC initiatives in South Africa. It was only the domestic political turmoil that exploded in South Africa in 1985 that led the Community to reconsider the Code and contemplate additional foreign policy actions. The period of benign consensus had come to an end and for the next two years the Community underwent a difficult and disruptive period of foreign policy revision.

Policy Conflict

The political necessity to be seen to be doing something in response to the mounting international anti-apartheid pressure provoked the Community into reforming and extending its South African foreign policy. However, this first attempt at foreign policy revision exposed the fragile nature of the collective consensus on South Africa. In March and April 1985 EPC statements were issued condemning the internal excesses of the South African military forces: in May Denmark took bilateral action outside EPC and prohibited all new Danish investment in South Africa. In response to the State of Emergency introduced on 22 July of that year the Community began to reconsider its existing foreign policy options and pressure within Europe mounted for something more explicitly instrumental and effective than the Code of Conduct. This first attempt at policy reformulation fractured, albeit temporarily, the facade of collective action; the French Government introduced additional unilateral action (the suspension of diplomatic ties and the cessation of new investments in the Republic). The potential disintegration of EPC was thwarted by the decision collectively to recall all member state ambassadors from Pretoria at the end of July with the purpose of advising the Political Committee responsible for South Africa on "measures to take to contribute to the abolition of apartheid" (Foreign Ministers, 1985b). One result was the decision to send an EC Troika and Commissioner to South Africa to gain direct knowledge and to present new policy recommendations to the Council of Foreign Ministers meeting of 10 September. At this meeting the Community reiterated its political foreign policy objectives calling for:

> the lifting of the State of Emergency, the immediate and unconditional release of Nelson Mandela and the other political prisoners, an end to detention without trial and forced relocation, a firm commitment by the South African Government to end apartheid and to dismantle discriminatory legislation, particularly the pass laws and Group Areas Act, and lastly real negotiations with the true representatives of the South African people, including those currently in prison. (Foreign Ministers, 1985b)

Therefore, almost exactly one year after the catalogue of escalating civil unrest in South Africa began, the EC recognized the necessity of increased pressure. The 10 September statement reflected the urgency of developing *ad hoc* policies into a more cohesive Community foreign policy (Holland, 1988a, pp. 35–6). The moderate content of the package was largely influenced by Genscher, the German Foreign Minister, who was able to placate the more radical demands of France. While intrinsically important for the development of EPC, many of the "new" measures were already in existence bilaterally; the innovation was that these were now to be harmonized and implemented through the Community. There were two types of collective actions adopted: positive and restrictive measures. The restrictive measures were:

- A rigorously controlled embargo on exports of arms and para-military equipment to the RSA.
- A rigorously controlled embargo on imports of arms and para-military equipment from the RSA.
- Refusal to cooperate in the military sphere.
- Recall of military attachés from the RSA.
- Discouraging cultural and scientific agreements except where these contribute towards the ending of apartheid or have no possible role in supporting it; and freezing of official contacts and international agreements in the sporting and security spheres.
- Cessation of oil exports to the RSA.
- Cessation of exports of sensitive equipment destined for the police and armed forces of the RSA.
- Prohibition of all new collaboration in the nuclear sector.
(Foreign Ministers, 1985b)

The so-called positive measures were more inventive and "reputed to have had a definite political effect on South Africa" (Nuttall, 1992, p. 234). The most important initiative was the creation of an assistance programme for "non-violent anti-apartheid organizations, particularly the churches" (Foreign Ministers, 1985b). Although modest in its original form, it is this emphasis on positive assistance that has increasingly come to characterize contemporary European policy. Other positive measures included educational assistance for the non-white community, and a programme to increase contacts with all sectors of the disenfranchised population coupled with a "programme to increase awareness among the citizens of Member States resident in RSA" (ibid.). Additional non-specific assistance was promised for the frontline SADCC states.

This compromise package of positive and restrictive measures engineered by Genscher almost collapsed at the last minute. The British Government felt unable to commit itself fully at this stage and included a "reservation" in the 10 September text. This stated: "the United Kingdom is able to support the general statement and the positive measures but wishes to give further consideration to the other measures proposed and believes it premature to come to a decision today on these matters" (quoted in Nuttall, 1992, p. 232). It was another two weeks before, "in the spirit of Community solidarity" that the UK lifted its reservation.

The reasons were explicitly intergovernmental. The Commission had proposed that the measures be enacted within the Community framework. This was opposed by the UK, Germany and Denmark and it was accepted that all the measures would be enacted on an "exclusively national basis" within EPC. The Commission was effectively excluded from the process, its role being confined to monitoring national implementation which, "in the absence of a uniform interpretation of what had been decided . . . proved difficult in practice" (Nuttall, 1992, p. 233).

The final aspect of the positive measures package introduced a reform of the Code of Conduct, or more precisely "adaptation, reinforcement and publicity" in the words of the EPC statement. The new Code was announced on 19 November 1985. For the first time an explicit political objective was stated, if a modest one; the Code was no longer the unique mechanism for achieving EPC goals, but now its task was "to make a contribution towards abolishing apartheid", reflecting the earlier criticism of its limited impact and peripheral relevance. There was a clear commitment in the revised Code for EC firms to encourage, assist and work with black trade unions, so that collective bargaining could be "in accordance with internationally accepted labour standards" (Department of Trade and Industry, 1986). Firms were also asked to increase training and advancement prospects for black workers and to "reduce the dependence of their companies on immigrant white labour" (ibid.). A wider range of social benefits were advocated such as medical, pension and insurance schemes for employees and their families, and in general EC firms were encouraged to "improve the quality of life of the black communities from which they draw their staff" (ibid.). In perhaps the most radical innovation, EC firms were asked to "encourage the setting up and expansion of Black businesses by sub-contracting, providing assistance for their Black employees to set up their own companies and preferential priority treatment in customer-supplier relations" (ibid.). There were procedural as well as substantive changes. A more detailed common reporting format was introduced; monitoring procedures were extended to allow each national parliament the opportunity to participate; the annual presidency summary was to be debated by the European Parliament and the Economic and Social Committee; all reports (national and Community) were to be made public; and finally, consultation between the diplomatic missions of the member states in South Africa was to be intensified and a separate annual report complied by these ambassadors.

One change in the Code that largely went unnoticed politically was in the method used to calculate the minimum acceptable remuneration levels. The revised Code *lowered* rather than increased these levels at the behest of the UK Government. Despite many of the useful improvements in the Code, it remained an oblique and increasingly irrelevant EPC tool. Less and less employees were covered as EC firms divested their interests. The growth of black trade unionism made this form of enlightened and benevolent paternalism especially archaic. Nonetheless, the Code retained its role, albeit a reduced one, as part of the EPC approach to the question of apartheid. Despite these and numerous other criticisms (Holland, 1989, *passim*) the Code entered into its second decade of existence.

The September statement also left open the question of further action, including sanctions, and only obliged the EC to monitor the situation regularly. This commitment did not result in any new policy initiatives despite a worsening domestic situation in the Republic. In June 1986 a second State of Emergency was introduced and stringent curbs placed on the media. With none of the policy objectives in any way met (indeed, the 1985 measures were only enforced as of 1 February 1986), the June 1986 meeting of the European Council exposed the acrimonious feelings and fragile consensus that existed between the Twelve, and "hammering out an EC response proved as tortuous as ever" (Lodge, 1986, p. 194). The Hague statement issued after the summit essentially repeated the rhetorical pressure on the South African Government; no new measures were introduced. A commitment to consider sanctions was however given, something the Community had previously avoided doing because of opposition from the British, German and Portuguese Governments. The statement committed the EC over the next three months to "consultations with other industrialized countries on further measures which might be needed covering in particular a ban on new investments, the import of coal, iron, steel and gold coins from South Africa" (European Council, 1986). This compromise failed to conceal underlying tensions. Most member states expected all of these sanctions to be automatically adopted after consultation had taken place: Britain (who assumed the presidency for the second half of 1986) and Germany did not.

Consequently, the eventual adoption of sanctions by the Community while enacted by consensus, was tardy and done with seeming reluctance (Holland, 1988a, pp. 38–9).

On 15 September 1986 the Community finally adopted a series of restrictive measures, although the modest inventory suggested at The Hague was not fully adopted. Further positive measures were also given increased support. Seemingly, EPC was operating according to the lowest common denominator principle. To summarize, the existing 1985 embargo on military, cultural and diplomatic contacts were bolstered by economic sanctions. Effective as of 27 September a partial ban on steel and iron imports from South Africa was implemented; one month later new direct investment in the Republic by EC firms was discouraged as was the import of gold coins (Krugerrands) from South Africa. The September statement also instructed the presidency "to seek consensus" on the ban of South African coal: no such consensus ever emerged.

As has been commented on extensively elsewhere, these Community embargoes were of greater symbolism than of direct economic effect for two reasons: their legal basis and their scope. First, while there is an implicit expectation of good faith on the part of the member states when enacting collective decisions, the chosen competence does have a disparate impact upon the implementation of common measures. The ban on iron and steel derived its authority from a decision under the European Coal and Steel Community Treaty (Council of the ECSC, 1986); the embargo on Krugerrands was enacted through a regulation under the Treaty of Rome (Council of Ministers, 1986b); but the policy designed to stem new investment was only based on a Council decision (Council of Ministers, 1986a): as such did not require identical legislative application or possibly interpretation across the Twelve (Holland, 1988b, *passim*). The legal point is an important one. Depending on the type of Community instrument chosen, varying opportunities existed for member states to take differing and equally valid interpretations on how adopted measures should be realized. Consequently, "the limited Community sanctions that were agreed were implemented neither simultaneously nor comprehensively by all member states, in spite of their obligation to do so" (ibid., p. 416).

Second, the economic impact of these Community measures were, to be generous, modest. Had the original Hague package of sanctions been adopted 16.5 per cent of South Africa's 1985 exports to the Community would have been effected (1,559.8 million ECU). Excluding an embargo on coal the combined value of the sanctions fell to a derisory 3.5 per cent (330.4 million ECU). South Africa had supplied almost one quarter of the EC's coal imports in 1985. Indeed, if the overall pattern for the 1980s is compared, trade increased significantly between Europe and South Africa (see Table 6.1 and supporting commentary for a more detailed discussion of trade including that for iron and steel for the 1985–89 period). After an initial drop in 1987, by 1989 overall imports from South Africa were back to their pre-sanctions average with Italy, the UK and Germany increasing their dominance of the markets (collectively from 57.3 per cent in 1986 to 66.7 per cent after three years of sanctions). For exports to South Africa trade actually grew between 1986–89 from 4,674 million ECU to 6,433 million ECU, with Germany followed by UK the leading exporters (46.0 per cent and 23.8 per cent respectively by the end of the decade). Official statistics suggest that trade in steel products fell to a third of the pre-1986 level (but there is a suspicion that trade was maintained through other mechanisms). At the time of the introduction of the 1986 sanctions the EC collectively imported 472 million kilograms of iron and steel products from South Africa; by the end of 1989 this had fallen to 166 million kilograms per annum.

What is noteworthy was that no official breaches of sanctions were ever reported. This, in part, may be because the adopted EPC sanctions were implemented and monitored by the member states: the Commission had no responsibilities in this respect nor any authority to invoke infraction procedures where breaches were suspected. Consequently, the phenomenal increase in the UK's South African imports in 1988 (to 55.9% from 19.5%) has not been publicly linked to any intentional breach in EPC policy by the UK. What can be concluded with confidence is that trade in Krugerrands came to a halt and those coins in circulation merely retained their gold content value. As for new investments, the authorizing Community legislation contained conflicting instructions. While demanding the member states "take the necessary measures to ensure that new direct investments . . . are suspended", this requirement could be complied with merely "by the issue of guidance", rather than legal compulsion. It is unknown to what extent breaches of this "guidance" by companies were discovered or even investigated by the respective member states (Council of Ministers, 1986a).

The record for positive measures (known as the "European Community's Special Programme for the Victims of Apartheid") is more favourable and less open to dispute. The idea of positive measures was originally floated in 1985 to counterbalance the introduction of sanctions (although no funds had been allocated since the September 1985 announcement). In the 1986 Hague communiqué the Community "underlined the importance they attached to the strengthening and more effective coordination of the positive measures being taken to assist the victims of apartheid". More importantly, DGVIII (Development and Cooperation) of the Commission who were to run the programme, were provided with a 10 million ECU budget for 1986.

The aims of the programme were to assist in the process of peaceful change by supporting non-racial activities, chiefly education and training, humanitarian and social aid and legal assistance, through non-violent organizations. This last stipulation was on the insistence of the UK Government who were still unconvinced of the commitment of the African National Congress (ANC) to forego the armed struggle. Initially, therefore EC funds were dispersed through four indigenous channels: the South African Council of Churches, the South African Catholic Bishops conference, the trade unions and the Kagiso Trust. Because apartheid was still in force at this time, the Special Programme focused on projects aimed at assisting individuals who had suffered from political repression: this included legal assistance and support for the dependents of people detained by the South African police, as well as more general humanitarian aid and development-focused education and training projects. Selected projects had to meet the Commission's prescribed guidelines, both positive (a commitment to non-racialism and democracy) and negative (no funding for South African Government related projects or facilities that they could legitimately be expected to finance, and no funds directly to political organizations) (Directorate-General VIII, 1986). However, even in this area of policy success there were some initial problems of implementation (Holland, 1988c). Nonetheless, the overall initial impact of the Special Programme has had a profound effect upon the Community's post-apartheid thinking. Development and assistance along the lines of the Special Programme came to dominate the Community's policy innovations for the rest of the decade (as illustrated below) and during the early 1990s (see Chapters 3 and 5).

Policy Compromise

The imposition of sanctions had been disruptive within the Community: maintaining that *status quo* rather than extending sanctions became the principle task after 1986. There was little enthusiasm for developing policy in the post-sanctions era. Critics have argued that this was essentially an alibi for the pervasive inability of EPC to act in a demonstrative way, whether in South Africa or elsewhere. The adoption of sanctions had served an end in themselves, at least from the Community's perspective. Where policy could go from this point was less clear-cut. British opposition to enhanced measures proved a fundamental constraint. For example, at the Hannover June 1988 European Council the presidency made the following innocuous comment in response to South Africa's legislative ban on the external funding of opposition groups: it merely noted that "the enactment of the proposed Bill designed to deprive anti-apartheid organizations . . . of financial support from abroad would place additional strain" on relations. Originally, the communiqué had called for the withdrawal of all EC member state ambassadors and a ban on South African Airways flights to Europe. Both these conditions were excised on British insistence (*Keesing's*, 1988, p. 36307).

Similarly, other new approaches that were advocated failed to gain unanimous support. One such attempt was the idea of a Charter of Political Principles to frame the constitutional requirements of a post-apartheid South Africa. Consensus in the Council of Ministers was missing. Another failed initiative, this time introduced by the Danish presidency, was for a Community sponsored all-party conference: consensus on who should attend could not be reached. Thirdly, as already noted, successive presidencies also inherited the obligation of seeking a consensus on the introduction of coal sanctions: none came even close to achieving this. In defence of this apparent policy moratorium, clearly there needed to be a period in which the EC could evaluate the effect of its 1985/86 policies. Policy innovation simply for the sake of appearances was not required. The use of sanctions as a Community policy instrument found few converts and no real zealots over the next few years. Collective démarches continued to represent the sum total of Community action. Alternative strategies were needed.

One such option was suggested under the Belgian presidency of 1987. A return to the regional policy of southern African development was advanced, inverting the normal secondary status of regional policy. An extension of funds and their more effective deployment became a new Community theme and the EC made concerted efforts to stabilize the conflicts that then existed in the SADCC region (principally Angola and Mozambique). The change was also indicative of EPC maturity: policy had progressed from the use of sanctions as a policy instrument to a more inclusive positive and negative strategy that encompassed the region as a whole and established a policy framework that was complementary rather than contradictory in focus.

A second option revolved around the comparative success of the existing operational positive measures. In contrast with the dissatisfaction and difficulty of constructing a consensus on putative sanctions, the widespread support for these measures was strong. The emphasis in Community thinking towards the end of the 1980s came to focus on developing similar additional measures, rather than attempt to engineer a new and probably imaginary consensus for further sanctions. From 1986 onwards the Special Programme increased its assistance to the victims of political repression; funding rose to 20 million in 1987 and thereafter incrementally to a level of 30 million by 1990.

In contrast to these innovations, the Community's Code of Conduct continued to be employed during this period in its revised form. Its relevance was increasingly challenged as EC firms accelerated their divestments. For example, at its peak in 1980/81, the Code covered 129,000 black workers employed by British companies alone; this had shrunk to 53,900 by the time of the 1989/90 report. Similarly, taking the Twelve collectively, in the ninth synthesis report (which covered the twelve months from July 1987 to June 1988) only 88,479 black employees were covered, compared with 121,155 in the sixth report (1984/85), the final year of reporting under the original unrevised 1977 Code guidelines (see Table 2.1). Despite its reduced scope, the role of the Code in the post- sanctions period was not downgraded. For example, addressing the European Parliament in June 1988, the

Greek presidency on behalf of the Community restated that "the Code is an important instrument of our policy which aims to eliminate completely any policy of discrimination in the economic and social sectors" (*EPC Bulletin*, 1988, 88/205).

An examination of the record of the Code in the post-sanction era suggests that faith in its utility constituted a rather perverse loyalty. As the accompanying Table 2.1 illustrates, from 1985/6 to 1987/88, British companies were almost entirely responsible for the reduction in the Code's coverage. Twenty seven UK companies either reduced their holdings or divested their interests resulting in the reduction in the total of black workforce of 16,500: the corresponding decline for the Twelve collectively was fifteen companies and 17,143 employees. Despite the ban on new investments in the Republic, during this period two Community member states actually increased their number of subsidiaries reporting – from fourteen to twenty-three in the case of France, and from 93 to 105 for Germany. (The explanation, however, may not necessarily be that new firms began operating, but rather these firms had previously refused to comply with the

Table 2.1 Synthesis Reports on the Code of Conduct for Community Companies with Subsidiaries in South Africa 1985/6–1987/8

	Number of companies			Number of black employees		
	1985/6	*1986/7*	*1987/8*	*1985/6*	*1986/7*	*1987/8*
Belgium	5	5	2	24	24	19
Denmark	7	7	5	270	793	158
Germany	93	94	105	19200	18900	19300
Greece	2	2	2	39	39	38
Spain	1	1	1	310	310	387
France	14	15	23	1974	2236	1806
Ireland	–	–	–	–	–	–
Italy	1	1	1	112	133	137
Luxembourg	–	–	–	–	–	–
Netherlands	14	11	10	4527	4441	3955
Portugal	2	2	2	66	78	79
UK	126	109	99	79100	70300	62600
EC12	265	247	250	105622	97254	88479

Source: Presidency of the European Community (1990).

Code's voluntary reporting requirements.) Focusing on the 1987/ 88 period, the synthesis report summarized the accompanying ambassadors' report and noted the following "successes":

> the Code has had an economic and social impact in South Africa through its contribution to an improvement in the standard of living of black employees of European companies and to the promotion of the principle of racial equality. . . .
>
> The ambassadors believed that the main purpose of the Code, namely that European companies not exploit their black employees and that their presence serve to undermine apartheid rather than bolster it, had been achieved. It was felt that the Code remains a useful instrument in promoting change and makes a real contribution to the abolition of apartheid both in the economy and in South African society as a whole. (*EPC Bulletin*, 1990, 90/101)

As noted elsewhere, the Community interpretation was somewhat myopic. As the report itself demonstrates, despite a decade of operation many of the minimum requirements had yet to be achieved. Universal recognition of black trade unions was absent; the use of migrant labour continued to represent 10 per cent of the Community's black workforce; 2 per cent of employees were still paid below the recommended minimum "supplemented living level (SLL)"; and "a small number of companies . . . had not yet achieved full desegregation" as required by section 6 of the Code (Presidency of the European Community, 1990).

It was to be expected, then, that critics from both the right and the left remarked on the Code's growing inappropriateness. The right for what they saw as its unwarranted interference and imposition of additional and uncompetetive costs; the left because of its implicit paternalism. However, the Code's resilience has been remarkable and it continued to play a policy role well into the 1990s. Establishing collective policies in EPC demands unanimity: but so does the decision to scrap any existing common approaches. Creating a consensus to withdraw a policy is no less difficult than it is to create one. Consequently, it was not until the creation of a transitional government and a fixed election date were established in South Africa in mid-1993 that the Twelve accepted that the Code had outlived its purpose and should be rescinded (see Chapter 4 for further details).

Despite the lack of policy development, from 1988 to 1990 South Africa regularly appeared on the Community agenda, at the levels of the European Council, Council of Ministers and the European Parliament. The accompanying Table 2.2 provides the data for parliamentary questions, EPC declarations and other statements made by the Twelve over a period of six presidencies. During the German presidency South Africa was raised at every Question Time addressed to the presidency and several longer parliamentary debates were held. In the declarations and press statements released, rhetoric held sway over substance and repetition over policy innovation. For example, in its opening statement of activities to the European Parliament in January 1988, the German presidency reiterated the Community's commitment to dialogue and the release of political prisoners stating that the "apartheid system cannot be reformed: it must be dismantled immediately" (*EPC Bulletin*, 1988, 88/025). One month later the first of two German presidency EPC declarations was issued in which the Twelve "vigorously condemn[ed] the new

Table 2.2   EPC Statements on South Africa 1988–90

Presidency Form of Action	1988		1989		1990		1988–90 Total	
	D	E	Es	F	Ir	I	n	%
Questions & Statements in European Parliament	20	27	16	6	11	5	85	54.8
Press releases	2		2	1		1	6	3.9
Messages		1	1			1	3	1.9
Declarations	2	4	4	4	3	2	19	12.3
European Council conclusions	1	1	1		1	2	6	3.9
Report on European Union		1					1	0.6
Joint declarations/ other formal statements	3	10	3	5	4	7	32	20.7
Code of conduct report	1		1		1		3	1.9
Presidency total	29	44	28	16	20	18	155	
Annual total		73		44		38	155	100.0

D = Germany; E = Greece; Es = Spain; F = France; Ir = Ireland; I = Italy.
Source: *EPC Bulletin* (1988–90) vols 4–6.

manifestation of political suppression" whereby South African organizations peacefully opposed to apartheid were prohibited from engaging in political activities (88/050). The second declaration issued on 14 June appealed for the reopening of proceedings against the Sharpeville Six who were under stay of execution for political activities. In its concluding "balance sheet" statement to the European Parliament just two days later, the German presidency could only note that the Twelve had "intervened in a whole range of individual cases to safeguard human rights in South Africa" (88/168); specific policy successes were notable by their absence.

During the Greek presidency, the topic of South Africa was raised 44 times, an increase in part explained by the greater number of statements made at the United Nations General Assembly. However, the tone of the new presidency was more forthright: in the Greek presidency's opening programme address to the Parliament apartheid was described as an "inhuman policy", South Africa was accused of systematic regional destabilization and warned of "a serious deterioration" in EC-South African relations (88/204). Similarly, representing the EC at United Nations General Assembly, the presidency condemned South Africa "whose policy of apartheid runs counter to all the principles of the United Nations. By its very nature the apartheid system is particularly repugnant since it violates in such a gross, unique and flagrant way basic human rights" (88/313). However, although Greece clearly belonged to those member states who were critical of the limited nature of Community action, the inability of the presidency to go beyond the existing consensus was underlined. In answering an oral questions in the Parliament, the Greek presidency stated: "the Presidency will make every effort to promote the decisive attitudes within the context of the Community, in relation to South Africa. . . . Of course, the results of our actions, . . . depend on the concurrence of all the Member States, and that is not something the Presidency can guarantee in advance" (88/255). Effectively, Community policy was to remain one of "persuasion and pressure". The two earliest declarations (July and August) called for the release of Mandela who had already been incarcerated for 25 years and whose health was the subject of concern; the third declaration opposed the extension of press censorship through the banning of the *Weekly Mail*; whereas the fourth declaration issued in late November

1988 was, finally, evidence of the success of "persuasion and pressure" – the commutation of the death penalty for the Sharpeville Six. While welcomed, this achievement stood in stark contrast with the ineffectual Community pressure in other outstanding contemporary issues. During 1988 the EC failed to secure abolition of the prohibition on seventeen anti-apartheid organizations to carry out peaceful activities that had been imposed in February of that year; curbs on the media remained in force; South African legislation was adopted preventing the external funding of anti-apartheid organizations; and the historical demands for the unbanning of political parties and freeing of political prisoners remained illusory.

In 1989 Spain and France shared the presidency. South Africa remained a Community external relations priority for the Spanish presidency and in their January address to the European Parliament the inadequacy of existing policy was noted, albeit obliquely. Thus the presidency stated:

> With the Commission's support, we shall endeavour to improve the coordination of our national programmes of positive measures to help the victims of apartheid . . . Although our restrictive measures are clearly effective, they are not on their own sufficient. Consequently, the Presidency will also endeavour to increase the scope of provisions in the 'Code of Conduct' for our undertakings in South Africa. (89/012)

The inclusion of the Commission was a welcomed acknowledgement of the more inclusive nature of foreign policy in the post-SEA era. Less satisfying was the substance behind the commitment to enhance the Code. No procedural or practical changes were ever adopted, whereas trade between the EC and the Republic remained largely unaffected by the 1986 sanctions. This situation led one member of the European Parliament to question whether the EC had decided to replace "the sanctions policy, with a development of the Code of Conduct policy" (89/082). Despite two joint démarches opposing further press censorship, in February 1989 two newspapers, *Grassroots* and *New Era* were suspended for three months by the South African authorities. An additional sixteen organizations were banned from engaging in peaceful anti-apartheid activities. In April a further démarche was made calling for the non-renewal of the existing State of Emergency: this was followed by another declaration in June in which the Twelve deplored the South African Government's decision to do just that, underlining – if any were needed – the increasing ineffectual nature of Community influence in the region.

Cumulatively, these events of the first half of 1989 made the Spanish presidency one of the least successful since the mid-1980s. In their own words, the presidency saw the South African response to the demands made by EPC as "absolutely pessimistic and negative. . . Unfortunately, the results of our efforts and those of other countries and of world opinion continue to be very limited, but the policy of exerting pressure on the South African Government will continue" (89/155). The Community's minimum demands for reform remained ignored by Pretoria: These were:

i)   lifting the State of Emergency;
ii)   abolition of all discriminatory legislation;
iii)   ending of detention without trial;
iv)   the unconditional release of detainees, including Nelson Mandela;
v)   the ending of forced removals;
vi)   lifting the ban on those organization who peacefully oppose apartheid;
vii)   the legalization of the ANC, PAC and other political parties; and,
viii) the establishment of a constructive national dialogue involving all political groups without any form of discrimination. (89/155)

The French presidency in the second half of 1989 inherited this policy malaise; superficially, the low level of parliamentary questions answered by the French presidency seems to reflect this continued dilemma. However, while there was a gross reduction in rhetoric, the substance of the four declarations issued indicated the concerted development of Community policy and reflected the first tentative signs of reform under the new de Klerk-led South African Government. The first three declarations replicated the existing pattern of *post facto* condemnation. The first objected to the enactment of the Foreign Funding Act designed to impede the functioning of the EC's positive aid programme; the second condemned the latest example of forced removals; whereas the third declaration opposed the threatened banning of a Community funded anti-apartheid newspaper, *New Nation*. However, in the December 9 declaration issued by the European Council at their Strasbourg summit, the seeds of policy innovation as well as of a decline in South Africa's resilience were in evidence. The declaration noted that 1989 in both South and southern Africa had been "of such importance as consistently to demand the attention of the Twelve" and while the signs of reform were "welcomed", they remained "still insufficient with respect to the immense task posed by the dismantlement of apartheid" (89/318). By way of encouragement, the Community decided to extend its involvement in positive measures while leaving the restrictive measures untouched. The declaration concluded:

> With a view to preparing for the developments which are inescapable in South Africa, this programme will be strengthened over the next two years by granting new scholarships for study in Europe and in the multiracial South African universities . . .

> The Community and its Member States have, moreover, decided to maintain the pressure that they exert on the South African authorities in order to promote the profound and irreversible changes which they have repeatedly stood for and to reconsider it when there is clear evidence that these changes have been obtained.

Although the Community had been calling for fundamental change and the release of Nelson Mandela for almost fifteen years, this last declaration indicated, finally, a degree of prescience. Within two months Mandela was released and the reform process of the 1990s had begun. This process is discussed in detail in the following two chapters.

It is not necessary here to revisit the saga of EC sanctions against South Africa in any greater detail. What this chapter has emphasized is the key components of EC policy. First, despite national differences, EC policy remained, until 1990, unified and collective in nature. Second, a range of economic instruments have been developed by the EC as legitimate foreign policy tools; indeed, reservations over using Community instruments for EPC were removed and a precedent established that has now become normal practice. And third, the content and the "effectiveness" of the policies adopted have suggested "symbolic" rather than "real" policy objective (Holland, 1991). Arguably, the rationale driving EPC and South Africa was not exclusively external in focus, but reflected internal EC issues pertaining to integration.

Importantly, the 1977–1989 period witnessed a metamorphosis in policy. Initially EPC was limited to essentially a single policy (the Code); during the 1980s this simplicity was replaced by a series of interlocking policies which, by 1990, were tantamount to a more comprehensive and complex EPC approach. Credit for the domestic reforms introduced by the de Klerk Government (which commenced in February 1990) rightly belongs to a variety of international and South African actors. The Community played a part, if not a leading role, in this process. Perhaps reflecting the disappointment of failing to lead international opinion, since the release of Nelson Mandela and the progressive normalization of South African politics, the EC has become the most active international actor. How to structure Community relations with the new post-apartheid South Africa has gradually replaced the punitive aspects of the previous policies of EPC.

As the following chapter argues, this transition has not been without conflict and a new policy consensus was not initially present. Chapter 4 examines the Community's internal policy making actors who were involved in this process of policy reformulation, whereas Chapter 5 outlines the content of the new policy. The process of foreign policy making in the EC has usually been tortuous, especially while this was governed by the consensus rule of EPC. In this respect, the reform of the Community's South African policy follows a typical path. What is perhaps unique, however, is the success of the Community in securing the transition from sanctions to positive measures to a broader programme of development assistance. In this respect the South African case suggests a Community foreign policy that has the potential to be flexible, effective and innovative. Such a characterization of EPC in the 1990s stands in sharp contrast to the perceived inadequacies of Community action in the Gulf war and in the former Yugoslavia. As a practitioner and commentator on EPC has noted:

The difficulties the Ten, later, Twelve, experienced in reaching agreement on sanctions detracted from the considerable achievement of their South African policy. The positions of the Member States were wide apart, and yet EPC provided a mechanism which resulted in a substantial European position . . . Political Co-operation produced a position which was the median, not the lowest common denominator, of the different national positions. (Nuttall, 1992, p. 237)

3 From Cooperation to Joint Action: 1990–1994

This chapter presents an overview of events (focusing specifically on Community, and latterly of Union, involvement) stretching from 1990 until the 1994 election. The shift from punitive European policies to a new cooperative engagement is the hallmark of this period. In addition, the implications of South Africa as a topic of joint action under the provisions of Title V of the Maastricht Treaty are explored in terms of policy making and institutional relations. This analysis of the practical operation of a joint action contrasts the former EPC process with the new expectations and assumptions of CFSP. The very newness of the proedure and the choice of South Africa as one of the first joint actions reflected the "experimental" nature, making an assessment of the process difficult. As the following discussion demonstrates, policy making was conducted simultaneously with institution building as the structures necessary to manifest CFSP joint actions only emerged as the result of experience, trial and error.

THE REFORMULATION OF POLICY: 1990–94

As demonstrated in the previous chapter, the late 1980s had been a period of policy frustration and stagnation. The events of 1990 provided the Community with the opportunity to progress beyond this self-imposed foreign policy moratorium. In 1990, the year of the eventual release of Nelson Mandela, the Community presidency was held first by Ireland and then Italy. Without an Irish Embassy situated in South Africa diplomatic representations made on behalf of the presidency were conducted through the Italian embassy. Although convoluted and inelegant, diplomatic substitution is a common necessity of EPC's global function and does not, *per se*, dilute the impact or coherence of the Community's foreign policy *persona* in any significant way.

It was perhaps appropriate that the policy momentum should begin to strengthen under the presidency of Ireland, one of the

EC's most vociferous anti-apartheid critics. Remarkably, the Irish were in the position of issuing three declarations, not of condemnation as was invariably the case, but of support for reforms. On 5 February the Community "welcomed" the reform programme outlined by de Klerk (*EPC Bulletin*, 1990, 90/051). On 13 February the release of Nelson Mandela was "warmly" welcomed and seen as "without doubt a most important contribution to the establishment of that climate the Twelve consider necessary for the initiation of genuine negotiations with the black community" (90/073). And on 9 June the EC "greatly" welcomed the lifting of the four year-old State of Emergency (Foreign Ministers, 1990). A fourth Declaration concerned the ninth synthesis report on the Code of Conduct covering the period 1987–88.

Policy adaptation over these six months commenced with the 20 February Dublin EPC meeting where the first two de Klerk initiatives were discussed. Partial progress beyond the existing declarations was made, though not without difficulty. Given the continued State of Emergency and imprisonment of political prisoners there was agreement that while welcome, the promise of reform was insufficient. No consensus on lifting any of the restrictive measures was possible, despite British enthusiasm. There was agreement that the positive measures favouring the black population should be further reinforced and that cultural and scientific cooperation could resume provided that the objective of such contacts was to contribute to ending apartheid. Lastly, it was agreed to send a fact-finding Troika to South Africa in April to report back to the Twelve on prospects for "promoting the launching of a national dialogue" amongst all political parties in South Africa (90/128). The Troika were encouraged by the prospects for substantive talks especially after the success of the first official ANC-Government meeting in May 1990. The Troika report was discussed on 18 June by the Foreign Ministers of the Twelve and the subject of a long statement attached to the conclusions of that month's European Council meeting.

In the six months since the previous European Council meeting in Strasbourg, both real and the potential for change in South Africa had accelerated rapidly, more so than at any time in the previous forty years. Mandela was free and the process of releasing all political prisoners appeared in motion; political organizations were unbanned; the State of Emergency was lifted (except in Natal); and, the Government had stated a commitment to a non-racial democracy and a willingness to commence negotiations on the future of South Africa with all representative groups. The statement was even handed in its praise for both Mandela and de Klerk and set as the Community's objective:

> the complete dismantlement of the apartheid system, by peaceful means and without delay, and its replacement by a united, non-racial and democratic State in which all people shall enjoy common and equal citizenship and where respect for universally recognized human rights is guaranteed. . . .

> It is the intention of the European Community and its Member States to encourage by every means available to them the early opening on negotiations leading to the creation of a united, non-racial and democratic South Africa. (90/269)

Looking forward to the economic needs of a post-apartheid South Africa the statement acknowledged the need for external financing and "positive action . . . to rectify imbalances". In this vein the EC committed itself to increase funding for its positive measures programme, and "to adapt the programme to the needs of the new situation, including those connected with the return and resettlement of exiles". In an attempt to balance the seemingly irreconcilable demands of the anti and pro-sanctions proponents within the Twelve (the UK and Portugal, on the one hand, and Ireland and Denmark on the other), the statement concluded with typical EPC flexibility and accommodation. The 1989 Strasbourg decision to maintain the pressure of existing measures "to promote the profound and irreversible changes" desired, was coupled with a new "willingness to consider a gradual relaxation of this pressure when there is further clear evidence that the process of change already initiated continues in the direction called for at Strasbourg".

Assuming the presidency for the second half of 1990, the Italian Government was charged with monitoring and engendering this process of reform and Community policy transformation. Successively, individual pillars of the apartheid system were dismantled, beginning with the abolition of the Separate Amenities Act. Perhaps anticipating the sensitivity of the reform process and wishing to create an appropriate negotiating environment, the second half of 1990 saw a decrease in Community statements other than at the United Nations General Assembly and special meetings devoted to human rights, racism and apartheid. Two declarations were issued in August: the first noted "keen satisfaction" with the outcome of ANC-Government pre-negotiation talks (90/302); the second called for the cessation of domestic violence which threatened the reform process (90/038). The European Council "Conclusions" issued in Rome at the end of the Italian presidency contained an annexed "Statement concerning South Africa" in which the next phase of Community policy development was advanced. The European Council agreed that only after the legislative repeal of the Group Areas Act and the Land Acts, would the Community "proceed to an easing of the set of measures adopted in 1986." Commenting on the need for economic stimulation in the Republic, the European Council determined "[A]s of now . . . to lift the ban on new investments" and to strengthen and adapt even further the positive measures designed to assist the "victims of apartheid". In addition, the Community stated that its policy would become more adaptable in its response to the "requirements related to the return and resettlement of the exiles" (90/472).

Both presidencies of 1991, Luxembourg and The Netherlands, were preoccupied with the drafting of the Maastricht Treaty on European Union. The limited personnel and diplomatic resources of Luxembourg made policy initiation difficult and during the Luxembourg presidency the principle objective was to focus discussion on the lifting of existing measures by consensus rather than introduce any radical innovations. An EPC press release from the General Affairs Council of 4 February 1991 announced that "the Community will prepare the necessary steps" with respect to its commitment to ease sanctions (General Affairs, 1991a). In response to de Klerk's reform proposals of 12 March, the 15 April General Affairs Council meeting agreed to lift the remaining 1986 sanctions (despite Danish reservations) as the conditions laid down at Rome "for the repeal of restrictive Community measures had been fulfilled" (General Affairs, 1991b). However, the statement noted that in certain member states the necessary national procedures for lifting the regulation suspending the import of gold coins and the decision suspending certain iron and steel imports were not in place. Achieving this necessary national approval proved impossible in Denmark. In

July 1991 the Danish Government failed to win parliamentary support for this decision, and this in effect blocked the legal removal of Community sanctions as the lifting of sanctions has to be unanimous within EPC. Consequently, the status of EC sanctions remained ambiguous throughout 1991. Certain member states, such as the UK, voluntarily lifted the collective sanctions, while others waited for a resolution of the Danish dilemma. Under these uncertain circumstances, coupled with the urgency to engineer consensus in the intergovernmental conferences at Maastricht by the end of 1991, the Dutch presidency acted as a policy *interregnum*.

In terms of diplomatic statements, throughout 1991 the Community commented favourably on the return of refugees, the signing of the National Peace Accord and on the tenth synthesis report on the Code. It also issued critical *démarches* on the continued imprisonment of political prisoners and the alleged involvement of the SADF in instigating violence. In December the announcement of the CODESA (Convention for a Democratic South Africa) process was welcomed by the Community as "a milestone on the way to a united, democratic and non-racial South Africa", and an invitation to participate as observers was accepted. At the 10 January 1992 Council meeting under Portuguese leadership, the decision to lift the Community sanctions on the import of iron and steel and Krugerrands finally took effect after the Danish Government withdrew its reservations on the repeal of the sanctions (General Affairs, 1992a). Similarly, the 6 April Council meeting lifted the ban on the export of crude oil to South Africa that had been in place since 1985 (*Survey*, April 1992, p. 98), and bans on sporting, cultural and scientific links foreshadowed for abolition since 1990, were at last formally removed. To replace this rapidly disappearing EPC sanctions policy, at the Guimaraes "Gymnich"-style meeting the Danish Government proposed that the EC adopt initiatives to reduce tension and violence in South Africa, such as supervision of the security forces, police training and monitor electoral processes. It was agreed to deploy observers in the Republic to study possible areas for future action. This was followed by an EPC statement on 23 June directed at the growing danger of violence undermining the reform process, particularly in light of the Biopatong massacre and the resultant withdrawal of the ANC from the CODESA process. In the "Conclusions" of the

Lisbon European Council a few days later, the Community welcomed the South African Government's decision to allow foreign observers to participate in the Boipatong investigations and underlined "the absolute need to ensure an effective control of the police and security forces". A resumption of the CODESA process was again urged so "that South Africa should not lose the substantial progress already made in that forum" (*Agence Europe*, 1992, no. 5760, p. 12). The Community's persistent urging for restraint had little effect on either the level of violence for the remainder of the year or on the ANC's boycott of CODESA which lasted until April 1993.

The rejection of the Maastricht Treaty in the Danish referendum of 2 June 1992 provided the Community with its greatest internal crisis since the infamous "empty chair" crisis of 1965. The assumptions about closer foreign policy coordination were suspended while the member states grappled with the implications of the Danish decision. Under these difficult internal circumstances, the time was not auspicious for advancing anything other than cautious foreign policy options based on consensus. One of the Danes' prime concerns had been over the expanding and majoritarian nature of foreign policy under the Maastricht Treaty.

The UK assumed the Community presidency for the second half of 1992 and initiated a Troika to South Africa for 2–3 September. The most positive outcome of the visit was the agreement to send a team of fifteen EC observers to the Republic in line with UN resolution 772. This team, known as ECOMSA (the EC Observer Mission to South Africa) arrived in late October 1992. It comprised of police officers, lawyers and economists and was instructed to cooperate with the National Peace Secretariat and other international observers already in the country. Their task was "to seek by their presence in situations of potential conflict, to prevent violence, defuse tension and promote peace" (Foreign Ministers, 1992). An additional six police specialists from the EC were also assigned to the Goldstone Commission investigating political violence. The EC underlined this commitment to facilitating the peace process in a December EPC statement which encouraged the "renewed momentum to negotiations designed to secure South Africa's peaceful transition" (*Agence Europe*, 1992, no.5869, p. 6); but no new policy proposals were presented.

Policy initiative on South Africa was one of the incoming Danish presidency's main external programme objectives. The early months of 1993 saw a continuation of the violence. In March, the role of ECOMSA was restated as "the mandate to observe the situation on the ground in areas most affected by violence and to facilitate dialogue between the relevant parties in order to defuse potential situations of conflict when needed" (Foreign Ministers, 1993). Less than two weeks later leading ANC figure Chris Hani was assassinated, to which the EC responded yet again with an EPC statement. The murder was condemned and "a thorough investigation' called for with the EC offering "to help in any way it can" with an appeal to all parties "to redouble their efforts to reach a negotiated settlement" (*Agence Europe*, 1993, no.5959, p. 3). In the final week of the Danish presidency the Community further condemned the right-wing attack on the CODESA delegates at the World Trade Centre in Johannesburg and reiterated its call for a speedy resolution of the multiparty negotiations (*Agence Europe*, 1993, no.6011, p. 4). In contrast, against this seeming tide of political violence, April saw the opening of the constitutional conference providing renewed hope for a negotiated settlement. The General Affairs Council decided to send the Danish Foreign Minister and president-in-office, Petersen, to South Africa. During the visit (27–29 May) he met with de Klerk, Botha, Mandela and Buthelezi and underlined the EC's commitment to supporting the process of democratization, and particularly encouraged the speedy setting up of a transitional authority and the agreement on the date for multiracial elections. Once such an authority was in place, Petersen suggested that all remaining sanctions would be lifted, the Community would assist with the reconstruction of the economy and would provide expertise in election organization (*Agence Europe*, 1993, no.5992, p. 4).

On 9 June 1993, during the last month of office, the Danish presidency proposed a reorientation in Community policy, fulfilling their original objectives set out in their initial presidency programme. After consulting with the Council of Foreign Ministers meeting in Luxembourg, Peterson, on behalf of the presidency described the new approach. He stressed that it was necessary for the Community to adjust its policy concurrently with developments in South Africa towards majority rule and democracy. Once the Transitional Executive Council (TEC) was established the Community indicated that a combination of measures would be taken. A new development cooperation initiative would be launched; support for the electoral process provided; discussions would commence on the future economic relations between the EC and the Republic; the EC agreed to advocate South Africa's case for the normalization of relations with the World Bank, International Monetary Fund and other international bodies; a full Commission Delegation would be opened; the ban an military attachés to South Africa would be lifted (with the objective of promoting the democratization and integration process in the security sector); the freezing of official contacts and international agreements in the security field was to be discontinued; and, reporting under the Code of Conduct discontinued and replaced by annual ambassadorial reports on developments in the equality of labour practices (General Affairs, 1993: for the full text, see Appendix document 3).

The "new" approach outlined in June 1993 was a typical example of the Community giving its belated political blessing to existing informal practice, The statement gave an EPC rubber stamp and formal legitimacy to the general *status quo* that had developed since February 1990. There was not a fundamental change; rather the process had been one of constant adaptation to changing circumstances and demands. The emphasis shifted from the limited brief of assistance to "victims" to a broader involvement in health and education programmes with housing and human rights an emerging sector of EC concern. The real Community policy departure was to take place from late 1993 onwards as the EC responded to South Africa's new "transitional" status.

The one area where policy initiation was evident was in the commitment to assisting the electoral process leading to the 27 April 1994 election. From July 1993 this became the dominant policy element. There was an enormous demand for observers during the election campaign to guarantee fairness at the ballot boxes. The EC committed itself to making a significant contribution to this number (through the channel of the member states primarily). Here, the experience of Community involvement in Namibia and Angola was of use, although South Africa presented its own unique set of electoral challenges. To launch this process the EC earmarked 5m ECU for its Special Programme to help electoral education. Allied to this electoral facilitation role, the EC agreed to recommence its funding assistance for the non-establishment press. The programme, part of the earlier positive measures, had been suspended in June 1992 after British objections to this use of funds. It was realized that successful elections demanded a pluralistic media environment. Funds were directed through DGVIII to the Independent Media Trust who, according to strict and agreed upon criteria, selected newspapers for funding.

Additional funding for the South African programme was neither ruled out nor guaranteed: the budget had risen from 10m ECU in 1986 to the 1993 level of 90m ECU, a figure that constituted the EC's largest contribution for development projects to any single country in Africa. Cumulatively, the EC provided 255m ECU, representing more than 50 per cent of all overseas aid in the period. An increase to 100m ECU was proposed for 1994 which was raised by a further 10m by Parliament, quite an achievement in the wider context of the Community's overall budget constraints and competing demands from other developing areas. The 1993 statements express the EC's commitment to South Africa during the transition process (lasting presumably until 1999 at the earliest). However, South Africa will be in competition with eastern Europe for investment and assistance and these closer geographical demands seem likely to result in a gradual reduction in development aid for South Africa.

In late May 1993, two weeks prior to the EPC statement, this "new" approach had been foreshadowed in a Development Council meeting declaration. The new "framework for action" entitled, *Future Development Cooperation with South Africa* sought to build on the existing programme of positive measures (see Appendix document 4 for full text). Any future negotiated programme of assistance would "be based on the established development priorities and policies" of the EC, in particular emphasizing "democratization, rule of law, human rights, good governance and popular participation" (Development Council, 1993). The actual content and application of the programme was not specified. This did not signify empty rhetoric or a lack of commitment for implementation; quite the opposite. These were intentionally left unspecified to provide the necessary flexibility to take account of the changing circumstances, needs and future government policies. Flexibility was to be promoted through decentralized management that was programme oriented and the continued use of NGOs, community-based organizations and even through those bodies established by the transitional government. Future EC policy would reflect the overall development of the domestic economy, levels of poverty and the pace of democratization. No special status was to be conferred: South Africa was to be treated in the same manner as other EC development programmes. In line with this approach the new EC development objectives were set out as follows:

– to support the peace structures and initiatives;
– to support the transition to a democratic government, including support for voter education and other preparations for elections;
– to support institution and capacity building . . . and policy formulation, thus promoting consensus on development issues between the parties involved and to strengthen capacity in order to allow the implementation of social programmes as soon as possible;
– while continuing actions of the kind undertaken in the framework of the positive measures, to implement activities of longer term nature within a number of focal sectors of special importance for the economic and social development of the vulnerable groups of the population. (Development Council, 1993)

In contrast to the late 1980s, in the 1990s a broad consensus developed over the appropriateness of EC policy. The bitter disputes that divided the Twelve in 1986 vanished. The last contentious issue was in July 1991 (over media funding); since then there had been policy harmony. Consequently, the leadership and agenda-setting role of the presidency became less crucial to policy innovation than was previously the case. Thus for the second half of 1993 the Belgian presidency simply followed the common line as delineated by the Danish presidency and the Commission. Understandably, the dominant preoccupation was with addressing the forthcoming election. To this end the Belgian presidency organized a Troika "Taskforce" to report on the alternatives for assisting the election process. The Troika reported in late September and a Council decision was taken on 8 November. The recommendations were generally accepted and the report provided the basis for the European involvement in the 27 April 1994 election.

The extraordinary European Council meeting of 29–30 October convened by the Belgian presidency to address the Community's priorities on the eve of the final implementation of the Treaty on European Union (which became effective as of 1 November 1993) determined, for the first time, that South Africa would be adopted as a topic for "joint action" under the auspices of the Union and the provisions of CFSP. The South Africa decision was one of the five initial foreign actions agreed to under the Treaty, the others being the promotion of peace and security in Europe, the Middle East, the former Yugoslavia and elections in Russia. The presidency conclusions noted that:

> The CFSP will be developed gradually and pragmatically according to the importance of the interests common to all Member States; the European Council asks the Council, as a matter of priority, to define the conditions and procedures for joint action to be taken in the following areas:

> . . . Support for the transition towards multi-racial democracy in South Africa through a co-ordinated programme of assistance in preparing for the elections and monitoring them, and through the creation of an appropriate co-operation framework to consolidate the economic and social foundations of this transition. (European Council, 1993)

The inclusion of South Africa as a topic for common action was more than symbolic; as noted in Chapter 1, such a commitment lends itself to the possibility of majority voting and the question of South Africa was now governed by the binding provisions associated with a joint action. At this stage the scope of the common action was not defined: divisions existed over whether it would be inclusive of all bilateral relations (including trade and development) or limited to joint action concerning the elections. However, the designation of South Africa as one of the first joint actions was emblematic of the high degree of consensus that existed in late 1993 on the appropriateness of European policy: had this not been the case, South Africa would not have been elevated to this new level of collective decision-making.

This new found consensus towards South Africa even extended to the view of the European Parliament. Under its provisions for debating topical and urgent debates, a resolution was passed on

29 October that called for the development of both the economic and political relations with South Africa. In particular, it called for the Special Programme to contribute to housing, employment and education issues, and for the Twelve to play a leading organizational role in voter education and in the monitoring of the 1994 election. This was further emphasized in early December when the Foreign Affairs Committee adopted a recommendation requesting that the European Parliament be fully associated with the Union's election role (*Agence Europe*, 1993, no.6121, p. 4). Given the historic antagonisms that had existed between the Parliament's pro-sanctions lobby and the Council's past reactive stance, this new collegiality was indeed remarkable. However, Parliament's rediscovery of its South African interest contained the seeds for potential institutional conflict. In addition to its wish for full involvement in the election process, in mid-December the Parliament adopted recommendations that a framework agreement be adopted as a transitional stage to a bilateral cooperation agreement between Europe and South Africa. As suggested in the following chapter, the presumed intergovernmental nature of CFSP did not dissuade the Parliament from exerting its views.

On 17 November South Africa's interim constitution was finalized preparing the way for the TEC to be established on 7 December, considerably later than originally anticipated and less than five months ahead of the election. This development saw the new European Union issue its first joint statement on South Africa in which Europe's support for the election process and readiness to assist in "economic reconstruction and development" were emphasized (*Agence Europe*, 1993, no.6110, p. 6). The 6 December meeting of the Union's Political Affairs Committee was more circumspect in its recommendations and the resultant Council decision only specified details concerning the electoral involvement of the Union; the nature of the cooperation framework was left indeterminate, although internal discussions on this aspect of policy were to begin. (As Chapter 8 argues, the scope of the joint action was of considerable importance to the definition of competences both between the Commission and the Council and within the Commission itself.) The joint action was to consist of "advising, bringing technical assistance and training, continued support to non-partisan elector education, and supplying a large number of European observers in the framework of a global international effort by the United Nations" (*Agence Europe*, 1993, no.6123, p. 3). A further CFSP statement issued on 15 December confirmed that the two remaining EC sanctions (the ban on nuclear collaboration and cessation of exports of sensitive equipment to the police and security forces) had been lifted with the inauguration of the TEC. The normalization of diplomatic relations was sealed with the signing of a diplomatic accord on 14 December (between the South African Ambassador and the Director General of DGIA) which facilitated the formal opening of the Commission Delegation in Pretoria (*Agence Europe*, 1993, no.6131, p. 3).

Greece assumed the presidency of the Union on 1 January 1994 and while they inherited a clearly structured policy framework, many of the details – both electoral and developmental – remained under discussion. In late January a presidency Troika visited South Africa to discuss election monitoring and investigate the political situation. In the following month the first formal meeting between the TEC and the Commission took place. Quite how useful the meeting was, given that the TEC's mandate was to expire after the election in just ten weeks time, remains questionable. With the approaching election campaign, the EU's Electoral Unit finally became operational in early February; in addition, the European Parliament announced its intentions to send seven MEPs as observers (a figure that was later expanded to twelve). As the election date approached the topic of South Africa was a permanent discussion item on the CFSP agenda. A presidency communique was issued on 3 March welcoming further initiatives towards an all-inclusive elections and reaffirmed that the EU's was "firmly committed to assisting the transition on democracy . . . so as to ensure free and fair elections, as well as in its announced intention to assist in the country's economic reconstruction and development" (*Agence Europe*, 1994, no.6183, p. 4). To support this latter concern, at the 28 March Ioannina informal CFSP meeting it was agreed that a conference involving all the southern African countries would be convened in September in Berlin under the German presidency. This commitment underlined the continuing and longer term nature of the joint action. In parallel, on 6 April the Commission presented its proposals to the Council concerning the framework for future bilateral economic relations with the Republic; these proposals were adopted by the General Affairs Council of 18 April and provided the Treaty based mandate on which negotiations could commence after the election of the multiparty government (see Chapter 6 and Appendix Document 7).

Against this tide of positive EU involvement, internal problems within South Africa continued to jeopardize the normalization of relations. In early April the EU issued yet one more statement condemning the continued bloodshed and level of political violence in South Africa (*Agence Europe*, 1994, no.6207, p. 4). However, this was balanced by a 22 April communique that congratulated Mandela, de Klerk and Buthelezi for reaching an agreement that facilitated IFP participation in the election (*Agence Europe*, 1994, no.6218, p. 4). The eventual EU contribution to the elections saw 307 observers deployed, plus an additional 80 European police officers. The report of the European Electoral Unit concluded that despite some examples of intimidation and administrative inadequacies, overall the election was held in a "substantially free and fair" manner (see Appendix Document 6). Subsequently, on 4 May President Delors sent messages of congratulations to both President-elect Nelson Mandela and to F.W. de Klerk. The declared result gave the ANC 62.65 per cent; the National Party 20.39 per cent; and IFP 10.45 per cent. The EU foreign Ministers discussed the report of the Council presidency on the elections at the 16 May General Affairs meeting, reviewing both the successes and limitations of the joint action to date, as well as explored the future scope of the commitment to provide continued assistance to the transition process in South Africa.

Of course, a history of CFSP and EPC statements do not, in themselves, provide an inadequate assessment of foreign policy. The consensual gloss imposed on all statements often belies the significant policy differences and ignores conflicting bilateral action. Thus while the EC has retained its collective response in the immediate post-apartheid period, contradictions and cracks in the common policy prior to the enactment of the Maastricht inspired joint action, were in evidence. Before the release of Mandela Community policy could be summarized as being unified and consisted of the following instruments (see Table 3.1): economic sanctions on South African iron and steel exports, Krugerrands, and new investments; imposition of bans on cooperation/trade in military, nuclear, technology and police fields; a crude oil embargo; a Code of Conduct in labour relations; positive aid for the "victims of apartheid"; and, regional aid for

Table 3.1   EPC/CFSP Policy Chronology for South Africa

Policy	Date Implemented	Date Rescinded
Code of Conduct (original version 1977)	Sept. 1977	Nov. 1985
1985 Sanctions on:		
oil exports – paramilitary goods – senstive technology – cultural, sporting & scientific contact –	Sept. 1985	April 1992
1985 sanctions on:		
nuclear cooperation –	Sept. 1985	Nov. 1993
military cooperation –	Sept. 1985	Oct. 1993
exchange of military attaches –	Sept. 1985	Oct. 1993
Code of Conduct (1985 revised version)	Nov. 1985	Nov. 1993
1986 Special Programme	July 1986	–
ECSC Decision 86/459 prohibiting certain iron & steel imports	Sept. 1986	Jan. 1992
EC Decision 86/517 prohibiting new investments	Sept. 1986	Dec. 1990
EC Regulation 3302/86 prohibiting the import of Krugerrands	Oct. 1986	Jan. 1992
ECOMSA	Oct. 1992	–
Development Council framework	May 1993	–
Council Statement on post-TEC policy	June 1993	–
Accreditation of Commission Delegation	Dec. 1993	–
European Electoral Unit Observer Team	Jan. 1994	May 1994
Commission proposal for a New cooperation framework	April 1994	–

SADCC. The difficulties in achieving this consensus notwith-standing, the EC policy was generally cohesive and collective: there were no public breaches in the agreed adopted policy (despite Mrs. Thatcher's individualism). The contrast with the period immediately after February 1990 is sharp. Britain was first to adopt a bilateral position that was in conflict with the existing EPC policy (and was thereby in breach of procedures agreed to under the 1986 *Single European Act*). In early 1990 the UK announced its unilateral decision immediately to revoke its ban on new investments; in a belated attempt to repair the EPC facade, the December 1990 Rome European Council meeting decided jointly to remove the ban, only to be obstructed by the Danish Parliament that voted to maintain sanctions. Subsequently, all but two of the 1986 sanctions adopted within the EPC framework were lifted by the Community before the introduction of the CFSP, whereas the positive measures were maintained, albeit it in an amended form. Since defining South Africa as a subject for joint action, while Union policy has been both common and consensual, its content initially replicated rather than distin-guished it from EPC. As subsequent chapters show, the mixed nature of CFSP joint action on South Africa and the resultant cross-cutting of competences and Treaty boundaries, has made policy innovation conservative and policy consistency a precar-ious objective.

FROM POLITICAL COOPERATION TO JOINT ACTION: IS THERE A DIFFERENCE?

The development of contemporary policy towards South Africa can only be understood within the context of the transition from EPC to CFSP. The decision to treat South Africa as a topic for joint action had fundamental consequences for the structure of policy making, if not necessarily on the policy options adopted. As one European Union practitioner sardonically commented, it added pleasure to enjoyment! To conclude this chapter the procedural differences between EPC and CFSP are examined in detail providing a platform on which the policy implications discussed in Chapter 5 can be interpreted.

Chapter 1 gave a descriptive account of EPC's development. The reforms of Maastricht were seen as modifications rather than as revolutionary changes in procedure particularly given the separate "pillar" and intergovernmental nature of CFSP. However, the potential of CFSP was undeniable and the Belgian presidency report to the October 1993 General Affairs Council delineated the new expectations of the Union's common foreign policy. Of course, it remains to be seen whether these expectations are matched by reality; nonetheless, the presidency paper set the tone and style for the initial conduct of CFSP and was therefore instrumental in shaping the manner in which the South African case was perceived and handled. Initially, cautious pragmatism was to govern developments and common policy was to build on the practical experience of the existing EPC *acquis*. Continuity, however, did not imply stagnation: the "political ambition" of the Treaty was to create a common foreign policy "which marks a qualitative leap forward, and equip the Union . . . to rise to the challenges and seize the opportunities of the post-cold war world" (Presidency 1993, p. 16). The following characteristics of the CFSP were central to achieving both the ambitions of the Union as well as a successful joint action on South Africa. These are: the enhanced authority of Union to commit member states to common decisions; the development of an active policy in the pursuit of the objectives of the Union; unity and consistency in external action; unity in the global presentation of policy and increased visibility of the Union as an actor in the international community; and, greater efficiency in decision-making procedures. Each one of these is discussed separately below.

First, with respect to obligations and commitments, Article J.2 of the TEU establishes that with respect to Union decisions "on any matter of foreign and security policy of general interest . . . Member States shall ensure that their national policies conform to the common positions"; in contrast, the SEA describes common positions as "a point of reference for the policies" of member states. The difference is more than semantic: the Union requirements are binding once a common position has been adopted, an attribute never accredited to EPC. Furthermore, where joint actions are adopted (as opposed to just common positions) these "shall commit the Member States in the positions they adopt and in the conduct of their activity" (Article J.3.4), with the commitment underpinned by a rigorous and elaborate set of procedures for sharing information and prior consultation. This level of commitment is underlined by the direct involvement of the European Council in setting out the "general guidelines" for joint action. The highest level of political authority is the source for such binding commitment. This qualitative difference has important implications for the treatment of South Africa: in contrast to the policy of EPC that, while collective, lacked a solid basis for common action, the Union's decisions are expected to have the full support of the Twelve in every respect.

Second, echoing the aspirations of both the 1976 Tindemans Report and the 1981 London Report, the TEU finally commits the Union to a foreign policy that is more than a reactive response. CFSP is to be proactive and a system of forward planning and systematic appraisal of both means and objectives in common policies established. This involvement is not confined to joint actions, but is to have general application for all CFSP activity. Such a proactive approach will help facilitate quicker responses to international events, a characteristic that was occasionally absent from EPC. As the presidency report clarified, "a pre-established consensus among Member States on objectives in a particular area will facilitate rapid and coherent reaction to events when they occur" (p. 17). The responsibility for coordination and policy development will be shared between three actors within the Union's foreign policy structure. The Political Directors and the Political Committee (POCO) which can utilize existing national foreign policy analysis and development skills; the presidency supported by the Council Secretariat; and the Commission. It is anticipated that the Political Committee will assume the principle role. South Africa, and the other four joint actions, provides the test for this procedure. However, as argued elsewhere in this volume, the absence of contingency planning in the event of a derailment of the democratic process in South Africa stands in contradiction to the Union's active and systematic approach.

Third, Maastricht sought to confirm the Union's external involvement while recognizing the divided nature of Europe's global action. In that regard creating Union activities as well as Community areas of competence has done little to clarify Europe's foreign relations. Irrespective of the pillarization of competences, the Union's pursuit of foreign policy objectives would often by necessity need to combine diplomatic action with that in trade and development policy areas. Thus, "the global approach will be present from the early stage of policy shaping, particularly implementing joint action" (p. 18). More specifically:

> The "single institutional framework" which unifies the preparatory process through the work of Coreper and the overall responsibility for the conduct of the Union's external policy given to the General Affairs Council are intended to ensure that the objectives set out in the Treaty with regard to unity and consistency are achieved, while respecting the different legal nature of decisions taken under the various parts of the Treaty. (Ibid., p. 18)

Experience suggests that this may well prove wishful-thinking. In the early stages of the joint action on South Africa the decision on "an appropriate cooperation framework" was delayed while the respective competences of DGI (External Economic Relations), the Political Committee, the member states, the Council Secretariat and the presidency were clarified. Simply, under what framework – the Treaty of Rome or the Treaty on European Union – was action to be taken; what were the policy making implications of this; and, which bodies were responsible for policy initiation? Procedural questions were important. For example, at the simplest level, if issues were being discussed under the CFSP framework at the Working Group level, just English and French are used as the working languages facilitating debate and dialogue rather than imposing the constraints of simultaneous translations. More importantly, the procedural differences between pillar I activities (such as trade with South Africa) and pillar II activities (such as election observation) are only being resolved incrementally. Where groups have been merged from different pillars, the procedural solution has been experimental. Despite these difficulties of operating in *terra incognita*, the overall experience of the early months of CFSP discussions was positive but open to refinement. As discussed further in Chapter 4, the traditional role of the Commission in determining external relations was potentially the most seriously compromised. South Africa found itself in the precarious position of a being the subject of a coordination and competences experiment; the practice of joint action on South Africa addressed these organizational questions in an incremental and exploratory manner, a characteristic perhaps not best suited to either policy efficiency or appropriateness.

Fourth, is the related question of perception of the Union as a unified actor and its visibility within the international community. As noted in the introductory chapter in this book, the foreign policy identity of the former Community and current Union has suffered from the multitude of actors involved. It was often unclear with whom third countries should conduct a foreign policy dialogue. In an attempt to remedy this the TEU reinforces the focal role of the presidency "in presenting and defending the Union's positions and policies under the CFSP to the outside world" (p. 21), but perpetuates the fragmented nature of foreign policy leadership by involving, where appropriate, both the Troika and the Commission. Improved EPC behaviour at the level of diplomatic and consular missions of member states and Commission Delegations in third countries was promoted (such as exchanging information, joint assessments, and ensuring that common positions and actions are maintained). The assumption was that "unity in presentation and pursuit of action *vis-à-vis* the outside world will promote greater visibility of the Union as an actor on the international stage" (p. 22). While the Belgian Report acknowledged that "[E]fforts are needed to ensure that third countries fully appreciate this role of the Presidency", it is difficult to see quite how this and the general goal of unity were to be advanced under Title V of the Maastricht Treaty. Again, the South African case illustrates the complexity and diversity of the Union's foreign policy character. What was the appropriate level of dialogue? Exclusively at the government-to-government level via either the presidency or the Council? Or via the Commission or Delegation in Pretoria? Practice and behaviour will no doubt eventually establish the Union's international identity; however, South Africa encountered the handicap of dealing with a dialogue partner that was still in the process of defining its own operational procedures and *persona*.

The Final characteristic of CFSP distinguishing it from its EPC forerunner was the attempt to improve efficiency in decision-making procedures. Despite the distinct legal characteristics of CFSP and Community action, the Treaty provides for "unity in the decision-making process, through the single institutional framework" (p. 22). The seeming paradox is resolved, according to the Presidency Report, as the Council's way of operating will be applied to CFSP; in general, decision-making will follow the established Community method whereby policy will be derived from precise proposals, although this right of initiative is shared for foreign policy between the Commission, the member states and the presidency. The possibility of qualified majority voting – seen by some as a radical departure from past collective action – is more conservative in practice; the importance of consensus typical of EPC, will remain an important part of the CFSP procedure. While Article J.3.2 provides for "matters on which decisions are to be taken by a qualified majority", member states also declared that as far as possible they would "avoid preventing a unanimous decision where a qualified majority exists in favour of that decision" (p. 23). Consequently, the formal practice of majority voting may be rare, perhaps non-existant. Decisions will be made in the context of majority voting, but where the threat of a majority decision is best left untested. Again, the South African case will help to establish a precedent and much will depend on the initial choice and experience of defining and implementing common positions and joint actions.

In contrast to the generally *ad hoc* EPC approach to collective action, the mechanics and instruments of a joint action under the TEU are detailed and procedurally exact. First, the European Council decides at regular intervals where to issue new "general guidelines" which form the framework for joint action. On instruction of such "general guidelines from the European Council, that a matter should be the subject of joint action" the Council of the Union, acting on a proposal from any of the bodies with the right of policy initiation, decides on "the principle of joint action" (Article J.3.1) consisting of the main political and operational aspects involved. This includes the scope, objectives, means, procedures and duration of the joint action; what aspects of the policy can be determined by qualified majority voting (J.3.2); and how it is to be funded (J.11.2). The Council also is charged with the responsibility of the overall effectiveness of action. To that end, it considers proposals from the Commission that are necessary for the implementation of the joint action; determines the extent of member states action to be adopted; decides whether national means are to be at the disposal of the joint action; and, whether the joint action will be pursued independently or in concert with third countries or international organizations (Presidency, 1993, p. 24). All joint actions are to be specifically defined and as visible as possible within the normal constraints of confidentiality imposed on foreign policy making.

Thus the purpose and means of the joint action will be stated and the decision "may be published in the Official Journal" under the heading "joint action decided upon by the Council on the basis of Article J.3 of the Treaty on European Union" (p. 25). Where a common position would gain from being made public (in line with the Union's desire for visibility) declarations and press releases can be invoked.

As the description of the enactment of the joint action on South Africa given in the previous section shows, the designated procedures and instruments were followed precisely. The European Council of 29 October set the "general guidelines" and specified that South Africa should be adopted as a subject of joint action. Subsequently, the December Council defined the scope of the joint action (initial election monitoring to be followed by an appropriate cooperation framework); the general and specific objectives (to facilitate the success of the election process and to assist in the democratization and transition process); the means (election funding and deployment of personnel); procedures (the operation of an Election Unit responsible to the Commission); the conditions (the establishment of the TEC); and the duration of the joint action (the Election Unit was to stay until one month after the election's conclusion). Critics pointed to the contrast between the two aspects of the joint action: on the one hand, the highly detailed framework for election support, on the other hand, the almost total absence of specific details on the topic of a cooperation framework. This imbalance reflected the newness of the CFSP procedure had yet to be thought through as the appropriate framework through which to address external relations. It also reflected the reality of the *status quo*: prior to the decision on a joint action, the Community had developed a policy towards the elections that could easily be adopted under this new heading. Conversely, there was no equivalent existing policy on bilateral economic relations that could be adapted in a similar way. There was simply a policy vacuum that the CFSP was unable to fill at such short notice.

The institutional arrangements between the various bodies involved in foreign policy decision-making were also reorganized as a consequence of the CFSP provisions, in particular COREPER-Political Committee relations, the Council Secretariat and the European Parliament. While acknowledging the truism that CFSP is an intergovernmental activity and ultimately shaped by the member states through the Council, the institutional locus of decision-making can potentially be of profound importance. The relationship between POCO and COREPER cannot be adequately understood by exclusive reference to the Maastricht text. According to the TEU Article 151, COREPER is "responsible for preparing the work of the Council and for carrying out the tasks assigned to it by the Council", a situation indicating primacy in the decision-making structure. By way of confirmation, Title V of the Treaty states:

> Without prejudice to Article 151 of the Treaty establishing the European Community, a Political Committee consisting of Political Directors shall monitor the international situation in the areas covered by Common Foreign and Security Policy and contribute to the definition of policies by delivering opinions to the Council at the request of the Council or own its own initiative. It shall also monitor the implementation of agreed policies, without prejudice to the responsibility of the Presidency and the Commission. (Article J.8.5)

Quite how this arrangement will work will be determined by practice and initial experience rather than constitutional interpretation. The assumption was that a successful CFSP necessitated the centralization of decision-making in the Union Council under a "single institutional framework" (Article C) supported by COREPER and the Council Secretariat. Other actors such as the Commission and the Political Committee are not excluded, "but their roles are envisaged in relation to the Council-COREPER-Secretariat command and control centre" (Ludlow, 1993, p. 4). However, the initial signs were that the Political Directors and POCO would play the more influential role and this continuation of an essentially EPC practice was confirmed by the Belgian presidency report. Although the Political Committee's opinions are funnelled through CORE-PER to the Council, effective policy making appears to take place at this lower level with COREPER acting essentially as a rubber stamp for POCO initiatives. Day to day business, such as the preparation and implementation of CFSP positions and decisions that occur between the regular General Affairs Council meetings, is explicitly a POCO competence. Further, the presidency report makes provision for the Political Committee to meet "alongside the Council to give opinions where appropriate, which take into account the latest developments on the current political scene" (1993, p. 26): thus, the COREPER filter can be procedurally by-passed at the request of the Council.

The integration of the former EPC Secretariat into the General Secretariat of the Council is an innovation that, like the COREPER–POCO relationship, will be defined over time. However, it soon became apparent that the Secretariat would play a more demonstrative role than had been the case of the EPC Secretariat. The entry into force of the TEU saw all working parties become designated as Council working parties. On a pragmatic basis, these groups were to be merged to enhance consistency within a single institutional framework. Thus efficiency would be increased as single group agendas would cover CFSP and Community matters. South Africa benefitted from this rationalization, although allowing for CFSP and Community topics to be discussed on a single agenda by a merged working group did not, by itself, solve the problem of policy coordination or distinctions between competences. Except where confidentiality demanded, the existing Community work-ing practices were adopted for CFSP matters discussed in the merged working parties: reports were to assume the normal status of being General Secretariat documents; information was to be circulated among member state capitals, permanent representa-tions and the Commission via the COREU network; and, reports forwarded by COREU to both the Political Committee and COREPER.

The final institutional consequence of the TEU concerned the practical exercise of closer relations with the European Parlia-ment. As explored elsewhere in this volume, the Parliament is well-versed in interpreting the Treaty reforms to its advantage. The presidency report stated that the Union would "attribute the utmost importance to the obligation to inform, in concert with the Commission, and consult Parliament" as provided for in Article J.7. This is to be achieved by the presidency attending, where necessary, the meetings of the Parliament's Committee on External Relations, for the Council Secretariat regularly to attend all such meetings, by participating in plenary debates and providing written information. The presidency is responsible for organizing the procedures for consultation with the Parlia-ment "on the major aspects and fundamental options of the CFSP", including joint actions, and for informing subsequent

Council meetings of Parliament's "reactions, communications, questions, recommendations or resolutions concerning the CFSP" (p. 29). However, it remains to be seen how effective this consultation will prove; it may become more of a *post hoc* courtesy than a meaningful contribution to policy development. Again, the experience of South Africa as a joint action will help to determine whether these stated intentions have any effective substance.

To conclude, the historical summary of the unfolding transition to democracy that began in February 1990 and took more than four years to achieve, illustrated the difficult process of policy adaptation within the European Community. The unmaking of foreign policy, let alone its replacement by an alternative approach, is an arduous and procedurally intricate discipline. Achieving a consensus to repeal policy appeared to be no less hazardous than that needed for imposing a policy. Even under the Maastricht dispensation, the scope of Union action was to prove an area of disagreement. The assumed simplification and efficiency of foreign policy by majority voting appeared to be, at least initially, a federalist chimera. The designation of South Africa as a topic for joint action presented a paradox. On the one hand, it implied an intensification of the policy making process in keeping with the aspirations of the CFSP; yet on the other hand, the content of the joint action was modest and, at least externally, appeared not dissimilar to the former EPC approach to South Africa. Accordingly, questions can be legitimately raised about the relevance of the Maastricht reforms *vis-à-vis* policy towards South Africa. Plus ça change . . .?

4 The 1990s Policy Revisions: Institutions and Actors

The opening chapter of this book disaggregated the various actors in the policy making process; a similar approach is adopted in this chapter. The central question that stems from this approach is whether the disaggregation of actors and institutions necessarily implies policy fragmentation, or whether there is coherence between the different policy making components. Obviously, not all actors are of equal importance in the foreign policy process, and decisions, at least formally, are elite based emphasizing the intergovernmental nature of foreign policy coordination. The complexity of the member state inputs or the operation of the Council demands an analysis specifically dedicated to these topics. The focus of this chapter is not upon these prominent actors. While the Council of Ministers is constrained by member state interests, comparatively minor actors can and do have an influential role to play, either as suppliers of specific information (for example, third country delegations) or as watchful critics (such as the Parliament) provoking action for an otherwise recalcitrant EPC/CFSP procedure. Thus while acknowledging the exclusive decision-making role played by the Council, supported by COREPER, the Political Committee and the Council Secretariat, the pertinent actors examined here are: the Commission; member state third country delegations; ECOMSA and the Programme Coordination Office; the Commission Delegation in Pretoria; and, the European Parliament.

THE COMMISSION

With respect to the role of the Commission and EPC, the impression given in Chapter 1 was of a cohesive and effective politico-bureaucratic organization with clear responsibility and purpose. Yet, the appearance of the Commission as a unified actor is misleading. When represented by its President at the European Council or related forums, the Commission's position is unambiguous. Within the Commission itself such clarity can be obscured by competition between different Commissioners and their respective DGs for autonomy and exclusivity in certain policy areas. This tendency was acerbated in the newly appointed Commission that took office in January 1993.

The key political dilemma was the nomination and appointment of the former Dutch Foreign Minister, Hans van den Broek to the Commission's external relations portfolio: van den Broek had held The Netherlands foreign affairs portfolio from 1982–92 and only stepped down on the guarantee of a Commission appointment. This set the stage for an internal bureaucratic power conflict between at least three DGs and their Commissioners as to who spoke for the Community in its external and foreign relations. Was it van den Broek whose Commission responsibilities were defined as "external political relations" and "common foreign and security policy"; Manuel Marin, Commissioner for Cooperation and Development (DGVIII) whose brief includes Lomé relations; or possibly Sir Leon Brittan, the Commissioner responsible for external economic affairs? The solution adopted in May 1993 was to establish a new Directorate General responsible for external political relations (as distinct from external economic or development relations). The Directorate only began to function officially in the Autumn of 1993 (once the ratification issue in certain member states had been resolved). It was composed of six sections divided according to both geographical area and subjects. South Africa was designated as part of directorate D which incorporated sub-Saharan Africa, Latin America and the Middle East. Importantly, key desk officers who previously dealt with South Africa in both DGI and DGVIII were transferred to this new directorate. One interpretation of this reorganization is that bureaucratically the balance between the respective DGs changed with profound implications for policy advice and agenda setting. After September 1993 the necessary expertise for policy formation was primarily concentrated in DGIA, to a lesser extent in DGI (who were responsible for proposing the new cooperation framework), with DGVIII's role limited to the Special Programme.

Defining the precise competences for each DG with respect to South Africa was a sensitive issue and clearly there were areas of overlap and possible dispute. Organizationally, competences were discreet; however, the practice of working together was the only sound way of designating boundaries. The post-Maastricht approach was to recognize a three-tier structure with respect to the EC's global competences: a distinction was made between trade matters (DGI), development (DGVIII) and now political affairs (DGIA). DGIA was involved in all aspects of policy regarding South Africa, whereas the trade and GATT issues relating to the new bilateral economic framework were, technically, the exclusive domain of DGI, except where there were political overtones. Clearly, the potential for a conflict of interests existed here and there was an early indication of this competition in the drafting of the Community policy guidelines in September 1993 for supporting the transition to democracy in South Africa.

In comprehending the intricacies of Community foreign policy, intra-bureaucratic rivalry is of the highest importance. The changing EC policy towards South and southern Africa in the 1990s captures this central feature extremely well. In a sense the South African case serves as a litmus test for the success or failure of the Commission's reorganization. While CFSP is determined at the Community's highest political level, bureaucratic inputs into the policy making process are not to be dismissed: it is an influential factor that can determine exactly how a foreign policy is perceived and can therefore shape the possible type of response the Union can make. Whether South Africa is seen as a "development" issue, or as a third country "trade" issue, or more spectacularly as primarily a foreign policy "political" issue is a significant policy making factor.

The 7 December Council statement on the scope of the joint action posed a potential threat to the traditional competences assigned to DGI. The joint action contained a commitment to establishing an appropriate cooperation relationship; but under what framework was this to be conducted? Through the Union and the intergovernmentalism of CFSP, or through the traditional framework of external economic relations conducted under the auspices of the Community by the Commission? If DGI of the Commission did not control of the cooperation negotiations this would imply a major invasion of the Commission's external relations competences. The inclusion of economic cooperation within the joint action potentially diluted the role and authority of DGI as it incorporated the decision-making structure of Article J, and not just the Treaty of Rome. The Commission therefore substitutes, at least in theory, its exclusive right of initiative in external relations for a shared right with the member states and presidency. The maintenance of traditional as well as legal areas of competence in the face of Union joint action, will remain an area of contention as the *modus operandi* of the Maastricht reforms mature. This struggle illustrates the potential bureaucratic immobilism of conducting external affairs under a divided rather than unified legal procedure.

South Africa also provided an illustration of the maturity of EPC and of the Commission's legitimation as a participant. The innovation of creating an external "political" affairs portfolio to complement the existing "economic" external relations confirmed both the Commission's growing political involvement, and, in one sense, the final abandonment of the spurious dichotomy between economics and politics that had been the defining characteristic of the much of the early history of political cooperation. The acknowledgement of a specific CFSP responsibility for van den Broek underlined the evolving nature of the Commission under the Maastricht Treaty: with the ratification of the Treaty delayed until late 1993, South Africa became one of the first areas to explore just how this new arrangement would work in practice. It provided a clear case study for examining a Community policy that cut across the Commission's policy sector demarcations. While the overlap between policy spheres has been a typical "spillover" theme since the origin of the Community, South Africa provided an extreme example and tested the ability of the Commission to coordinate policy and maintain internal consistency. Thus the question of consistency is not just between the various institutions and actors involved in the foreign policy process, it also relates to intra-Commission policy making.

If this situation was complicated and challenged policy consistency, the abolition of the EPC Secretariat and the creation of a new directorate within the Council Secretariat specifically for external relations and CFSP, succeeded in exacerbating matters considerably. The General Secretariat is responsible for providing the Council presidency with additional inputs: this new directorate was a potential threat to the Commission's policy making and policy initiation role. The EPC Secretariat had been relatively small, was exclusively intergovernmental drawing staff from the member states in accordance with the Troika procedure. A policy planning function was implicitly forbidden by the member states in their 28 February 1986 decision "which made it plain that its task was to assist the Presidency and that it had no autonomous attributions of its own" (Nuttall, 1992, p. 20). Nonetheless, its establishment did mark "an important change in the ethos of EPC, which became more bureaucratic as it became more efficient" (ibid., p. 257). The new Council Secretariat directorate was introduced on 1 January 1994 and was composed of twenty-four staff: twelve permanent Council Secretariat employees and twelve seconded from member states for periods ranging from three to five years. In addition to the Director General, there were two deputies for external relations and one for CFSP matters. In further contrast with its forerunner, all twenty-four staff salaries, travel and administrative budgets were funded by the Council Secretariat, not the member states. It remains to be seen whether this enhanced expertise in external relations and CFSP will make a significant impact on the role and effectiveness of the Council presidency. The implicit threat is on the Commission's policy implementation and advisory role. The Council Secretariat could prove to be a challenger for both DGI and DGIA: arguably, the division between DGI and IA will weaken the influence of the Commission *vis-à-vis* the Council Secretariat. Just at the time when the Commission decided to split external political and economic competences, the Secretariat adopted the opposite strategy and combined these under the same directorate. The calibre of their respective staffs and the emerging "foreign policy cultures" unique to each will determine the medium term outcome of this new and additional point of policy competition. While competing policy options are generally associated with better policy decisions, this may be at the cost of consistency within the various component parts of the Union's new foreign policy structure.

The political role of the Commissioners may be of potential importance in future Union policy. As noted above, the division of the external relations portfolio together with the involvement of the DG responsible for Development presents the potential for the South African policy to become enmeshed within an intra-bureaucratic battle over areas of competence, prestige and authority within the Commission and between Commissioners. A less conspiratorial interpretation suggests that this potential bureaucratic conflict is unlikely. The record shows that the various DGs responsible for South Africa have been successful in cooperating internally and coordinating external relations and development policy. It is tempting, but wrong, to assign the Commissioners themselves with a directly political policy making role. Throughout the history of Community policy on South Africa there are no examples of inter-DG disputes having to be resolved at the level of the Commissioner. Any such conflicts have been resolved internally at lower levels of coordination.

The divisions within the Commission as well as between the Commission and the other actors in the Community foreign policy making structure are important to the issue of agenda setting. Who controls the South African question? How is it defined? Where is policy made? One way of approaching this central debate is to examine the Commission's role within an agenda management theoretical framework. This approach has been used in the past to illustrate the complexity of EPC and South Africa (see, Holland, 1987; 1988a, Chapter 7). The agenda management approach posits that policy definition is a prerequisite for problem solving. The logic is simple: a decision as to the ideal or most effective policy choice is dependent on how the issue is perceived. At best, a wrongly or poorly defined problem prohibits an informed discussion of options: at worst it can suggest a completely inappropriate perspective and solution. Two stages within this process are instrumental: first, the problem definition itself; and second, the process of agenda management of the problem so defined. As one commentary stresses, it is this latter condition that is crucial as some policies are intentionally formulated in such a way simply "to remove (or exclude) an issue from the political agenda, involving no real attempt to solve a particular problem" (Stringer and Richardson, 1980, p. 23).

In past studies of EC policy towards South Africa the agenda management explanation has been used to powerful effect. Up until 1984 the "problem" had been effectively defined out of existence as:

The EC displayed the Code of Conduct which sought to remove apartheid; they acted in unison; in consequence, a potentially volatile and divisive political issue was simply re-defined in non-contentious terms and legitimately removed from the political agenda. (Holland, 1988, p. 148)

Despite the failure to exclude the issue from political debate after 1984, the agenda management perspective retained its analytic utility as a persuasive approach for the 1985–89 period. Redefining the issue as a foreign policy problem took time, and to that extent those member states who had been instrumental in the mis-definition of the problem earlier were successful in "buying time", delaying as they did the imposition of economic sanctions until the end of 1985. Even this concession saw the solution to the problem mis-defined: the limited sanctions chosen could not lead to the realization of the Community's prime policy objective: the abolition of apartheid.

In these earlier periods those responsible for the problem definition were the member states and, but to a much lesser extent, the Commission. With the composite effect of the SEA and the Maastricht process, the Commission's role as an agenda manager has significantly increased in foreign affairs, particularly in the case of South Africa. The internal competition within the Commission for foreign policy influence (specifically including the South African example) as described in the first section of this chapter correctly identifies the continuing relevance of an agenda management model for understanding Union policy. What is the correct definition of the post-1992 South African issue? Is it a continued foreign policy problem? A development issue? A question of aid? Or should the problem really be defined in terms of a normal third country economic trading relationship? Thus the key agenda managers have become the bureaucratic actors – the Commissioners responsible for the respective DGs – usurping to a significant degree the role of the political actors who controlled the problem prior to the 1990s. This change was a consequence of the general policy consensus that existed at the political elite level from the early 1990s onwards and their willingness (or acquiescence) to allow the Commission a dominant policy initiative role. Though this competence was to be shared under the Maastricht provisions, contemporary EC-South African policy has been tantamount to the Commission's policy domain. The policy disputes that do occur, the debates about defining the problem and setting objectives, are primarily within the Commission bureaucracy and no longer between member states, resulting in a remarkable bureaucratization of a foreign policy issue.

The first evidence of the different definitions of the South African issue was evident in mid-1993 when Commissioners Brittan and van den Broek each outlined their policy initiatives for a new South Africa. At this stage which, if either, of the two views would predominate had yet to be decided. The occasion for this rare public example of competing Commission policies was the first ever conference devoted to the topic of the EC and South Africa organized by Forum Europe in Brussels. The South African Government, ANC and other political organizations attended and presented their views. The intervention of two addresses from the Commission was indicative of three things: the division within the Commission itself; the importance of the South African question; and, signified by his absence, the declining influence of Marin, Commissioner for Development. This third point is perhaps the most significant as it was emblematic of DGVIII's inability to define South Africa within an exclusively development framework such as the Lomé arrangement.

The key distinguishing elements of each approach can be summarized as follows. Van den Broek attempted to place South Africa within a broad foreign policy perspective and cited the recent European Council declaration on South Africa as the current Community position. The scale of the EC's existing commitment (especially that provided through the Special Programme administered by DG VIII) was emphasized, as was the new policy of supporting the organization of the election and providing observers. However, van den Broek was hesitant to specify a particular framework for a new relationship: rather he called for an "in depth reflection" on the part of the Community so that once a non-racial South Africa was in place appropriate frameworks could be agreed upon. The nearest the Commissioner got to stating EC policy objectives was an awareness that growth and business confidence were needed to alleviate the social problems of poverty and inequality. The main thrust of the address, however, was the necessity for regional stability and South Africa's role as a regional partner. In this respect, the advantages of regional integration along a Community inspired model were outlined and an offer to "provide advice and cooperation" to achieve this given (van den Broek, 1993, p. 10).

In contrast to the broad canvass and generalities outlined by van den Broek, the complementary address by Sir Leon Brittan provided a precise and uncompromising assessment of the economic dilemmas that confronted a future democratic South Africa. First, mythical expectations were exposed: South Africa's potential as a regional catalyst was challenged; the belief that massive international and Community aid would be forthcoming was rejected; and the presumption that foreign investment would automatically return questioned. A "sober look at the reality of today's South Africa" was called for that recognized the limited role that the EC can play, the need for sound economic growth and policies to enhance foreign investor confidence (Brittan, 1993, p. 1). Thus Brittan advocated a competitive business environment, the end of import substitution and the dismantling of all forms of protectionism, much of which had been in operation contrary to GATT requirements. A market economy based on the principles of good governance could only provide the needed political stability which was the prerequisite for growth. Within the recognition that South Africa's solution lay with the Republic itself and not with Europe, a broad framework for cooperation was called for highlighting: a political dialogue encompassing regional security issues and human rights; trade and investment provisions; continuing development assistance in the form of the existing positive measures; enhancement of the democratization process together with a Community role in voter education and monitoring the conduct of the elections.

These contrasts not withstanding, there was also a notable similarity in approaches presented by Brittan and van den Broek which collectively further underline the marginalization of a development-centric approach. Both sought to limit the aid and development role of the EC and emphasized the necessity for business and trade to act as the catalyst for improved social conditions. Both were in agreement that the exact nature of the new relationship was less important than a commitment to normal economic relations. The definition of South Africa as an exclusive development issue was replaced by one that combined various strands from formerly distinct policy areas. Flexibility and multi-level relations were the new demands.

DGIA's ability to lead the Commission perspective was significantly constrained by the delay in realizing its complete staffing establishment. Despite being introduced in the new Delors Commission of January 1993, it was almost eighteen months before DGIA was near to being fully operational with a staffing level of around 250. The problem was a combination of lengthy procedures for the transfer of staff from other DGs and attaining additional funding for new appointments. Consequently, while

DGIA was involved in framing the joint action, it was considerably disadvantaged *vis-à-vis* DGI. For example, as late as January 1994, on average only 30 per cent of staff assigned to geographical directorates were in place. In directorate D (which included responsibility for South Africa) four out of ten assigned positions were filled at this time. Given that this directorate was responsible for Latin America, Africa and the Middle East, the modest personnel resources posed considerable limitations.

Without pre-empting the commentary of Chapter 6, the eventual decision on the shape of future European-South African relations suggests two interpretations on the outcome of this intra-Commission confrontation. One alternative argues that DGI successfully retained control over its legitimate scope of external economic relations and established its co-authority with DGIA in foreign affairs. Alternatively, the outcome was characterized as a result of compromise and indicated a new intra-Commission cohesiveness born out of external institutional challenges, particularly from the Council General secretariat. Whichever alternative is preferred, clearly the role of the Commission as a foreign policy actor has been reinforced.

MEMBER STATE MISSIONS IN THIRD COUNTRIES

From the Brussels perspective, the majority of documented past EPC coordination took place through the restricted COREU network that links the presidency, member states and Commission. Outside the COREU communications EPC coordination took place through regular (bi-monthly) meetings of the various geographical and sectoral Working Groups (such as the Africa Working Group) which prepare, by consensus, the meetings of the Political Committee (composed of the member state Foreign Affairs Political Directors or equivalents). Their decisions are eventually endorsed by the Twelve acting within the framework of political cooperation (sitting usually as either the General Affairs or Foreign Ministers Council). The outcome can take the form of declarations, definition of a common position, policy recommendations, etc., and is represented through the presidency.

While acknowledging that Community foreign policy is primarily Brussels-centric and political elite driven, the expression of common policies by the member state embassies in third countries can make an important policy contribution, both as a source of information and of innovation. In tandem with the signing of the SEA, the procedures for what was then EPC coordination in third countries became formalized in the 28 February 1986 decision of the Council of Foreign Ministers. It stated:

1. Member State's missions and Commission Delegations shall intensify their co-operation in third countries and international organizations in the following areas:

(a) exchange of political and economic information;
(b) pooling of information on administrative and practical problems;
(c) mutual assistance in the material and practical sphere;
(d) communications;
(e) exchange of information and drawing up of joint plans in case of local crises;
(f) security measures;
(g) consular matters;
(h) health, particularly in the field of health and medical facilities;
(i) educational matters (schooling);
(j) information;
(k) cultural affairs;
(l) development aid.

(Foreign Ministers, 1986, Pt. II.1)

Furthermore, member state ambassadors and, where applicable, Commission representatives in third countries were instructed to "meet regularly in order to co-ordinate their views and prepare joint reports, either on the request of the Political Committee or on their own initiative when the situation requires" (Pt. II.2). The Political Committee was also empowered to call for periodic reports from third country member state missions "with a view to strengthening" cooperation (Pt. II.3). Lastly, embassies were to provide "help and assistance" to other EC nationals who were without representation in a specific third country (a provision that was subsequently enhanced and incorporated in the Maastricht Treaty). (Pt. II.4). There has been no formal revision of these procedures since 1986; in general their application has become widespread.

An earlier review of the level of diplomatic coordination between the member states represented in South Africa focused on three presidencies: in chronological order (1986/7), those of the UK, Belgium and Denmark. From this analysis the following conclusions were drawn. First, EPC procedure seemed "relatively neglected in South Africa" when contrasted with the high level of involvement on the part of member states in Brussels (Holland, 1988a, p. 128). The "importance" of the issue for the Council and the member states was not reflected, at least procedurally, in Pretoria. While joint meetings were held at Head of Mission level, informal cooperation was the more important avenue. Second, sharing of information – political and economic – was limited, reflecting the natural competition between a number of member states in their bilateral relations with South Africa. Third, the embassies played "only a nominal role in the positive and negative measures adopted by the Community", with the application of the Code of Conduct the major involvement in policy (ibid., p. 127). Fourth, for the smaller states, the role of the presidency was limited locally; consequently "EPC as a procedure was not utilized fully" (ibid., p. 128). The rationale used to explain this behaviour drew on three elements. The abnormal relations between the EC and South Africa made, by definition, "normal diplomatic activity fairly meaningless . . . The very 'political' nature of the South African issue has largely rendered the procedure for EPC redundant" (ibid., p. 128). The argument of size was also crucial: the Belgian embassy operated with a minimal diplomatic staff and Denmark was not officially represented. And lastly, the tradition of strong bilateral ties between principally the UK, Germany, Portugal, and The Netherlands and South Africa tended to undermine the *communautaire* perspective.

These conclusions regarding EPC third country procedures during a period of sanctions exposed a significant degree of bilateral freedom. EPC was not an exclusive activity at the expense of bilateral relations, but a complementary one running "parallel to, rather than in unison with, political cooperation" (ibid., p. 130). In summary:

there seems to be no necessary link between intensified political cooperation and the relative importance' of a third country.

. . . while it still remains the case that diplomatic cooperation cannot exceed the limits set by the national governments in EPC, in the South African example the emphasis was inverted. Political cooperation was significantly lower than that exhibited in Brussels.

. . . many of the administrative and procedural recommendations remained untried by the EC delegations in South Africa. (Ibid., p. 130)

To balance these reservations, it was also clear that a new diplomatic "norm" of consultation had taken root: diplomatic attitudes, if not concrete procedures had changed.

These conclusions were based on the three presidencies spanning June 1986 to December 1987. To estimate how, if at all, political cooperation had developed in South Africa during the 1990s, an analysis of the same three presidencies – those of the UK, Denmark and then Belgium in the revised chronological order – was undertaken (covering the period June 1992 to December 1993). In many respects the changes were remarkable, in others a natural continuation and progression in political cooperation occurred.

First, both the formal and informal levels of cooperation were intensified. Perhaps understandably given the nature and content of EPC, informal contact became intense and possibly of greater impact than the established formal procedures. The First Secretary responsible for EPC of the host presidency was in almost daily contact with his or her counterparts. Taking the British presidency as an example, it was seen as the task of both the Ambassador and the First Secretary to brief the other EC embassies, particularly those with comparatively small contingents, on the daily political developments. Obviously, the size of the UK Delegation made this task easier – they could afford the luxury of having a representative attend every daily session of the CODESA negotiations at Kempton Park. But it is emblematic of the new ethic of shared political information that this procedure had become normal practice, and the informal exchange of information was characteristic of all member state presidencies during the early 1990s.

Size of delegation no longer appeared necessarily to be a positive indication of involvement. The two most important policy announcements of the post-sanctions period (the May Development initiative and the June policy statement) occurred under the auspices of the Danish presidency, despite the delegation in South Africa having a diplomatic complement of just two individuals. In fact "smaller" countries can often have a distinct advantage over larger ones in specific cases of foreign policy. The traditional priority placed on South Africa by the Danish Government and various political parties and lobby groups emphasized this topic within EPC. Given the relative small scale of the diplomatic resources at the presidency's disposal, it was much more likely to rely on its third country mission for policy innovation than, say, one of the larger traditional countries with South African interests. Further, the embassy's relationship with the Africa desk in Copenhagen went beyond the normal level of cooperation; almost daily contact made the policy input direct and influential and, consequently, the presidency a resounding success. Thus the size of the Danish and Belgian missions (three for the latter) does not, by itself, disadvantage their presidencies impact or involvement when compared with the British Delegation which remains the largest EC representation.

For both large and small embassies alike, holding the presidency is an administrative strain. The presidency is responsible for producing all drafts of documents and the pressure can be intense, especially in a politically volatile environment like South Africa. For the smaller embassies, it is generally the case that no additional staff are deployed to assist with the presidency: additional assistance may be provided for the larger delegations. For this and other related reasons, the prospect of annual presidencies periodically raised in Brussels is met with a degree of horror by most, if not all, third country delegations. The current *modus operandi* copes with the present situation; any extension of the presidency would necessitate a fundamental revision on how this was managed and conducted in all locations. The current burden has been lightened somewhat by the 1993 decision to abandon the formal reporting of the Code of Conduct. This activity was particularly onerous for member state missions with significant commercial relations in South Africa. Rather than spend time collecting and collating individual and summary reports, member state diplomats can devote greater energies to encouraging bilateral investment without the perceived imposition of the Code upon European business activity.

A distinction has to be made between the sharing of political as opposed to economic information. At the political level there is almost complete sharing of information: a limited range of issues remain exclusively bilateral, but these are very much in the minority. For example, bilateral aid to the ANC, or another political organization, would not be considered as part of the EPC collective process. In general, political dialogues between member state missions are frank and open. While personal chemistry between diplomats is an obvious advantage in fostering this process in South Africa, there has developed an almost institutionalized atmosphere for the informal dissemination of common political knowledge. This stands in contrast with the level of exchange of economic information. Many member states have competing economic interests and it is in these areas that traditional diplomatic behaviour understandably remains. The major competitors in this respect are the UK and Germany, both of whom have substantial levels of trade with South Africa and are natural rivals for business. In addition, Italy and some of the medium and smaller EC states also have both traditional as well as new interests with Pretoria: France, in particular, increased the strength of its embassy for explicitly commercial reasons. Thus CFSP operates as a political concept, not an economic one.

With the lifting of the Community prohibition on cross accreditation of military attachés between member states and Pretoria (effective from 6 October 1993), both the UK and Germany resumed the military relationship and had attachés in place before the end of the year. The rationale was partly strategic, partly to assist the peace initiative, but also partly economic. Military sales were integral to both countries external business interests. In this respect there was some resentment over the continuing French military relationship with South Africa through out the period of sanctions, most notably the sale of French military aircraft.

The formal operation of political cooperation assumed the following basic pattern irrespective of which member state held the presidency. Monthly meetings were held between member states at the level of Heads of Mission, with additional lower level meetings occurring on a more irregular basis. The presidency would circulate the agenda in advance: this would generally consist of a review of current political events; political issues for discussion; and, general business. No formal conclusions are drawn or a record ever kept: again, the principal purpose is to disseminate and share information. Subsequently, the presidency Head of Mission reports to the EC's Africa Working Group, who in turn advise the Political Committee and COREPER and in turn, the Political or General Affairs Council in Brussels. By way of example, the following items were discussed in the October Heads of Mission meeting under the Belgian presidency. The respective representatives reported on the recent European visit by Mandela (to Portugal, the UK and Belgium); the possible constitutional referendum as proposed by de Klerk was discussed; and, the EC's contribution to the election process was further examined in the light of the September Troika "Taskforce" report on the subject which was due to be discussed at a November General Affairs Council meeting in Brussels. This report examined options related to the number of observers needed, the number proposed by the EC, the financing of the operation and how the EC's contribution should be coordinated with the overall international contribution. While the member state embassies can provide certain initiatives, their work is controlled and dictated to a large degree from their home capitals. Therefore, some topics were excluded from consideration: for example, local views on the appropriateness of Lomé or an alternative bilateral association agreement were not canvassed.

Such a direct sharing of information and member state coordination is a necessary, indeed perhaps essential, function of the presidency. While in theory all joint information on the topic of South Africa should be copied to third country embassies via the COREU network, invariably this is not the case. EC Heads of Mission meetings serve to repair any information vacua that may have occurred. Consequently, there was a remarkable similarity in views among the Twelve and their diplomatic representatives. Only one outstanding issue was divisive: how to ensure the participation of Buthelezi and the Inkatha Freedom Party in the election process. Even this division was one of tactics, not substance, as there was consensus on the objective sought. To the one extreme it was seen as necessary to make further concessions in order to accommodate Buthelezi; to the other it was suggested that a firm EC stand would be more beneficial, with a range of Community opinion spread across these alternatives. Political cooperation at both the Brussels and local level had successfully engendered a collective and consistent approach.

From the third country perspective the historical emphasis has been on bilateral relations, rather than a Community focus. As was demonstrated in the sanctions period, the importance of EC-level action, the implications of the Single Market, and so on, were only vaguely understood by the then South African Government. However, during the 1990s there has been a growing awareness of the EC dimension in tandem with, rather than replacing, the traditional bilateral perspective. This process was complicated by the diverse nature of political authority in the transition phase in South Africa: formally, the Government remained the authoritative legislative actor; informally, the views of the ANC and CODESA were paramount; and, after December 1993 the Transitional Executive Council held joint responsibility. It was often unclear when and with whom Europe should or could establish a dialogue; or vice versa, how and on what basis these various South African representative bodies could formalize relations with the Community. The various member states also encouraged the creation of bilateral links, for example between the ANC and Britain or Germany, and to some extent unintentionally blurred the definition of the EC's unique relationship. In addition, the Troika had been used increasingly infrequently as a form of Community representation throughout the 1990s. This reflected the normalization of relations: with the release of Mandela, the removal of apartheid legislation and the gradual reduction in human rights abuses, there were simply less occasions on which it became necessary to issue joint démarche. Despite these handicaps the impact and publicity afforded to the Special Programme had done more to establish the EC's individuality than the previous policy of sanctions. European sanctions were a minor contribution in comparison with the actions taken by the international community: in contrast, the positive development measures established the Community as the leading international actor in the post-apartheid context.

An interesting feature of third country cooperation as expressed in South Africa is the high and intense level of interaction that has developed without the presence and catalyst of a Commission Delegation. Traditionally, Delegations regard the facilitation of formal EPC contacts as one of their tasks, ensuring, for example, that the member state embassies do convene regular meetings which the Delegation attends. Perhaps the intense political nature of South Africa guaranteed the operation of EPC irrespective of any Commission stimulant. The opening of a full Delegation (replacing the Programme Coordination Office) in early 1994 was not, therefore, in response to any absence of political cooperation or collective action. The member states and their respective presidencies had already institutionalized EPC/CFSP at a level that it was difficult to improve upon. Consequently, the opening of the Delegation was symbolic of a normalization in economic and trade relations than of any perceived defect in foreign policy coordination between the ten embassies of the EC with representation in South Africa (Ireland and Luxembourg were without representation prior to 1994).

Interestingly, the one member state to renew its diplomatic links with South Africa during the 1990s was Denmark. During the previous Danish presidency (June–December 1987) the representative role and presidency functions were carried out on Denmark's behalf by the embassy of the Federal Republic of Germany, the succeeding country to hold the rotating Community presidency (Holland, 1988, p. 127). Thus, the 1993 Danish presidency provided it with the first opportunity to directly engage in policy making and perhaps explains the particularly important role played by its embassy. The objective of the Danish presidency was within its six mouth tenure to persuade the EC to elaborate a policy for relations with the new South Africa: a double policy track was proposed – the removal of the remaining sanctions and a commitment to a broad-based development approach. Denmark was largely successful in both these aspirations: the removing of sanctions was agreed to in principle in the June statement (although enacted incrementally over the following months; and, the development content of the Special Programme was maintained, although a commitment to further development assistance through Lomé was not realized. In addition, in the Spring of 1993, the Danish presidency was the first to raise the issue of Community involvement in the election process. The subsequent Troika "Taskforce" that reported in September 1993 was the direct result of this initiative. Collectively, these contributions were tantamount to a substantial input and the Danish presidency can rightly be regarded as the most active in terms of policy innovation since the imposition of sanctions in 1986. And all this was achieved with a local diplomatic staff of two: no additional staffing was employed. In line with the comments already made on the influence of "size" and EPC coordination, arguably the smallness of the Danish Delegation proved a major asset. Consistency of line and interpretation were easier to maintain as the Ambassador was resident in Cape Town throughout the presidency and the First Secretary based in Pretoria. Each had a clearly defined representative role that made liaising uncomplicated. As the following section on the Programme Office suggests, significant policy impact can be achieved in third countries on incredibly limited human resources.

In conclusion, South Africa presents a very clear and good example of the developed and cohesive nature of EPC as expressed in third countries. In contrast with the comparable findings from six years earlier, EPC was no longer "relatively neglected" at the fringes, embassies did not play a nominal role, and EPC was characterized by a maximum rather than minimum utilization of the procedures for foreign policy coordination. The sharing of political information had become established, the comparative size of the different delegations was no longer an impediment to an effective presidency, and the changed political nature of the foreign policy issue produced enhanced consensus which reflected the "importance" of the topic. This latter contradiction of the 1988 findings supports earlier academic work that suggested that the relative "importance" of the third country was directly and positively related to the degree and effectiveness of cooperation (Bot, 1984, p. 155).

Two elements remained consistent over the period. First, bilateral ties and traditions were not subsumed within the collective EPC relationship, but continued to play an important role parallel with EPC. Second, the informal characteristic of political cooperation remained essential to its success and gave greater substance and effect to the formal organizational and procedural aspect of policy coordination. However, neither of these conditions should be interpreted as necessarily anti-*communautaire*: the political cooperation dialogue in South Africa has matured to the extent that bilateral interests are no longer seen as undermining or being incompatible with a collective approach; and, the intensity of cooperation has blurred what were previously important distinctions between formal and informal practice. One possible general explanation for this closer and increasingly effective EPC is the transition process in South Africa demanded a greater degree of information and discussion than is normally the case in third countries with stable political systems. No one actor had an advantage based on historical or culture links; the game was not zero-sum, but rather through EPC all member states could gain. This transition phase also gave greater opportunity to the presidency to launch initiatives, as indicated by the Danish experience.

THE PROGRAMME COORDINATION OFFICE AND ECOMSA

Past diplomatic relations between South Africa and the EC have been abnormal. No direct Community representation (in the form of a Commission Delegation) existed and for most of the 1980s contact with South African officials was limited to purely formal procedural duties. Prior to the 1990s none of the Commission officials responsible for policy towards South Africa had ever visited the country in an official capacity and informal diplomatic dialogue was discouraged. This situation persisted despite the existence of a South African Mission (established in 1971) attached directly to the EC in Brussels. Community representation within South Africa during this time was delegated through the country holding the six-monthly presidency, or occasionally (and often signifying a new crisis) through a visiting Troika. During the 1990s relations began to normalize and two developments signified the emerging institutionalization of relations: the establishment of a Coordination Office; and, the participation of the EC Observer Mission, ECOMSA.

The normalization of the relationship began to develop in February 1991 with the establishment of the Programme Coordination Office which assumed responsibility for the Community's Special Programme (see Chapter 5 for further details). The Office did not have the equivalent status or functions normally attributed to a full EC Delegation. First, it was staffed by three "Europeans" and four local project officers, making it considerably smaller than the average full Delegation. Second, the scope of its activities were limited explicitly to administering and coordinating the Special Programme. Third, its status was informal: it was not a diplomatic post, did not enjoy normal diplomatic immunity and therefore did not "represent" the Community formally. And fourth, it was funded out of the Special Programme budget and not the Commission budget as was normally the case.

Why was this unusual, indeed unique, form of association within the EC's global relations selected by the Community as the appropriate mechanism for establishing institutional relations? The choice reflected the political considerations and the hesitant consensus that existed for normalizing relations. Two competing tensions existed within the Community. On the one hand, the European Parliament had voiced its opposition to a formal relationship and its power of veto over new agreements was a decided threat; consequently, a less formal structure was considered in order to avoid parliamentary disapproval. On the other hand, a number of member states were unhappy about the existing arrangements for the supervision and execution of the Special Programme which, it was suggested, was too distant (organized as it was exclusively through the four South African NGOs) and lacked normal Commission oversight and control. No other EC international programme had such a distant line of command. Consequently, some form of direct accountability and Commission responsibility was requested particularly as a new direction for the Programme was needed to respond to the changing political context of the 1990s. The resulting compromise was the invention and establishment of the Coordination Office. It did not have any formal ties to the South African Government, did not invoke diplomatic status and therefore did not confer or even imply "recognition" of the South African authorities. Perhaps for this sensitive political reason the staff employed to undertake the EC's tasks were not Commission *fonctionaires* (permanent civil servants), but contract employees hired from outside the Commission hierarchy. It has to be acknowledged also, the three individuals chosen had considerable comparative development experience (for example in Namibia) and were ideally suitable. As noted above, staff funding through the Special Programme emphasized the informal position of the Coordination Office.

This creative solution was not without some internal contradictions. The Office's competences were limited to the Special Programme and it reported, at least formally, to DGVIII. The office was not officially responsible to the member states through

EPC procedures or for any other Commission activities. This formal delimitation was ignored in practice. Other Directorate-Generals in Brussels made requests to the Office for information which, although not part of its function, were accommodated. The head of the Coordination Office attended the regular Heads of Mission EPC meetings and was a full participant in the member state discussions pertaining to development. In theory the Office's precise role was informal and distinct; in practice institutional boundaries were blurred and it was an integrated aspect of Community behaviour despite lacking formal endorsement.

The second example of normalization and institutionalization became apparent in October 1992 with the arrival of ECOMSA. The task of this fifteen person group was to observe, to assist the peace process, and to work closely with the other international observer missions and with the National Peace Accord structures. This innovation, while initially modest in personnel, was indicative of both Europe's commitment to an involvement in all aspects of the South African process, and of its wider desire to become an active international actor. ECOMSA provided vital expertise which was put to great use in training and advising the European Union Election Unit on logistical and security matters.

Both these forms of institutionalized relations were precursors to a more traditional and comprehensive approach – the creation of full diplomatic, political and commercial relations realized through the inauguration of the EC's first Delegation in South Africa.

THE COMMISSION DELEGATION

The June 1993 Council statement for the first time publicly committed the EC to establishing a Delegation once the TEC was in place (although a decision in principle had been made and the Head of Delegation designate chosen almost a year previously). The eventual accreditation of the Head of Delegation to Pretoria in December 1993 and the actual opening of the Delegation in early 1994 was emblematic of the "normalization of diplomatic relations between the Community and its Member States and South Africa" (Commission, 1993b, p. 5). Normalization would also allow for a comprehensive and strong political dialogue (either bilateral – EC presidency–South Africa – or via the Troika) covering such questions as regional security, human rights and non-proliferation. And obviously, there were economic aspects related to normal bilateral economic relations. In another sense it was emblematic of a specially privileged status as EC Delegations are not situated in all, or indeed most, third countries and their location is coveted. Eventually, the informal structures that had characterized the limited past relations were to give way to the typical institution dialogues established between all EC Delegations and their third country hosts.

The Delegation planned an accredited staff of 25 (a quarter *fonctionaires*, the remainder locally employed staff), making it an above average sized Delegation. Logistical, administrative and practical problems delayed the effective establishment of the Delegation: as late as the end of May 1994 only a skeleton staff was in place. The first Head of Delegation, Erwan Fouere, had formerly served as the Commission representative in Mexico and was sensitive to the development needs of a first world–third world country. Whereas the Coordination Office was responsible directly and exclusively to DGVIII, the Delegation was under the control of the new DGIA which in November 1993, after a protracted inter-DG struggle, had usurped the former role played by DGI and assumed responsibility for relations with all the Commission's third country Missions. This involved some 700 Commission employees. From both a bureaucratic and a foreign policy perspective this change was important. While those staff seconded from other DGs (especially DGI and DGVIII) were still to be appointed by their respective Commissioners, DGIA now exercised the right to nominate the Head, Deputy Head, administrative and political staff in all the Commission's 110 third country Delegations. Prior to this, staffing decisions were broadly shared along geographical lines between DGs I, IA and VIII. In addition to DGIA's new appointment dominance, it was agreed with respect to

the right of co-management for the other officials, Hans van den Broek, Commissioner responsible for External Political Relations, will ensure the management of the personnel as a whole assigned to missions for the other Directorate Generals in so far as they are part of Delegations. (*Agence Europe*, 11 November 1993, no. 6105, p. 7)

The implications emanate far beyond the case of South Africa: career advancement for senior Commission employees through overseas posting as Head or Deputy Head of Delegation has come under the control of the Commissioner for DGIA and not the Commissioner for whom the individual my have previously worked. Whether intentional or not, a consequence this approach may be a deterioration in staff-Commissioner relations, divide and rule replacing loyalties that had previously been absolute and not shared. This break with past practice may be the focus of intra-Commission rivalry and conflict. It is too early to comment during its first year of operation, but the possibility exists that the vast majority of future Heads of Delegation may in fact be drawn exclusively from DG IA personnel.

The functions of the Delegation went beyond those narrowly defined for the Coordination Office and mirrored, in general, the typical role played by Delegations globally – those of communication, information, and the identification and promotion of EU and bilateral interests. In specific relation to South Africa, three basic policy pillars were identified: the framework for bilateral trade; raising the EU's profile within South Africa; and, development assistance. First, economic and trade liberalization within the context of GATT was the framework within which bilateral trade was considered. While the initial decision on the specific components of such a relationship were under discussion prior to the Delegations establishment and the determining decisions largely the purvey of DGI in Brussels, the Delegation was expected to be involved in defining the details of the framework once the core decisions had been made. For example, the Delegation would be instrumental in instigating dialogues with industrial and trade associations, chambers of commerce, and so on, in South Africa, fostering links with their European counterparts. Second, the Delegation sought to build on the existing sponsorship of black education by encouraging the development of tertiary level studies about the EU and the introduction of European Documentation Centres for both universities and public libraries. This information function was also to have a public focus and an EU exhibition was to tour the country to enhance public awareness of the Union as South Africa's largest development assistance donor and most significant trading partner.

Third, the existing Special Programme run through the Coordination Office and via the NGOs became the exclusive responsibility of the Delegation. The 1994 budget was 110m ECU and it was intended that this level of funding would be maintained at least through the tenure of the South African Government of National Unity. This transfer of authority was a potentially sensitive issue. Thus, the establishment of a Delegation has not only effected the Coordination Office, it brought into question the existing privileged role played by the four NGOs involved in the delivery of the Special Programme. There is an implied conflict of competences. In all other third countries where development issues form part of the EU's activity, these are conducted through the Delegation on a government-to-government basis. It was only South Africa's peculiar situation that made such direct contacts impossible and hence the invention of the NGO intermediary procedure. The Delegation began interacting with the Transitional Executive Council once it was set-up, although the TEC as such did not have a specific Development Committee but a general Foreign Affairs Committee. As an interim body, it was inappropriate to formalize a permanent agreement and structure. In the longer term, the continued viability of the NGOs will be determined by the quality of the service they deliver. However, since their initiation in 1986 the NGOs have matured considerably and have a significant advantage in terms of experience and expertise in the field. So long as the NGOs can deliver more effectively than alternative transitional or new government-to-government arrangements then they are unlikely to be replaced, at least in the medium term. Indeed, the new challenge may foster increased efficiency and this formerly "unique" EC development structure may provide a model for involvement in development issues elsewhere. The NGOs future lays mainly in their own hands.

Prior to its establishment, it was presumed that an additional, if temporary, function of the Delegation would be to assist in the organization of the election observers. The responsibility for the election monitoring, however, lay exclusively with the election unit established by the Commission. However, in practice the actual execution of the joint action marginalized the Delegation almost totally. The fact that the European Union Electoral Unit's handbook to observers failed to mention the Delegation in its list of European diplomatic missions to South Africa – but did provide information on the Norwegian and Swiss embassies – was indicative (if not intentional) of the dislocated relationship (see the Postscript for additional commentary on this point). Lastly, the Delegation's role was also tightly circumscribed geographically. Through the Lomé Convention the surrounding southern African states already had representation. The Pretoria Delegation was limited to South Africa and did not assume a regional role. Any form of regional accreditation or inter-Delegation coordination was a matter for medium-term policy development.

The expectations and requirements stipulated after the SEA concerning cooperation between member state embassies and Commission Delegations was discussed above. These conditions remained in force at the birth of the Pretoria Delegation; however, certain revisions in the light of implementation of the Treaty on European Union were being developed. The impact of Maastricht was on the reporting role of the Delegation; on strengthening the local aspect of coordination on CFSP; on their involvement in "joint actions"; and, in general, on the level of Commission involvement and participation in all matters as the thirteenth and equal partner in collective Union foreign policy. No new functions had been stipulated before the end of 1993; however, it seemed inevitable that once the new practice developed this new institutional relationship would be codified, albeit in a *ex post facto* manner typical of Community, and now Union, behaviour. In a practical sense, the new Delegation would expect to be reporting to Brussels on virtually a daily basis, rather than the normal monthly rotation. Other than an end of mission report submitted by every out-going Head of Delegation, no fixed reporting timetables exist. Each case is treated according to circumstance and demand.

THE EUROPEAN PARLIAMENT

Despite its formally constrained role in foreign policy, the European Parliament can through its debates and procedures for motions become a policy making actor. Some examples illustrate this characteristic well. First, the Parliament was instrumental in strengthening the provisions of the Code of Conduct. Second, two years later the Parliament introduced a special budget contribution for SADCC to counter regional destabilization perpetrated by South Africa. Third, the initiative to set up the Special Programme in 1985 came from the Parliament; what is more, the annual increase in funds allocated to the Special Programme not only require parliamentary approval, but have invariably been at Parliament's insistence. The 1994 budget procedure provided a typical example. The original Commission recommendation for 1994 was 90m ECU, the same as for 1993. At the December budget parliamentary review, the European Parliament increased this by 20m ECU and ear-marked 10m explicitly for the South African election process. However, at the second reading the Council rejected any increase creating the paradoxical position whereby the EU had approved a "joint action" in November 1993, but then vetoed the necessary funding to execute the policy. Such policy contradictions are not uncommon. The eventual resolution saw the Parliament increase total funding to 110m ECU with a special election budget line of 10m ECU included within the Special Programme funding. Fourth, during the 1980s the Parliament had been instrumental in promoting a policy of sanctions within EPC and in maintaining the issue of South Africa on the Council agenda. Resolution after resolution was passed calling for demonstrative action: without attributing cause or effect, the Parliament was a significant lobbyist for the final adoption of sanctions.

During the reform phase of the early 1990s the Parliament maintained its interrogative method, but rarely formulated detailed studies of relations with the new South Africa. However, the intensity of parliamentary questions declined and the focus of those asked changed from a concern with sanctions and EC policy, to that of political violence within South Africa and the Community's lack of involvement. The meetings of the auxiliary EC–ACP Joint Assembly were generally the more active policy forum. Prior to the Braun-Moser Development Committee Report of 1993, only two other parliamentary investigations were conducted in the 1990s: the October 1990 Development and Cooperation Committee Opinion on southern Africa, and the related December 1990 Political Committee Capucho Report which similarly focused on regional issues (Namibia, Angloa, Mozambique as well as South Africa). The Development and Cooperation Committee Opinion described a catalogue of predictable actions: increased humanitarian aid, food support, infrastructural development, training, commercial and trade cooperation. More innovatively, it called for the Community to encourage member states to cancel the region's multilateral as well as bilateral aid debt, and to "provide financial resources to encourage the development of democracy in South Africa particularly by the creation of democratic institutions" (European Parliament, 1990a, p. 32). More negatively, it stated that Europe should not consider opening a Commission Delegation before apartheid had clearly been abolished. Paralleling these concerns, the Capucho recommendations relating to the Republic reflected support for the early stage of the negotiation process coupled with concern for the heightened violence and a commitment to maintain existing sanctions "until there is clear evidence of profound and irreversible changes" (European Parliament, 1990b, p. 9).

The Parliament's role again became involved once the parameters of the new relationship became focused and South Africa was designated a "joint action" in November 1993. As these examples illustrate, the Parliament's foreign policy role has been positive, increasing funds and approving new projects. The negative power to prevent the adoption of a foreign policy action introduced by the Council of Ministers could not be exercised, making the Parliament a constrained, if benevolent, actor in the execution of foreign policy.

The SEA gave the European Parliament a significant new power that had future implications for determining foreign relations with South Africa: the ratification of new association agreements. Given the past absence of any formal agreement with South Africa, if any non-Lomé agreement were signed parliamentary approval would be required. While the Parliament had exhibited strong anti-apartheid views during the 1980s, its response to a new bilateral framework was largely an unknown quantity given that in June 1994 a new Parliament was elected, the political sympathies of which were unknown.

The South African case was a typical example of the weakness of the Parliament's SEA status. It was kept "closely informed" as required by the SEA, but its precise policy role remained largely at the mercy of the member states and the Commission. In that sense, the Parliament's involvement as a foreign policy actor is more significantly limited than that for most national parliaments. In response to this frustration with its circumscribed foreign policy competences, the European Parliament attempted to establish an expansive interpretation of its new powers described in the TEU. The general conclusion was that Maastricht added little constitutionally to empower the European Parliament in the area of foreign policy. Article J.7 states:

The Presidency shall consult the European Parliament on the main aspects and the basic choices of the common foreign and security policy and shall ensure that the views of the European Parliament are duly taken into consideration. The European Parliament shall be kept regularly informed by the Presidency and the Commission of the development of the Union's foreign and security policy.

However, this seemingly modest increased authority of the Parliament once again whetted the Parliament's appetite for a more intrusive role. As the Parliament had proven repeatedly since its first direct election in 1979, it was extremely adept at exerting the maximum influence from the smallest of constitutional concessions. An example of this tendency occurred as soon as the new Union adopted its first set of five "joint actions". These actions, announced by the Council on 8 November 1993, made no reference to consultation with the Parliament as required by Article J.7. The Parliament claimed that decisions on "the main aspects and basic choices" of the first CFSP common action (monitoring of the 12 December 1993 elections in Russia) had therefore been taken without prior parliamentary consultation. The Parliament's CFSP committee asked the Council *ex post facto* formally to amend its decision to associate fully the Parliament with the joint action and to involve it in the work of the Special Coordination Unit in Moscow established to facilitate EU election observation and monitoring. Extending the interpretation of its Maastricht authority, the European Parliament passed a recommendation that in future Parliament be consulted as soon as possible before the Council adopted any CFSP decision and a new inter-institutional agreement of procedure be concluded (*Agence Europe*, 1993, no. 6113, p. 4). This issue was taken up with the new Greek presidency in early 1994. Discontent was expressed with the existing procedure of two quarterly seminars between the presidency and the Parliament's CFSP committee because, as the chair of the committee Enrique Baron explained, "CFSP has its own dynamism which renders it necessary for the European Parliament to be closely associated with its elaboration" (*Agence Europe*, 1994, no.6145). Developing a workable but effective new inter-institutional arrangement could be achieved in a number of ways: through joint debates; a constant flow of information; and, more radically, to extend the existing co-decision procedure to include Parliament's voice in CFSP, or demand parliamentary approval for any CFSP joint actions. Such an invasive interpretation of consultation was not shared by those member states who assumed the Maastricht reforms had simply maintained and in no way extended parliamentary involvement with foreign policy. While the initial experience did not suggest any significant alteration in Parliament's involvement (a consequence of the truncated parliamentary year due to the direct elections in June 1994), the implications for all future common actions, including that with respect to South Africa, were fundamental.

The Council responded to Parliament not only by agreeing that in this first case of joint action constitutional procedures had been circumvented, but also by acquiescing. The Belgian presidency of the Council pleaded that "the apprenticeship of novelty had a price . . . speed had been required, whence a small short-circuit between the European Parliament and the Union Council. It will not be repeated" (*Agence Europe*, 1993, no.6114, p. 4). Without bestowing unrealistic expectations on the phrase "duly taken into consideration" (which sceptics argued could only ever be *ex post facto*), during the transition phase to the South African elections, Parliament recognized an opportunity to reinforce its constitutional position and play a more active foreign policy role. Two examples in December 1993 confirmed this tendency. First, at its plenary session a Committee on Foreign Affairs recommendation was adopted that called for the Parliament to be fully associated with the Union's joint action establishing an Electoral Unit. The timing was such that it was possible, given necessary cooperation, for Parliament to participate meaningfully and not be reduced to a rubber-stamping role. The Parliament insisted on contributing its own observers and was concerned that Europe's observation role should be adequately staffed. In particular, the resolution

> reaffirming that, of all the institutions of the Union, it is first and foremost for Parliament to monitor the conduct of elections in third countries and to deliver an opinion as to their democratic legitimacy.

. . . recommends to the Council of the European Union that, when adopting the joint action concerned, it involve Parliament fully in the European elector unit and in the liaison unit. (*EURO-CIDSE*, December, 1993, p. 5)

Second, at the same plenary session the Parliament adopted a report calling for the Commission to draw up a framework agreement as an initial step towards a full association agreement. It was also recommended that the Special Programme be widened in scope and that funds be increased to 110m ECU, rather than the 100m initially proposed by the Commission (*Agence Europe*, 1993, no.6131, p. 13).

Third, the Committee on Development and Cooperation "Report on the development prospects in South Africa and southern Africa" was presented. The motion for resolution stressed that the policy debate was structured within Title V of the CFSP provisions of Maastricht and the decision to treat the topic of South Africa as a joint action. The Report's rapporteur was the European Peoples' Party member, Braun-Moser. Nineteen recommendations were made, many of which reflected the Council and Commission *status quo*. Thus, the report committed the EU to sending election observers; advocated commencing discussions relating to the form of relationship in terms of trade and development cooperation; agreed that a new political and economic framework should take account of the SADC and Lomé dimension; called for greater SADC regional cooperation; and, supported South African membership of the World bank and the IMF. Where Parliament's views differed with those of the other Union institutions mainly concerned the form of the expected new framework agreement where the report favoured an agreement within the ACP–EC Convention. The report's development priorities focused on the need to coordinate with the domestic authorities and meet the needs as defined by local communities. It promoted the evolution of the Special Programme to meet these new demands and argued that "human resource development, housing, health-care services, water and sanitation projects, electrification and rural development" should constitute donor priorities (European Parliament, 1993, p. 6). The report also contributed to the regional integration debate. It supported the creation of a SADC joint parliamentary forum; the harmonization of customs tariffs and increased intra-regional trade; South

Africa's membership of the PTA; the exploitation of South Africa's transport and communications infrastructure; and encouraged the development of joint ventures for industrial development and job creation.

South Africa also provided an opportunity to explore Parliament's financial control over CFSP expenditure. As noted already, previously there had been a Council–Parliament confrontation over increasing Special Programme funding. In total, the exclusive CFSP budget heading provisionally allocated just 15m ECU for 1994, although accompanying measures could be partially, or totally, funded under related budget headings (as was the case for election monitoring under the Special Programme). Of course, an excessive use of this additional funding mechanism would lead to dislocation within the Union's other financial programmes. In setting the figure of 15m ECU it was impossible for the EU to forecast whether this would be sufficient (*Agence Europe*, no. 6153, p. 8). A Commission proposal of January 1994 argued against CFSP being funded on an *ad hoc* basis through national contributions, in favour of funding through the Union budget. However, the existing budgetary constraints agreed to at the Edinburgh European Council that limited maximum expenditure until 1999 had also to be observed. The problem was, therefore, a budgetary and a political one: first, support of existing joint actions had to avoid a reduction in funding for other external activities of the Union; and second, such joint actions funded through normal budgetary EU procedures must not be transformed, even partially, into intergovernmental CFSP actions. In this respect Parliament's budgetary role was of vital importance both to the Parliament's meaningful involvement in CFSP and to the progressive *communautarization* of joint actions. (As examined in greater detail in Chapter 8, the funding debate constituted a CFSP issue that transcended the case of South Africa and saw the Parliament in conflict with the Council.)

Despite calling for inclusion in the joint action, and specifically for involvement in the Electoral Unit, the European Parliament also established its own group of election observers. Twelve MEPs were selected representing four political groups (five each from the European Peoples' Party and the Socialists, and one each from the Liberals and Greens). They were to parallel the election monitoring role played by the Parliament in the first joint action

– the December 1993 parliamentary elections in Russia. Several exploratory visits were planned prior arriving a week or so before the vote. Although the December plenary meeting had called for Parliament's close cooperation in the Electoral Unit, in practice this did not transpire until after the Unit had been set up in South Africa in February 1994. Again, the novelty of the CFSP procedure meant that inter-institutional liaison was often neglected inadvertently and it fell to the Parliament to remind the Council and provoke coordination. In addition to the Parliament's own delegation, other MEPs were involved through the 200 strong AWEPAA election monitoring team.

The MEP observer mission were deployed for ten days (from 21–30 April) and covered three areas: KwaZulu–Natal, the Western Cape and the Eastern Cape. In their post-election analysis they declared the process "substantially free and fair" while acknowledging that there "had been logistical and organizational difficulties, which were understandable in the exceptional circumstances" (*Press Release*, 30 April 1994). In a gesture symbolizing the reincorporation of South Africa into democratic society, the Parliament extended an invitation to South African parliamentarians to observe the European Parliament's own direct election between 9–12 June 1994. In the plenary session immediately following the election the European Parliament called for concerted and continued EU support, both political and financial, to consolidate the new democracy. The joint resolution of the PSE, PPE and Green Groups called for an increase in the budget of the Special Programme and the speedy conclusion of a cooperation agreement. Parliament also recommended that a permanent European Parliament Delegation for Relations with the South African Parliament be created, but rejected a motion that advocated South African membership of Lomé (*Agence Europe*, 1994, no.6225, p. 4).

The roles played by these various actors and their institutional relations was not, of course, unique to the South Africa example. A parallel with the multilevel negotiating process of Lomé IV is striking. For Lomé, DGVIII, the DG responsible for policy initiation had to clear its proposals with the other directorates

particularly the External Relations Directorate (DGI), and the Agricultural Directorate (DGVI), between the Commission and the member states, between the member states themselves, between the Commission and the member states on the one hand and various lobby groups (including NGOs) on the other, and between the Commission, the member states and the European Parliament. (Ravenhill, 1993, p. 44)

Complexity is emblematic of Community policy making and South Africa was in no sense an exception to this rule. If anything, the example displayed greater complexities. This chapter has examined a number of participants in the policy making process. The focus has been on those institutions and actors outside the political decision-making forums (such as the Council, the Political Committee and COREPER). Clearly, the role of the Commission is of importance to CFSP particularly given the internal divisions examined above. However, the outcome of the negotiating brief to design an appropriate cooperation framework assigned to DGI will be crucial in determining the new role for the Commission within CFSP. The challenge is for the Commission to defend its traditional external economic role in the face of competition from within the Commission and from the member states. The exceptional circumstances of South Africa have historically made coordination between member state embassies in Pretoria a vital aspect of policy formation; the opening of a Commission Delegation will change this relationship as the normalization of institutional relations occurs (as has already happened with the merging of the Programme Coordination Office in Pretoria). Finally, while still a peripheral actor the Parliament's foreign policy views and participation cannot be ignored. Given the anti-apartheid history and actions of the European Parliament, a continuing role and interest in the shape of future relations is to be expected.

5 The 1990s Policy Innovations

Obviously the distinction between purely institutional development and policy innovation is an imprecise demarcation: they are in most circumstances related, if not mutually dependent conditions. Consequently, while the previous chapter sought to limit the discussion to institutional developments, there were implicit and explicit policy implications, best illustrated by the institutional reform of the Commission. Similarly, while this chapter considers specific policy innovations of the 1990s these are, where necessary, examined within an appropriate institutional framework. The policies discussed are, firstly, the Code of Conduct; secondly, the adaptation of the positive measures into a development programme; thirdly, election monitoring; and lastly, South Africa as a CFSP topic for joint action. As such, these policies are all directly concerned with South Africa: the related policies involving regional integration and an external bilateral cooperation framework are dealt with separately in Chapters 6 and 7. The previous discussion has shown that these policies were developed under both EPC and CFSP provisions: the consequences for policy making, however, were not uniform as the following discussion illustrates.

THE CODE OF CONDUCT

The oldest Community policy, the Code of Conduct, has always been a focus of controversy (Holland, 1989). By the 1990s some member states were advocating that it was no longer an appropriate mechanism given the removal of the legal framework of apartheid; somewhat ironically, the Code's functioning has been undermined by legislation that made it illegal to classify employees by race. It was also criticized for putting an additional burden on EC companies placing them at a competitive disadvantage. Despite these concerted attacks and British pressure for its

117

earlier abolition, the Code survived until 1993. However, it is anticipated that the general thrust of the Code's original interest in proper employment practices will continue to be an EC priority despite its abolition, and informal monitoring will take place by member state missions and the Commission Delegation in South Africa.

Critics of the Code's waning relevance presented a strong case. By the end of June 1991 the Population Registration Act which required the statutory obligation to maintain racially segregated staff records was abolished, together with the remaining so-called "pillars of apartheid" (the Land Act and the Group Areas Act) that had directly as well as indirectly affected labour relations; divestment had reduced EC involvement significantly (both in terms of the number of EC firms operating and in the number of black workers employed); and, the growth in black trade unions facilitated the return to normal bargaining relations that did not require the paternalistic over-sight of Community involvement. As the seventh annual UK summary of the revised Code stated, because of these changes "the future of the Code is under active discussion . . . changes are expected to be agreed soon to reflect the changed circumstances of South Africa" (Department of Trade and Industry, 1993, p. 1).

The eleventh synthesis report (1989/90) which covered the final year prior to the easing of the apartheid structures foreshadowed the diminishing focus for the Code. The report covered 241 EC companies which employed approximately 80,000 black workers. The report noted, *passim*, that "a very large majority" of firms accepted whatever form of representation the workforce preferred; non-racial criteria had become the norm for determining wages and employment; a "majority" of companies had total desegregation; and support for black business was increasing (Presidency, 1992).

The British reports provide an even better illustration of the general demise of the Code's utility. At the peak of British involvement (the end of the 1970s) there were 205 firms in South Africa: by 1991/2 this had fallen to just 100; there was a similar reduction in the number of black workers employed (from 134,000 in 1981/2 to 48,885 a decade later). The three most recent UK reports best illustrate this decline in comparison with the earlier period of the revised Code's application (see Table 5.1). The number of category "A" companies (those with a 50%

holding in a South African subsidiary and employing twenty or more black workers) dwindled to just 77 from 126 in 1985/6. The corresponding decline in black employment was from 79,100 to 48,885 by the time of the penultimate reporting period. Total desegregation was finally achieved in all 77 companies for the first time in the Code's fifteen year history; similarly, pensions, medical and insurance benefits and provisions for on the job training were comprehensively provided, once again for the first time. All but 500 of the 48,885 black employees (98.9 per cent) received at least the minimum SLL (supplemented living level) required by the Code. Although the form of representation varied significantly between companies, in 1991/92 all companies confirmed that all employees, irrespective of race, were free to choose the type of organization to represent their interests. While there was only partial application of other aspects of the Code, these areas were of generally less central importance. Ultimately, the Code was a victim of its own propaganda: one the one hand, its principle objectives had broadly been realized; on the other, European interests had fallen to such a level that the effect of the Code was peripheral to the question of multi-racial democracy. Hence, the successful application of the Code's requirements, in one sense, undermined its necessity and longevity. This, coupled with the new labour relations situation after 1992 and the continuing criticism by the UK and some other member states of the Code's inappropriate interference with normal business relations, fore-shadowed its inevitable abolition. As already noted, such a course of action was announced for the first time in June 1993, in one of the final EPC statements of the Danish presidency, although the formal suspension was only confirmed five months later in the context of the Union's CFSP joint action.

Despite these criticisms, the removal of the Code's reporting requirements may lead to a deterioration in EC labour practices. It was certainly the case for some UK firms that the threat of adverse publicity was as important a stimulus for good labour relations as was any moral commitment to ending apartheid. With the removal of this openness there is no effective independent watchdog to monitor practices. It seems unlikely that the new Delegation will become significantly involved given the intergovernmental nature of the process. Nor are the various member state embassies in a position to conduct investigative work: even under the Code they were totally reliant on the data

Table 5.1   Revised Code of Conduct: UK Reports 1985/6–1991/2

Reports Year	1985/6	86/7	87/8	88/9	89/90	90/91	91/2
Total no. of Reports	160	128	120	111	107.9	101	100
No. Cat. 'A' reports	126	109	99	93	87	80	77
No. of other reports	34	19	21	18	20	21	23
No. not reporting	2	0	0	1	1	2	2
Representation							
No. of blacks employed (000s)	79.1	70.3	62.6	63.3	53.9	54.5	48.8
No. of firms:							
– using liaison committees	73	70	60	57	53	53	50
– confirm freedom of association	114	100	96	92	87	80	77
– signed direct recognition agreements	49	46	44	46	44	46	46
– signed direct collective bargaining agreements	40	38	33	32	31	33	36
– promoting the Code	35	31	35	35	33	31	33
Employment							
No. firms using migrant labour	36	21	17	13	9	6	5
No. migrants employed (000s)	11	11	10	8.2	4.5	5.5	6
No. firms accepting principle of equal pay for equal work		124	*	98			
Desegregation							
No. firms with total desegregation	76	67	62	64	65	78	77
No. firms with desegregation in workplace	117	100	87	82	70	78	77
Fringe Benefits							
No. firms providing:							
– housing	92	78	72	67	62	57	50

Table 5.1 *cont.*

Reports Year	1985/6	86/7	87/8	88/9	89/90	90/91	91/2
– transport	48	43	32	32	27	23	22
– pensions	117	102	94	90	85	79	77
– insurance/medical	116	103	93	89	84	76	77
– funeral grants	33	33	29	23	29	31	33
– advisory schemes	23	23	25	17	14	15	18
– clothing	33	29	20	20	22	20	22
– retirement awards	42	44	33	29	28	29	29
– loans	32	32	27	23	21	22	22
– recreation	37	31	35	23	16	18	19
Advancement No. firms providing:							
– on the job training	124	108	99	93	87	80	77
– external training	100	95	86	81	77	69	70
– apprenticeships to all races	52	42	34	33	36	29	29
No. of firms with no overseas recruitment		44	*	*			
Pay No. of employees paid at/above SLL5/HDL(000s)-n	76.1	68.4	61.1	62.2	52.4	53.8	48.3
%	96.2	97.3	97.6	98.3	97.2	98.6	98.9
Black Business No. of firms:							
– providing contractual assistance	*	35	34	31	29	25	25
– supporting the National African Federated Chamber of Commerce	*	10	10	12	8	8	8
– supporting the Small Business Development Corporation	*	14	15	15	14	10	10

* = not known.
Source: Department of Trade and Industry (1993).

produced by the individual companies. Without any such similar data a true indication of labour rates, for example, may be difficult to ascertain. A reconsideration of the Code may be one of the issues that may need to be addressed in the second half of the 1990s. Conversely, all member state delegations resident in South Africa have welcomed the demise of the Code essentially for practical reasons: it significantly reduces the workload, particularly for the smaller missions.

THE SPECIAL PROGRAMME AND DEVELOPMENT

The initial broad consensus and general success of the Special Programme encouraged the development of this aspect of policy during the 1990s. Following the unbanning of political organizations and the repeal of apartheid legislation in South Africa, as of 1 October 1991 the Commission in consultation with the partner channels, reoriented the Special Programme to make it more appropriate to the changing political situation in the country. Whereas earlier assistance had been concentrated on a variety of projects to alleviate the effects of repression, the new approach involved creating an "integrated, coherent development programme targeting interventions in key areas and sectors" (Directorate-General VIII, 1992). To facilitate this more intense level of involvement the Commission opened its Programme Coordination Office in Pretoria. Consequently, the former exclusive role played by the four "channels" in South Africa was replaced by a more diverse partnership structure. This expansion in both the Community's profile and its scope of activities has been probably the most important policy development prior to the creation of majoritarian government in South Africa.

The original aim of the Special Programme was to assist in the abolition of apartheid by encouraging peaceful change through a range of development initiatives directed through non-governmental and non-violent organizations in South Africa. Direct support to political parties was prohibited. Projects supported were required to promote the concept of non-racialism, democratic practices and enjoy broad-based local community support. The structure chosen for the implementation of the programme reflected the peculiar situation of South Africa. With no direct representation in the country and with formal links with Pretoria inappropriate given that the programme was focused on assistance to the "victims of apartheid", four "channels" were selected to act as conduits for project proposals, assessment and the distribution of funds. This approach was unique within the Community's experience and was viewed initially with some reservation by a number of member states.

The main partner in implementing the programme was the Kagiso Trust, an independent development agency established as a direct consequence of the 1986 EC measures. Before Community funds could be effectively dispersed, it was necessary to assist in the strengthening the capacity and organization of the indigenous development structures which were comparatively immature and marginalized. Thus in the early years of the programme, the EC concentrated on enhancing the development agency infrastructure in South Africa and to that end provided technical and administrative expertise for three of the four channels (Kagiso Trust, South African Council of Churches and South African Catholic Bishops' Conference). This was designed to increase project identification and management capacity. Training was also provided by qualified professionals in such areas as urban development, local government, health, education and legal services, and through specialized research institutes. The fourth channel, the International Confederation of Free Trade Unions is not exclusively a development agency, had its own organizational structure was used only infrequently by the Community (Commission, 1993a, pp. 9–10).

The first funding phase of the Special Programme ran from 1986–91. The focus was on three development topics – education and training, humanitarian and social projects and legal support – a total of 402 projects worth 130.7m ECU were funded (see Figure 5.1). Education and training took almost half of the total expenditure in this period (with university bursaries the largest recipient of support). Humanitarian and social support accounted over 40 per cent of funds and assistance here focused most directly on those affected by apartheid. Legal assistance was provided to individuals and organizations who lacked resources to pursue politically motivated legal cases, and to human rights groups. Community funding "proved crucial during the period under the State of Emergency (1985–1990) when bannings and detentions without trial were widespread in South Africa" (ibid., p. 10).

Figure 5.1   Special Programme Commitments by Sector, 1986–91

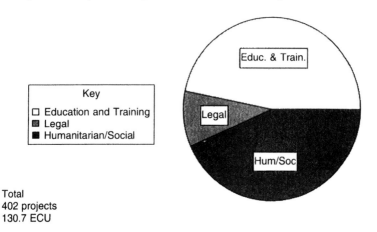

Key

☐ Education and Training
▦ Legal
■ Humanitarian/Social

Total
402 projects
130.7 ECU

Source: Commission of the European Community (1993a).

Figure 5.2   Special Programme Commitments by Sector, 1991–93

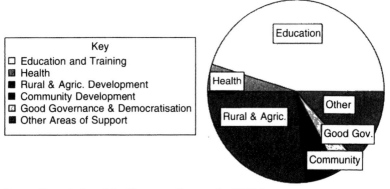

Key

☐ Education and Training
▦ Health
■ Rural & Agric. Development
■ Community Development
▨ Good Governance & Democratisation
■ Other Areas of Support

Source: Commission of the European Community (1993a).

The second phase of the Special Programme was in response to the political reform process symbolized by the release of Nelson Mandela. While maintaining its original objectives the programme began a transformation into a more specifically development-based orientation. This meant that human rights support gave way to a greater emphasis on the process of democratization and good governance and the previously diverse nature of the programme evolved into a more coherent sector-based and coordinated development programme. Thus the aims of the Special Programme grew into the following seven specific commitments to:

a) support sustainable long-term development initiatives for the most marginalized communities and areas;
b) support the reconciliation process by building a consensus on the nature of South Africa's development problems;
c) assist in coordination, consultation and cooperation between the varied development agencies so as to maximize the use of limited resources;
d) continue to enhance the managerial, organizational and implementation capacities of the NGOs and other groups so that development assistance becomes increasingly efficient and therefore effective;
e) promote affirmative action programmes within development groups in line with the racial and gender composition of South Africa;
f) support research into new policy initiatives which can lead, in time, to a comprehensive national development policy frame-work; and,
g) promote "bottom-up' rather than "top-down" development strategies by including wherever possible local communities in planning and implementing projects. (Ibid., pp. 12–13)

This redefinition in programme objectives required structural adaptation too, particularly since the opening of a Programme Coordination Office in Pretoria in February 1991 finally allowed the Commission to become directly involved in project identification, assessment and monitoring. Thus the existing four channels no longer acted as the exclusive intermediary agents after 1991. The medium-term viability of this diversity remains questionable given the establishment of a full strength Commission Delegation in 1994. However, in the first two years of the redesigned programme (1991–93), the NGOs remained the dominant focus for channeling resources to sponsored projects. Projects were selected on an individual basis by the Commission (DGVIII) on advice from the Coordination Office and in consultation with the member states. To assist the EC in its priorities, independent external and local studies have been regularly undertaken which review the effectiveness of past assistance by sector, establish current needs and outline future involvement. In this way the programme was constantly adapting and its continued relevance ensured.

As can be seen from Figure 5.2, in contrast to the first period of operation, between 1991–93 EC involvement has diversified across five distinct sectors: education and training (which remains the largest commitment at 83m ECU); rural and agricultural development (36m); good governance (13m); health (7.7m) and community development (7.2m). Beyond these specified priority sectors *ad hoc* support has been given to isolated projects. For example, 10m ECU were provided for the UNHRC programme for the repatriation and resettlement of South African political refugees. The following section provides a brief outline of the type of projects that have been funded by the EC in each of the main five sectors (for a detailed description see, Commission, 1993, *passim*). While the scale of South Africa's development problem is immense, Europe's commitment is significant and broadly focused. Since 1991 the programme can legitimately claim to have been a substantial success and a positive contribution to erasing the social, economic and cultural consequences of apartheid policies.

Education and Training

An education crisis in South Africa is one of apartheid's most destructive legacies: the scale of the problem has meant that the Community has devoted almost half of its financial contributions to this sector. The aims of the EC are to provide additional support in order to maximize the impact of existing state resources as well as to generate new initiatives that could provide models for national-level education. While the programme covers education from the pre-primary level, the greatest percentage of funds was devoted to tertiary support. In 1993 alone, the EC provided bursaries to more than 7,000 black students (worth a total of almost 20m ECU)(see Figure 5.3). Bursaries are provided for disadvantaged students to study courses that match the development needs of the country, namely the natural sciences,

Figure 5.3   Commitments: Education and Training Sector, 1991–93

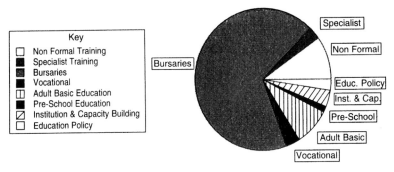

Total Committed 1991–1993: 83 million ECUs

Source: Commission of the European Community (1993a).

engineering, management and administration, accounting, economics, agriculture and teacher training. A further 3.4m ECU was spent from 1991–93 on specialist training programmes "designed to meet the particular needs of South Africa's transition to democracy", and in 1992 alone 1.6m ECU was spent on tertiary level public administration training for the future generation of civil servants. Another key educational area currently funded is research into the restructuring of the South African educational system and educational policies to meet the needs of society. Similarly, the EC supported institutional development and capacity building and placed an onus on extending adult and non-formal education to overcome the low skills level of a substantial percentage of the population and the unacceptably high illiteracy rate (which has been calculated at more than 45 per cent for the black population) (see South Africa Foundation, 1993, p. 113). A total of 6m ECU was committed to adult basic education projects from 1991–93. Conversely, the Community was also actively involved in pre-school education with 900,000 ECU allocated for this purpose since 1991. Teacher training is another key area of Community involvement particularly in the areas of mathematics and science education. Finally, 2.8m ECU was committed from 1991–93 towards promoting employment through vocational training. Most recently the EC provided the services of an international reference group to assist the South African National Training Board in restructuring vocational and technical training. Most estimates put black unemployment rates at above 40 per cent and growing.

Rural and Agricultural Development

As the development focus of the Special Programme became more pronounced after 1991, greater funds were channeled towards the rural and agricultural sector. The aim of funding is "to improve living conditions" and to break the apartheid created dependency culture by helping "people and communities to become productive". As shown in Figure 5.4 eight distinct project areas have been supported to:

i)   provide water and sanitation to the poorest communities;
ii)   establish a major, integrated, regional rural development programme that is responsive to and involves local communities in planning and project implementation;
iii) support for a micro projects programme;
iv)   assistance to small scale community based development projects;

Figure 5.4   Commitments: Rural and Agricultural Development Sector, 1991–93

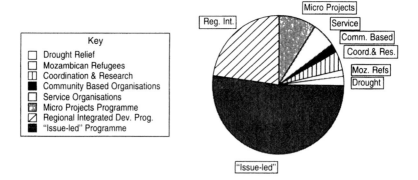

Key
☐ Drought Relief
☐ Mozambican Refugees
⊞ Coordination & Research
■ Community Based Organisations
☐ Service Organisations
▨ Micro Projects Programme
▨ Regional Integrated Dev. Prog.
■ "Issue-led" Programme

Total committed 1991–1993: 36 million ECUs

Source: Commission of the European Community (1993a).

v) support for technical and service organizations which assist local communities;

vi) support for Mozambican refugees in South Africa;

vii) emergency drought relief; and,

viii) support for research and coordination on rural development, agriculture and land issues.

The first three projects sectors together account for four-fifths of the 36m ECU spent between 1991–93. All three were notable for the insistence on involving the local populations in every phase of the project cycle – from the original idea to final implementation and maintenance. Water and sanitation was a particularly pressing priority given South Africa's drought prone areas and estimated 8 million rural population without access to clean water or sanitation. The short-term objective was to provide these services to one million people in the worst areas over a three year period: the longer tern objective was to establish a framework that will facilitate sustainable development of water and sanitation services. Typical of EC development involvement, the emphasis was on local participation at all stages of project design and execution. Over a two year period 13.5m ECU was earmarked for this programme alone.

The second project sector was designed to allow local communities, with the assistance of NGOs, to initiate comprehensive regional development schemes. In this way it was hoped to promote large scale sustainable development in some of the most marginalized areas in the country. Currently, this part of the programme only operates in Natal/KwaZulu: 10m ECU has been committed. The approach was unique within South Africa: it consisted of economic development through support for production, particularly small agricultural holdings; infrastructural development to provide a firm base for other development projects; and, social and institutional development which entails support for education, health and social welfare projects and training in the management of local development initiatives. The micro-projects sector of the programme was operated on a pilot basis in the Eastern Cape/Border region and was assigned funding of 4.5m ECU over a two year period. The value of the scheme, however, was not its monetary contribution alone: it encouraged local participation (such as labour) in each micro-project which was then augmented by EC technical support. The range of micro-projects was considerable, although the dominant focus was on support for social infrastructure (particularly those related to women) and agricultural activities. The remaining five project sectors had a total of 8m ECU devoted to them. The smallest sector was support for Mozambican refugees (400,000 ECU) and emergency drought relief (687,000 ECU).

Good Governance and Democratization

This political aspect of the Community's development pro-gramme has become central to the more traditional socio-economic concerns. While somewhat unusual, increasingly the EC has linked its international aid and development programmes to political issues, particularly human rights and good govern-ance. This can be seen in the terms of the Community's Lomé relationship with the 70 ACP states and in the European Council resolution on "Human Rights, Democracy and Development" adopted on 28 November 1991. Thus although South Africa presented certain unique demands, the inclusion of good governance and democratic conditions as development criteria have been applied in comparable cases elsewhere.

Commitments within this sector, amounting to some 13m ECU for the years 1991–93, were divided between four areas: voter education; human rights and democracy; conflict resolution; and, media funding (see Figure 5.5). The bulk of the funding was spent on voter education, registration programmes and the training of election monitors. Obviously, the EC's commitment to these issues accelerated the closer the first democratic non-racial elections became. Conflict resolution – in terms of resolving disputes as well as dealing with the underlying causes of conflict – constituted the second area for assistance (2.7m ECU 1991–93). Support was channeled through a variety of the existing resolution pro-grammes in operation: for example, through the Community Dispute Resolution Trust, the Independent Mediation Service of South Africa, the Independent Projects Trust and to committees run under the auspices of the National Peace Accord. Defending human rights and promoting good governance was the third most funded area (a total of 1.7m ECU since 1991). Both the original and the reformulated positive measures programme provided the financial opportunities for legal redress for the under-privileged

Figure 5.5   Commitments: Good Governance and Democratisation
Sector, 1991–93

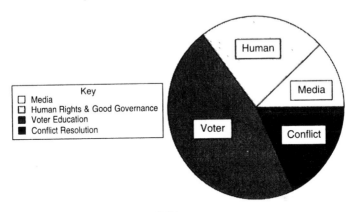

Key
☐ Media
☐ Human Rights & Good Governance
■ Voter Education
■ Conflict Resolution

Total committed 1991–93: 13 million ECUs

Source: Commission of the European Community (1993a).

which otherwise would not have existed. New initiatives included
"projects that seek to encourage the development of a culture of
respect for the rule of law and observance of human rights under a
new constitutional dispensation" (Commission, 1993a). The final
area was support for media plurality through the Independent
Media Diversity Trust. This was established to provide
alternative media sources to the mainstream South African press
which is owned exclusively by two companies. The Community's
commitment to the media can be traced back to the original 1985
positive measures when five black South African papers were
sponsored. The 1991–93 funds were used to secure the commercial
viability of various newspapers and for training young black
journalists. Other groups were also created to monitor impartiality within the State broadcasting structures in an attempt to
"level" the playing field. In total, 1.5m ECU was devoted to
support for an independent and pluralistic media.

Health

Prior to the removal of apartheid legislation one of the major
concerns of the EC was not to perform development tasks that

were rightly the responsibility of the South African Government. As the EC's involvement in the health care sector illustrates, this inhibition has disappeared and the Community has worked with parastatal organizations where appropriate. The Community was involved in promoting a unified health system determined by the principles of equality, accessibility, affordability and efficiency: as such the emphasis shifted from a "curative" philosophy to an approach that stressed the socio-economic origins of South Africa's health problems which primarily afflicted the poor, those environmentally deprived, uneducated and female population groups. Consequently, the whole range of Community development policy impinged on its health care policy through the general commitment to social up-liftment. Of the 7.7m ECU earmarked for health between 1991–93, support for preventative primary health care took virtually half the funds (3.7m ECU) (see Figure 5.6). This focus was on those groups who lacked basic health and sanitation facilities and provided where possible local health and nutrition clinics as well as the training of local medical personnel. Again typical of the EC's overall programme strategy, often the health policies were in response to local initiatives and were combined with local participation. Health research was the second major component of the programme: in particular, the EC

Figure 5.6   Commitments: Health Sector, 1991–93

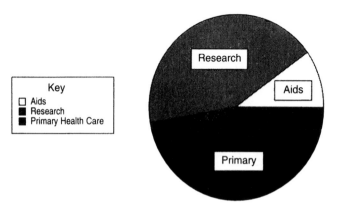

Key
☐ Aids
■ Research
■ Primary Health Care

Total committed 1991–1993: 7.7 million ECUs

Source: Commission of the European Community (1993a).

has been instrumental in campaigning for improvements in occupational and industrial health and safety. The final aspect of the health programme was the fight against AIDS. The Community assisted in promoting AIDS awareness and educational projects, inter-organizational linkages, support for the National AIDS Convention of South Africa and the promotion of HIV codes of practice. A total of 400,000 ECU were assigned to this sector (see Figure 5.6).

Community Development

This was the smallest sector of Community activity (amounting to 7.2m ECU) and incorporated four elements. In descending order of expenditure, these were: assistance for trade unions; youth work and the homeless; micro-enterprises; and urban development and local government (see Figure 5.7). The objective of Community funding in these areas was "to help regenerate South Africa's urban centres and tackle the major development challenges in the country's towns and cities in a way that is sustainable and that involves local communities in the development process" (Commission, 1993a). Both the physical and social infrastructures of cities were included. Thus, for example, assistance to trade unions was

Figure 5.7   Commitments: Community Development Sector, 1991–93

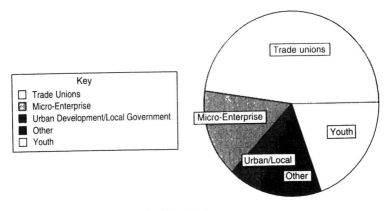

Total committed 1991–1993: 7.2 million ECUs

Source: Commission of the European Community (1993a).

designed to increase the ability of those organizations to represent the interests of their members and thereby directly enhance community well-being: some 2.1m ECU was committed to trade unions from 1991–93. The EC's youth policy was designed to combat the influx of unemployed, poorly educated, homeless "street kids" into urban areas. Support totalling over 1m ECU focused on providing shelter, subsistence and educational and training opportunities through which these marginalized youth could become viable economic members of society. Micro-enterprise covered support for a wide range of small business projects within various black communities. This was a comparatively new, but increasingly important, aspect of EC activity, and accounted for 600,000 ECU under the new Special Programme budget. This approach reflected the EC's awareness that economic growth was the key to South Africa's development. Assistance was focussed on those areas that could have wider economic repercussions. Development policy is no longer about simply giving assistance or direct aid, but about establishing the conditions and infrastructure within a society to secure long-term improvement that can be self-sustaining.

These projects undertaken during the 1990s significantly helped to establish the EC as a benevolent and concerned international actor in South Africa. The contrast with the criticism of the EC prior to 1986 as an organization more interested in maintaining favourable economic ties than in promoting social justice and human rights could not be more explicit. While the economic relationship continues to grow, the emphasis in Community relations with South Africa has increasingly become structured within an appropriate development framework. Community funding priorities illustrate this change of priorities. The Special Programme has experienced a remarkable growth in its budget since the initial 10 million ECU were allocated in 1986 (see Table 5.2). In 1991 this had risen to 60 million ECU and increased further in 1992 to 80 million ECU making the Special Programme one of the largest development programmes ever implemented by the EC globally and the largest single programmable development programme in Africa (Houtman, 1992, p. 420). The EC has become the single largest international donor of external assistance to South Africa: in 1992 the EC was the leading donor with 80m ECU, followed by the USA (60m ECU) and Sweden (40m): additional, bilateral assistance from five EC member states

Figure 5.8   Growth of Special Programme, 1986–94

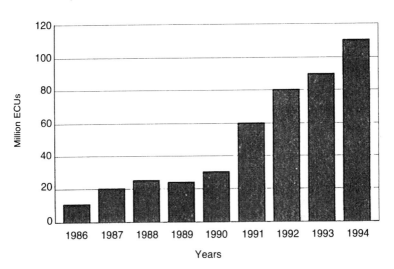

Source: Commission of the European Community (1993a).

amounted to almost a further 60m ECU (Commission, 1993a, p. 7). For 1993 the Community figure rose once again to 90m ECU and the budget for 1994 was raised yet again to 110m ECU. In total, from 1986–1992 covering both phases of the Special Programme 536 projects were sponsored at a cumulative cost of 246 million ECU.

In summary, the new measures within the Special Programme constituted a coherent, targeted sectoral-based development initiative for the most needy sections of South African society. EC assistance alone is, of course, insufficient; however, the initiatives begun, if replicated at a national level and with both State and international funding, can provide an appropriate and effective panacea for South Africa's existing apartheid inheritance.

The consequences for the NGOs of a "new" Community relationship with a democratic South Africa were significant in three ways. First, with the establishment of a Commission Delegation in 1994, the historically exclusive aid distribution role played by the NGOs was usurped. Second, after the installation of the TEC the

Community indicated that certain state structures could be used, a reversal of the existing approach which forbade (at least theoretically) such contact. Any such decision, however, will be made in a "gradual and cautious manner" and NGOs seem likely to retain their predominance in the short-term at least. Third, the longer-term implications for the NGOs are perhaps more serious. The four channels established in 1986 were primarily concerned with the dispersal of funds; their roles were as financial trusts in the absence of a European presence. The Commission Delegation in Pretoria has reclaimed this normal Community function and the NGOs will have to develop more traditional roles appropriate to a normalized domestic situation. The NGOs served an essential and unique function, but one paradoxically dependent on the structure of the apartheid system. The Commission document outlining the Special Programme went to great lengths to praise the role of the NGOs and to defend their future utility. However, despite an assurance made by Commissioner Marin in 1993 that this unique and innovative form of "partnership with NGOs and of 'people oriented' development will remain an instructive one not only for development in South Africa, but throughout the world" remains questionable (Commission, 1993a, p. 6). The seeming inevitable duplication of roles may well lead to eventual rationalization and a more traditional government-to-government relationship.

The Community's initial approach lacked focus, a result of the fact that there was no central indigenous body with whom the EC could discuss and establish development priorities. The April 1994 election created a legitimate Government and for the first time a bilateral discussion on development needs became possible. The focus of the development programme will, naturally, remain under constant review; however, the concentration on core projects that emerged during the early 1990s looks set to continue to dominate future projects. After the initial boost in both funding and project involvement it seems probable that the European focus will be limited even more rigorously to highlight its most effective contribution, in such areas as vocational training, education, development of the informal sector and micro-enterprises. What seems less likely is for the EC to follow its SADC strategy of involvement in infrastructural programmes. These will remain the exclusive responsibility of the Government of National Unity.

ELECTION OBSERVATION

The extraordinary October 1993 European Council meeting committed the new European Union to an electoral role that went beyond simply observing the conduct of the South African election. The pre-mission report of the Taskforce Troika that visited South Africa from 27 September 5 October was originally intended to be exploratory. However, the pressure of time as well as the comprehensive nature of the analysis meant that this single report became the sole basis for the Working Group and the final Council decision. As the report noted, the elections were important not only for the establishment of democratic institutions, but also as a further step towards consolidating democracy in the southern African region as a whole. Hence the importance attached to free and fair elections by the international community, and a willingness to contribute to the electoral process. The twenty page report addressed the following questions: the role of the EU; the size of delegation; the funding of the operation; and the coordination of the EU's contribution with that of the international community and the UN. On 7 December the TEC invited the EU, together with other international bodies, to observe the election; the subsequent December Union Council decision gave the EU a legal mandate under TEU Article J.3 to undertake election observing, which closely corresponded to the recommendations and wording of the Taskforce report.

The role played by the Community was shaped by the new demands of "joint action" of the Union, and the clarification of South Africa as such was both of symbolic and practical importance. The symbolism suggested that the international role that the Union was defining for itself was to be a global one, not limited to Europe's immediate geographical concerns. South Africa constituted the Union's first test in a non-European zone; consequently, success was crucial to the future potential of CFSP. The practical effect was that policy towards South Africa assumed the binding authority conferred through the Treaty on European Union. In addition, it illustrated in a real sense the importance that was placed upon the transition process in South Africa by the Twelve. The timing, of course, was fortunate: as noted already, the 1990s had seen a convergence of member state views on South Africa and a new explicit policy consensus dominated. In a sense, therefore, by 1993 South Africa was an obvious candidate for common action, something that would have been impossible just a few years previously. And yet, this consensus was more at the level of principle than practicalities. The 29 October Council decision only gave a general outline of the joint action, delineating two aspects: the immediate election process; and the longer-term appropriate economic and social framework for bilateral relations. It was left to the 7 December Council to further specify the scope of the joint action: the question was to what extent were trade relations and development assistance to be discussed as part of the joint action, rather than left within their existing policy frameworks. Some member states, such as the UK, questioned whether the decision on joint action covered all EU–South African policy, arguing that the scope of joint action was limited to the election process. The majority of member states took a more inclusive view. The result was a compromise reminiscent of EPC behaviour: the election role was specified and enacted as a joint action, whereas the wider cooperation issues were left for a future agenda. While this example is specific to the South African case, the broader implications are more significant. The question of defining the scope of a common action will become one of the major tests of the future CFSP, and one determined by political choices.

This dispute not withstanding, one element of the new approach consisted of "a co-ordinated programme of assistance in preparing for the elections and monitoring them" (Council, 1993). The wording of the December decision was important. While recognizing it was the responsibility of the South African authorities to conduct the election, the Union was willing to be involved in preparation and observation as directed. The decision referred to "preparing" and "monitoring": while the EU's role was not to supervise, the contribution implied somewhat more than simple observing. Consequently, the Union's role was not seen as peripheral or short-term and involvement extended over three months. Originally, it had been hoped to despatch the Electoral Unit (known locally as EUNELSA – European Union Electoral Unit in South Africa) in early January 1994: departure, however, was delayed and it only became operational during early February. The introduction of the European Union Observers was staggered. The original Taskforce report envisaged a minimum of 312 individuals, twenty-four from each member state and the Commission. The first fifty-two were to arrive in January

1994, and a further 100 the following month; the remainder arriving a few weeks prior to the election date. However, the December Council decision amended this strategy and the commitment of personnel was deferred and delegated to EUNELSA in consultation with the Commission. This procedure was not in fact followed as the figure of 312 was confirmed in late January (before EUNELSA was established) as the EU contribution. The revised schedule saw the observers sent in four waves – 10 February (52 observers); 1 March (104 observers); 1 April (104); and, 14 April (the remaining 52 observers). The Observers were accredited to the South African election authorities and had diplomatic status under UN Resolution 772. It was envisaged that half of the observers would depart immediately after the voting and another quarter after the election count and certification of the result. The remainder, together with the administration, were to remain in South Africa for a further month after the election. The Union argued that effective involvement had to constitute more than a snap-shot of the election week itself. Thus involvement was with the entire election process, not just with the monitoring of ballots cast. The lead-up to the election, the role of the media and instances of political intimidation were all crucial to an assessment of the extent to which the election was deemed "free and fair".

The December Council decision confirmed that funding of Observers was to be split between the Commission and the member states, a procedure that reflected the general CFSP principle of shared financial competences as set out in TEU Article J.11. Member states were responsible for funding both travel and salaries of their respective observers from Europe to South Africa; once there, all local expenses were to be funded from the 1994 Special Programme budget which had an additional 10m ECU allocated explicitly for the election. The Taskforce estimated that the costs would be in the region of 7.2m ECU. These funds were in addition to the 5.5m ECU already assigned to the electoral education programme in 1993. Thus no new budget line had to be introduced to accommodate this action, avoiding possible technical and political complications. All personnel, including the EUNELSA leader, were appointed by the Commission on the basis of nominations from the member states. In practice, this neat procedural distinction became blurred and one of the few areas of contention in the joint action. In Maastricht terms, the difficulty was in using pillar I finances for pillar II objectives. Indeed, some member states, and not just the small states, complained that the joint action was too expensive and they were unwilling to supply their full complement of observers.

The December General Affairs Council decision defined the Union's assistance to the electoral process as that of

> the provision of advice, technical assistance and training, continued support for non-partisan voter education, and the provision of a *substantial number of European observers* as part of an overall international effort co-ordinated by the United Nations. (Council, 1993, Article 1.1) (my emphasis)

The justification behind EU involvement was threefold. First, by observing it was hoped that confidence in the elections would be created and the transparency of the electoral process assured; second, EU participation was seen as a partial deterrent to those groups who might try to interfere with the conduct of the election; and third, EU involvement provided domestic and international credibility for the outcome of the election.

The Union decision confirmed that EUNELSA would be led by an experienced high-ranking politician knowledgeable of South Africa. The announcement of the candidate to fill this post was considerably delayed from the original November date until 21 January 1994. This did not reflect any great disagreement over the various candidates, but rather once again illustrated the experimental nature of CFSP procedures and the mixed nature of joint actions. Member states were responsible for nominating candidates to the Commission who then made their recommendation back to the Council as part of the required consultation process. The eventual selection of the Dutch former Minister of Defence and of Justice and current Professor of Law, Jacob de Ruiter, provided the group with the necessary independent and non-partisan profile. He was assisted by a French candidate, Warin, who had extensive diplomatic experience and UN expertise as deputy unit leader. The remaining nine member of the Unit consisted of the head of administration and advisors in the fields of elections, legal issues, elector education, media, training, conflict resolution, security and logistics. These individuals were nominated by member states and their collective experience was diverse: for example, one individual had been responsible for organizing elections in Northern Ireland and another had been involved in the Lebanon. EUNELSA was operationally independent and reported back to a Troika-Commission Steering Committee which operated in Brussels and South Africa. The task of the unit, which was established on 24 January and dissolved one month after the election, was extensive (see Appendix document 5). It was to consult with the South African Independent Electoral Commission (IEC) on "the nature and scale" of the European Union's involvement; assist in devising "proposed guidelines and Code of Conduct for observers"; liaise with the UN on the coordination of international observers; coordinate the deployment of the Union's observers; assist in the establishment of national and regional coordination centres for observer operations; help local NGOs; provide support, if asked, in "monitoring of the security forces responsible for the election process"; and, advise and assist in "the monitoring of the media" (Council of the European Union, 1993, annex, para.2). The scale of involvement was consequently under constant review despite a figure of 312 observers having been agreed to. While respecting the decision's commitment to a "substantial number of European observers", depending on circumstances the Union's involvement could increase, or diminish, on the advice of EUNELSA. There was also the related issue of coordinating the EU observers with those from the European Parliament and from the member states.

The final level of involvement was close to the original figure with a total of 307 Observers being deployed in all nine South African Provinces. An additional fourteen MEPs were assigned and integrated into the overall EU deployment. For pragmatic reasons, the final deployment schedule was amended: 41 Observers arrived on 15 February; 85 on 1 March; 111 on 4 April; and the remaining 80 on 14 April, less than two weeks before the election. Technical assistance in the form of personnel was also provided to the IEC in the fields of security (112 European police officers were assigned during the last weeks of the campaign), mediation, analysis, logistics, election administration and to the Independent Media Commission. In total, the EU assigned 450 people as part of the election joint action. Total funding worth R40.5m was provided: voter education received a grant of R30.5m and R10m was given to the IEC electoral fund to provide financial assistance to parties contesting the election (EUNELSA, 1994, p. 9).

The European contribution to the international election observers team while not insignificant, was comparatively modest. The UN agreed to send 1,778 observers although the bulk of these were deployed only on a short-term basis. Other contributions came from AWEPAA (200), the Commonwealth (70), the OAU (50). In total, there were approximately 2,800 observers making the EU's contribution equivalent to one in every nine international observers. If observers from NGOs are included, then over 5,000 observers were involved (*Agence Europe*, no.6149, p. 4). However, a crude quantitative assessment of the EU's observer role misses the qualitative aspect of the involvement. The extended deployment of three-quarters of the EU's observers facilitated an intimate exposure to the complexity of the election issues in South Africa and provided sufficient time for contacts and confidence to be established. The EU's mandate was to cover the electoral campaign as a whole, not just the voting process. A better indication of effectiveness is to count the number of observer days involved rather than the gross number of observers deployed. By this calculation the 307 European Observers provided the equivalent of 15,000 observer days.

The overall coordination of the international observers was organized through steering groups linking the various teams under the auspices of the UN. However, the mandate of both the European and the international observers was limited: the responsibility for the conduct of the election rested exclusively with the IEC established in November 1993. Even where malpractice occurred, observers were not empowered to intervene, but just to observe and report. Given the fact that there were some 8,000 voting booths in operation, clearly the monitoring procedure had to be selective and attempted to focus on the most volatile of areas. In general this lead to some rural areas being excluded from any international monitoring procedures, although the normal national election monitoring did take place. In total, 2,233 voting stations were visited by EU Observers during the election period (EUNELSA, 1994, p. 1).

The Taskforce report outlined the expected problems in achieving a legitimate election result. Of greatest concern was the lack of confidence in state structures, in particular the security forces. Ideally, international observers should have been located at all voting booths. The delay in establishing the TEC resulted in the IEC only being able to operate for four months prior to the election. The logistics of running the election were profound. Some 23 million voters were enfranchised, the vast majority voting for the first time; voter registration was impossible; and, there were potentially serious problems relating to voter identification. The impartiality and ability of the Home Affairs Department responsible for the election organization did not go unquestioned. Concerns were also expressed about the state-controlled media and, unavoidably, the role of violence and intimidation.

While the report's concerns were largely supported by the Electoral Unit's experience, the post-election EUNELSA statement emphasized that "overall, the election was a remarkable achievement" (p. 5)(see Appendix 6 for the full text). The assessment noted that the campaign had been "generally free and fair but the voting process less satisfactory" with 24 per cent of the voting stations visited by European Observers reporting insufficient materials such as ballot papers, ballot boxes, and voters' ink, and in 10 per cent procedures were imperfect. Violence and intimidation did occur in specific areas during the election but nowhere near the scale anticipated: in the majority of the country the election was conducted, by South African standards, in comparative calm and tranquility. The State of Emergency declared in Kwa-Zulu Natal, township violence in the Witwatersrand area and restricted access to the former homelands of Bophutathswana and Ciskei constituted the core of intimidation. Typically, intimidation took the form of parties being prevented from campaigning in certain areas: bombing and sabotage by right-wing extremists cost 21 lives during the election week and caused disruption, but did not derail the electoral process or undermine the validity of the result. In general, all the major parties were guilty of transgressions and while any form or threat of intimidation and violence constitutes a blemish on the democratic process, the EUNELSA assessment concluded that the incidents that did occur during the campaign did not materially effect the result.

Given that the IEC had only sixteen weeks to establish the entire machinery for conducting the election – the production of all election equipment and materials, selection and training of personnel, the location of voting booths and the distribution of ballot materials – the organization was commendable if flawed. Particular problems were associated with the suitability of some polling booths, issuing of voting documents, voter education programmes as well as with the distribution of essential election materials. The count presented the greatest logistical challenge and the IEC's administrative competence in this area was the least impressive. The earlier concerns about the impartiality of the media and the security forces proved unfounded. Indeed, the South African Police played a constructive role in safeguarding the election.

With the disbanding of EUNELSA in May, one aspect of the joint action was successfully completed. The other aspects of the joint action were not so precisely defined temporally and gave an open-ended commitment on the part of the Twelve. While the practical execution of the EU's new role as an election observer exposed some procedural deficiencies, the overall experience enhanced both confidence in and the expectations of joint CFSP actions. (These deficiencies and recommendations for improvement are outlined in the Postscript.)

SOUTH AFRICA AS A "JOINT ACTION": POLICY GUIDELINES 1993–4

As noted in the opening paragraph of this book, the context against which the above policy changes occurred was the change from EPC by the European Community according to the SEA, to joint action of the European Union as governed by the Maastricht Treaty. Because policy towards South Africa has been developed over several years the topic straddles the EPC–CFSP divide. The change in the content of policy was not a result of the change from Community to Union, or from EPC to joint action; rather it was a response to the changing dynamics in South Africa. As previous chapters have shown, many of the changes in policy that became incorporated in the Union's joint action after 1 November 1993 were developed much earlier. In that sense the transformation into Union was coincidental, rather than instrumental, although once defined as a joint action policy was expected to be conducted more cohesively.

Why was South Africa chosen as one of the initial five subjects for common action? Several, perhaps obvious, reasons played a role. First, South Africa was a natural choice; there was an extensive history of collective action under EPC. Second, since 1991 there had existed a broad policy consensus, something of a rarity in European foreign policy. Third, topicality and the pure chance of timing were involved: the South African issue was of renewed international importance in the Autumn of 1993 coinciding with the final launching of the CFSP. Fourth, its inclusion alongside the more direct European interests of the other four joint actions intentionally signified the European Council's commitment to the global role of the Union. Fifthly, South Africa offered what appeared to be a comparatively easily achievable success given the existing European policy consensus and apparent democratic progress being maintained in the Republic. It presented a much needed antidote to Europe's other foreign policy disappointments. Lastly, though related, it presented to the new Commissioner for External Political Affairs a high profile and relatively low risk initiation into foreign policy.

On 29 September 1993 the Community issued its policy guidelines in support of the transition to democracy in South Africa (see Appendix document 2 for the complete text). As noted previously, this was a joint document written by DGIA, DGI and DGVIII, which was first submitted to the full Commission for approval before being sent to the Council for discussion. The purpose of the document was to propose the necessary steps for the normalization of the EC's relations with a democratic South Africa and it was the basis behind the presidency conclusions of October 1993 that designated South Africa a joint action. The guidelines set-out a three-stage phased policy approach that responded to the acceleration of the democratization process. Thus actions to be taken were listed; a) once legislation establishing the TEC was enacted; b) once the TEC was established and operational; and, c) once multiracial elections had taken place and a democratic government was installed. The TEC provided the Community with the first opportunity to establish a political dialogue with an official representative body for consultation across a wide range of issues. The nature of this relationship was determined, of course, by how the TEC actually operated in practice. As the introduction to the guidelines noted:

> The progress achieved in the constitutional negotiations has opened-up the possibility of developing a more integrated EC policy targeted on the creation and strengthening of democratic

structures; on the encouragement of sustainable economic policies; on the progressive integration of South Africa into the world economy; and on the continuing support to the development of historically marginalised communities. (Commission, 1993b)

The rationale for sanctions no longer existed and the progressive normalization of relations became the new policy perspective.

(a) Actions taken after the enactment of TEC legislation

The first action outlined was European support for the "complete lifting of trade, financial and investment sanctions by the international community" and thereby facilitate the reincorporation of South Africa into the world economy. Thus the progressive removal of trade and economic sanctions that had begun in 1990 was to be completed and South Africa's participation in both World Bank and IMF programmes supported. Second, two actions were proposed within the existing framework of the Special Programme. One aspect focused on the emerging electoral process. Ensuring a successful democratic election was important not only to South Africa, but also the EC and the international community: consequently, support beyond the existing commitment of 5.2m ECU was offered including monitoring of the election. Further, the Commission gave a commitment to continue with its support and involvement in ECOMSA (both financially and in terms of personnel). The second aspect built on the broader development cooperation element governed by the Special Programme. The scale of the economic and social problems facing the new South Africa were such that foreign assistance was "necessary to stabilize the next political dispensation". Efforts beyond the existing level of aid were needed. Thus the guidelines committed the Community to a policy of at least maintaining the Special Programme funding "during the whole period of political transition".

(b) Actions taken once the TEC is operational

The second phase of Community policy was originally intended to become operational once the TEC was in place. However, the delay in its establishment together with pressure from member states to accelerate the process actually saw two aspects of the guidelines implemented prior to the formal launching of the TEC on 7 December 1993. First, the guidelines foreshadowed a review of the two EPC sanctions that remained (restrictions on military attachés and security cooperation). Second, the Code of Conduct, the suspension of which had first been raised in June 1993, was to be discontinued. However, the sanctions were actually lifted on 6 October 1993, almost two months before the TEC was in place, and the Code had effectively been halted after the June announcement.

The remaining initiatives within the guidelines came into force only after 7 December. First, the Commission opened its first Delegation to South Africa symbolizing the normalization of relations (see Chapter 4 for details). And second, exploratory discussions concerning the longer term relations between the EU and South Africa began, providing the necessary preparatory groundwork for the formal negotiations anticipated for after the elections. The discussions took three forms. First, it was anticipated that the EC would establish "new lines of communications in the political field" with a new South Africa which would become "over time . . . a major political interlocutor for the European Community". Second, developments in trade and economic relations were foreshadowed. However, here European comments were uncompromising and demonstrated that the normalization of relations meant treating South Africa by internationally accepted trading standards: preferential consideration to compensate for the disadvantages of apartheid's legacy were not to be expected. The framework for future trade policy would have to respect obligations under GATT as well as be consistent with the EC's existing trading agreements, both regionally and globally. The influence of DGI in the text of the guidelines was clear:

South Africa must be left in no doubt that, in order to restore much needed trade and inward investment . . . it needs to send a clear confidence building message to the business community worldwide. There is no better way of doing this than for South Africa to intensify its efforts to dismantle, as a matter of priority, such trade barriers as export subsidies, import surcharges, formula duties, high level and low number of tariff bindings and to commit itself to a market economy that welcomes foreign investments. (Commission, 1993b)

Within these conditions, the guidelines empowered the EU (through DGI) to enter into preliminary dialogue with the TEC. The difficulty was, however, the comparative unprepared-ness of the TEC to participate in such a debate. No clear ANC position on trading relations had emerged during 1993: in contrast, the Commission had drafted its own confidential working paper on the possible options available in November 1992, one year before the TEC was established (see Chapter 6 for further details).

The third long-term economic issue addressed was that of development cooperation, and here the perspective of DGVIII was dominant. Again, the thrust of the proposal was for "preparing the eventual normalization of relations in this field". In keeping with the guidelines overall regional awareness and closer economic ties within the region were emphasized. Just as for the question of an economic framework, by the end of 1993 no clear perspective had emerged from South Africa about how it perceived the development relationship. The issue of Lomé membership was a topic of speculation, not informed opinion. The guidelines did attempt to stimulate that policy debate within the Foreign Affairs Committee of the TEC by suggesting the following innovations.

> Special attention should be paid in this respect to promoting regional projects which would benefit from regional funds made available to southern Africa under the Lomé Convention as well as from the Special Programme for South Africa.

> One concrete and immediate possibility would be that, at the request of the ACP States concerned, South Africa should be allowed to export to these countries on the framework of Lomé financed Import Support Programmes being implemented in the SADC countries. (Commission, 1993b)

Despite these regional considerations, the guidelines revealed nothing concerning prioritizing regional as opposed to South African needs. While the two are obviously linked, the linkage can be as much a source of conflict as of complementarity. The joint origin of the guidelines contributed, quite understandably, to different emphasizes, and potentially to contradictions within the overall policy. South Africa's choice of bilateral framework may not be necessarily the best framework for the region. This crucial issue for post-1994 European relations are addressed fully in Chapter 6.

(c) Actions taken after the election of a democratic government

Here the guidelines only stated that depending on the extent to which the discussions with the TEC had been fruitful, the Commission if authorized by a Council directive, could commence negotiating "in order to prepare a comprehensive long-term agreement, encompassing the whole of bilateral relations". These guidelines addressed the criticism that the Community was allowing its policy towards South Africa to drift. It established a logical three-phased approach that acknowledged the complexity of reinventing relations with South Africa and was at one level sensitive to the regional perspective. However, the guidelines could obviously only provide a broad framework and the policy detail was left essentially undefined. While this was a logical response to both the emerging situation and a reflection of the as yet to be decided South African position on a range of external issues, this policy vacuum also possessed the potential to produce policy conflict. The document reflected also the consensus position established between DGIA, DGI and DGVIII and some of the implicit points of contradiction were left unresolved. The balance between South African and southern African policy is an issue that will remain on the Community agenda for the second half of the 1990s. The guidelines in themselves did not solve the inherent contradictions.

In conclusion, the policies of the 1990s witnessed a passing of the old and the emergence of the new within the context of the transition from EPC collective action to CFSP joint action. The Community's original policy of the Code of Conduct and the punitive sanctions of the 1980s were replaced by the Union's positive policies. These consisted of three distinct components. Two, the Special Programme and Europe's electoral role, have been discussed here at length. The third element, the development of an appropriate cooperation framework, dominated the four months of 1994 that led up to the South African election, and it is this aspect of the Union's joint action that the next chapter examines.

6 A Framework for Relations with the New South Africa

Historically, the European Community never had formal relations with South Africa: a normal complementary bilateral relationship, in terms either of trade or political relations, has been absent. At a superficial level, both trade and diplomacy suggested the appearance of normality. The EC was South Africa's largest single import market and the EC provided a consistent, if small, level of exports. Investment, too, was largely European. Diplomatically, ten member states operated embassies in Pretoria and South Africa was accredited to several EC countries as well as to the Commission in Brussels. Yet this appearance belied the abnormal nature of the relationship that had existed since 1977. As the earlier chapters in this book illustrate, until 1993 the relationship was confrontational and restrictive: sanctions, codes and diplomatic declarations were emblematic of both this political and economic abnormality. The task for Europe and South Africa was how to establish a "normal" political and trading bilateral relationship leading into the twenty-first century.

From 1992 onwards the Commission began to consider various options for a future trading relationship, and more implicitly, the content of a new political relationship. The Community approached these topics with a comparatively open mind: there was no hidden agenda and no specific framework was to be unilaterally imposed. Conversely, this did not imply that the EC was prepared to accept whatever type of new arrangement suggested by South Africa. A compromise based on the most suitable framework for South Africa's needs and for the Community's interest was sought. This process of normalization proved relatively drawn-out largely because of South Africa's prevarication over its preferred future economic classification under GATT. The choice was between retaining its existing

"developed nation" classification, or negotiating a down-grading
to "developing" or "country in transition" status. However, prior
to South Africa's decision, the Community had already examined a range of possible new relationships to manage bilateral
relations.

In contrast, the scope of the new political relationship was less
contentious and witnessed a speedy consensus. Obviously, during
the "abnormal" phase of relations the EC prohibited any direct
links with South Africa and between Commission officials and
South African diplomats based in Brussels. Indeed, the ban on
informal diplomatic contacts in Brussels was unique within the
sphere of the EC's international contacts. When representation
was required, this was executed by the Council presidency on
behalf of the Community, or occasionally through visiting
Troikas. The first step towards a normalization of political
relations took place in February 1991 with the opening of the
Commission Programme Coordination Office in Pretoria. Thus
for the first time the Community was directly established on South
African soil, although at this time the Office did not have
diplomatic immunity and its role was highly constrained. It was
not in any sense a Commission Delegation as found elsewhere in
the world and the Coordination Office was responsible for the
management of the revised Special Programme projects (see
previous chapter).

The June 1993 announcement that a full Delegation would be
established once the transition to democratic election had begun
signified the final normalization of political relations. As already
noted, it represented possibly a privileged relationship as EC
Delegations are not situated in all third countries. Following
examples elsewhere in the world, normalization would also allow
for a comprehensive and strong political dialogue to be
established. This would cover questions of regional security,
human rights and non-proliferation. This process may take the
form of annual bilateral meetings between the twelve, or a Troika,
and the future South African Government. Normalization of the
political relationship will also affect some of the existing structures
and process that were specifically created to accommodate the
"abnormal" period of relations. In particular, as discussed in
Chapter 5 the role of NGOs is under threat. While Europe is
unlikely to completely renege on this specialized partnership given
the widely acclaimed success of the NGOs, a normal relationship

will see a greater use of government structures to deliver the EC's development initiatives. Signs of this metamorphosis were evident by 1993.

DEVELOPING THE BILATERAL AGENDA

The central dilemma for Brussels was how to activate the necessary debate about bilateral relations: prior to 1994 the ANC were essentially unprepared, and until the TEC was finally created in the last month of 1993 there was no authoritative democratic interlocutor that the Commission could use to initiate a dialogue. Again, the phased approach of the Union's joint action illustrated this political constraint. Exploratory talks at a high official level could only commence once the foreign relations sub-council of the TEC was operational, and formal Ministerial contacts and decisions were excluded until after the April election. Initiating the dialogue proved awkward, despite the best of intentions. Although operational by 7 December 1993, it was 14 February 1994 before the TEC sub-council could find time to schedule the first meeting with a Commission delegation. (The presidency Troika that visited South Africa in late January 1994 was not involved in the negotiations on bilateral economic relations.) This delay was more indicative of the untried nature of TEC procedures and the extensive scope of the foreign affairs portfolio than any intentional neglect of the European connection. However, the delay was frustrating for the Commission who were ready and waiting to enter into dialogue, particularly as the sub-council had already scheduled a visit to the UN in New York (4–12 February) and to the OAU in Nairobi (18–23 February). To facilitate this first meeting the Commission delegation travelled to South Africa. The sub-council consisted of just six representatives drawn from the multi-party talks; the Commission was represented by Mr. Giola, the Deputy Head of DGI and the other *fonctionaires* from DGI, VIII, III and IA who were responsible for the South African portfolio, collectively a team of about a dozen officials.

Despite the leading political role assumed by the Danish presidency, Denmark was typical of the majority of member states in that they held no strong views on the appropriateness of Lomé or of another form of association agreement between the Community and South Africa. This disinterest in the Council of

Ministers was somewhat remarkable and gave the Commission an increased role in the foreign policy making process. The Commission's proposals were not met by direct confrontation in the Council – consequently, its control of the policy agenda made the Commission at least *primus inter pares* on this occasion. The October 1993 European Council announcement to include the democratization process as one of the first CFSP topics did not contradict this relationship despite the Commission's shared right of initiative under the Treaty on European Union. The European Council decision did not set out a new political framework to shape policy, but rather (as is often the case with such announcements) it reflected current thinking and was influenced strongly by the Commission's input.

The Commission was in an unenviable position. On the one hand, it risked being accused of tardiness in allowing the bilateral debate to remain undeveloped until three months before the election date; on the other, they risked charges of preconditioning the outcome prior to negotiations by imposing a European agenda. The Commission was keen to avoid even the suggestion of neo-colonial insensitivity by dictating the framework of the new relationship. Hence the dilemma. As remarked elsewhere in this volume, the public silence on the part of the Commission was not indicative of a policy vacuum: as early as November 1992 DGI produced a paper that signified the beginning of the process from the Community's perspective. This was complemented by a revised paper circulated to the Council in mid-January 1994. Moving beyond this level of preparation was seen as inappropriate until the TEC responded. Informal contacts were instigated during 1993, particularly when Mandela or other representatives of the ANC visited Brussels, as well as de Klerk and members of the National Government, although most of this process was low-key and not open to public scrutiny. The two conferences held in Brussels on the question of the EC and South Africa (in June and October 1993) were especially useful in providing a non-political or diplomatic forum where contacts could be made and at least initial policy options explored. From the Commission's perspective, the onus first lay with South Africa to define its position, thereby empowering themselves and establishing policy objectives that could later be matched with an appropriate bilateral economic framework. Only then could the Commission effectively respond. But again, this begged the question of time and resources: in the transitional phase where perhaps rightly the TEC saw other domestic issues as priorities, arguably it was incumbent on the Community to initiate the process by suggesting a possible economic framework. The risk of being accused of dominating the negotiations (a familiar claim within the Lomé framework) was the price to be paid to avoid delaying the process until after the April election. The Commission and the TEC fell between two stools; although they did initiate discussions in February 1994, the value of meeting the TEC at such a late stage was marginal. Effectively, the bilateral cooperation framework was only addressed in May 1994.

The November 1992 DGI report prepared at the request of EPC was the first attempt to identify the main issues that the EC needed to address in shaping its future policy towards the Republic and presented a survey of the various available economic frameworks to structure a new, normalized relationship. The report was sensitive and insisted that its discussion did not preclude or prejudge other options or policy initiatives that could develop. An analysis was given of South Africa's "predicament" in terms of the political transition, the economic crisis, violence and radicalism. Against this background, political, development, regional and trade issues were elaborated and a synopsis presented of the different economic frameworks that were viable. The reports conclusions and recommendations are summarized below: all quotations are from the report which remains a confidential document.

South Africa's Predicament

From the perspective of November 1992 DGI was remarkably prescient politically and warned that the transition to a new constitution would be "longer and harder than expected" and cautioned for a measured and patient response. The timing with respect to up-grading bilateral relations (economic and through the opening of a Delegation) was recognized as crucial. Interestingly, the ending, when appropriate, of the two-track development approach through which NGOs insulated the positive measures from any government-to-government contacts was also foreshadowed. In keeping with the general international approach, it was advocated that "conditionality should have a prominent role in the forging of new bilateral/multilateral ties with South Africa". The report characterized the economic situation rightly as a structural crisis, the origins of which went beyond the global recession and reflected the cumulative effect of sanctions, capital outflows and inflation. The disinvestment campaign and the lack of international investor confidence were identified as giving further impetus to the existing philosophy of import substitution and the high concentration of monopoly capital producing an inward rather than export oriented economy. Unemployment levels of above 40 per cent had become the norm. Annual economic growth in the region of 6–7 per cent was needed merely to match the population growth of 2.5 per cent: estimates put growth at below 1.5 per cent. These structural weaknesses gave a gloomy medium-term scenario anticipating a continuing decline in per capita real income. The inability of any new Government adequately to fulfill black expectations was seen as both a source of potential social unrest and for improvised, short-term and ill-advised economic policy choices, such as the option of a redistribution policy. To compound matters, the endemic level of violence and the culture of radicalization was depicted as a powerful deterrent to both local and foreign investment.

Issues Facing the New Relationship

South Africa was regarded by the Commission as a candidate for establishing a post-electoral political dialogue. The question of South Africa's arms production capacity (the parastatal organization, Armscor) also highlighted the sensitive topic of regional security. Questions of human rights, borders, minorities and non-proliferation were also considered specifically with respect to the terms of conditionality the Community might consider requiring. The scale of the immediate development needs (health, housing, education, social services, etc.) called for massive financial support and it was recommended that the Community's existing programme would need to be strengthened and eventually embodied within a single framework of relations (replacing the *ad hoc* system devised in 1985). The regional development implications and the need to look for a viable regional framework was emphasized. Closer economic links between all countries in southern Africa were regarded as the key to longer-term regional security and development and essential if the potential danger of economic polarization around South Africa was to be avoided. Stable and sustainable development for South and southern Africa were mutually dependent with regional trade complementarities crucial. Achieving such a balanced complementarity was to prove the greatest challenge to the 1994 policy decisions. If regionally based industries are to develop then an agreement on sharing access to the European market between the SADC ACP states and South Africa is needed, implying mutual cumulation in the rules of origin. As the document stressed only by approaching South Africa and SADC countries within either a compatible, or a single, policy framework, will Europe be able to contribute effectively to stable economic development.

The document raised the question of preferential access for South African exports in a way that confirmed the dilemma set by dividing the political and economic competences of external relations. Simply, the decision whether or not to grant preferences was not just an economic issue, but an eminently political one "that should logically precede the choice of the appropriate legal framework". Within this constraint, it was acknowledged that the structure of South African trade posed a Janus face: it bore both remarkable similarities to a typical developing, as well as to a developed economy. Its developing characteristics are evident in health and education statistics and the low ranking in the UN's Human Development Index. South Africa's economy displays a reliance on primary products typical of developing nations. For example, the mining sector alone accounted for up to 15 per cent of GDP and roughly two-thirds of export earnings (of which gold contributed a massive 70 per cent). Agriculture represented around 10 per cent of GDP. In contrast, South Africa's manufacturing sector contributed some 25 per cent of GDP; however, this sector is only viable because it benefits from high protective tariffs without which it would be internationally uncompetetive; these same tariffs limit South Africa's export potential as they are clearly contrary to GATT requirements and would face anti-dumping charges. Consequently, Europe's single market seemed unlikely to be an important focus for South African manufactured exports: only certain agricultural goods had export potential. It is only the regional, and possibly continental, market in which South African manufactures can successfully compete. In contrast, South Africa possessed an industrial capacity, a financial sector and a communications infrastructure comparable to a developed nation. The overall assessment was that there was no pressing *macro-economic* argument for granting South Africa across-the-board trade preferences; any such concession would reflect a *political* decision.

The Commission document concluded with a review of the options available for trade and economic relations which covered reciprocal versus preferential trade arrangements. Reciprocal arrangements would treat South Africa as a normal developed trading nation whereas a non-reciprocal arrangement would offer preferential access to the Community's single market. The reciprocal options considered Most Favoured Nation (MFN), bilateral trade and cooperation agreements, free trade or customs union arrangements and association agreements; non-reciprocal arrangements covered Generalized System of Preferences (GSP) treatment, Lomé membership and an innovative approach, associated Lomé status. (These options were subsequently revised in a 1994 Commission paper – see below.) The Commission forewarned of the complexity of the choices and the difficulty posed to policy analysis. These, and other options, are discussed in detail in the next section.

Coinciding with the adoption of the joint action, although not a direct consequence of it, in November 1993 DGI began to readdress its policy position. Subsequently a revised DGI document on trade policy options for future relations with South Africa was transmitted to a Council Working Group on 21 January 1994. Independently, DGVIII presented a report on development options and DGIA issued a composite paper that included issues concerning the political dialogue to the Working Group. The report presented a refinement of the European position; however, the analysis reflected broad conceptual issues rather than detailed specific product concessions. Again, the Commission approach was confined to identifying the different problems associated with each option, and consciously avoided a prescriptive recommendation of any one particular option. All options were problematic in some aspect, although not equally so. The analysis confirmed that while Lomé remained on the agenda, from a DGI perspective it presented the most serious difficulties with regard to GATT obligations.

Over the 1992–94 period, the DGI position moved to accepting South African status as either a developing country or a country in transition. However, the extension of full developing country concessions was not proposed. Although Article 18b of GATT allows developing countries to impose protectionist tariffs, the Commission view was that such a choice was politically misguided as the South African economy should be encouraged to dismantle protectionist practices, not extend them. At best, specific developing country instruments could be applied to South Africa on an *ad hoc* basis. Rather than apply an existing framework, consensus emerged around adopting and combining specific approaches from a variety of existing cooperation agreements negotiated with third countries. In particular, the 1993 new cooperation agreement with Israel was seen as an important model.

Perhaps the greatest policy development was the recognition that an interim limited framework agreement with South Africa might be the preferred option. Such an agreement could be negotiated comparatively quickly and provide the foundations on which a more developed cooperation policy could subsequently be developed after 1994. The time involved in negotiations at the European level should not be under-estimated. The process requires the Commission to obtain a mandate from the Council to commence negotiations which, once concluded, have to be discussed by the member states before being ratified through COREPER, the Council and the European Parliament. The potential for delay (both intentional and inadvertent) is considerable. Even a limited interim solution could take several months to finalize, whereas a comprehensive agreement that took account of GATT and existing third country agreements could easily take several years to conclude. If the EU's joint action was to be effective, some form of agreement, no matter how imperfect, had to be in place before the end of 1994.

THE TRADE RELATIONSHIP OPTIONS

The precondition for the kind of trade relationship to be chosen was that EU–South African relations would have to be complementary with relations with the SADC region. The September 1993 Commission paper for the Council stressed this requirement. Past policy had always attempted to reconcile a southern African concern with a South African policy, even if the equation was often imbalanced. Consequently, the 1993 policy innovations were consistent with the Community foreign policy framework espoused since the 1970s. Regional integration and complementarity were to remain the guiding principles. Within this context a variety of options were canvassed by Europe, South Africa and other interested third parties. As one senior Commission representative expressed it, the Community was faced with a puzzle: ". . . the puzzle being, how best can we insert a new South Africa into that complex web of relationships, to the best advantage of South Africans, their closer neighbours, and their other economic trading partners – without hurting anybody" (Pooley, 1992, p. 1).

There were six basic variations on the form of bilateral relationship that would lead to the normalization of trading relations in 1994. The onus lay with South Africa: namely, whether the Republic was to retain its GATT designation as a developed country or whether a new classification as a developing, or "country in transition" was to be proposed. The implications were that if South Africa retained its developed status then almost any non-reciprocal arrangement granted to South Africa's exports would, under any legal framework, be incompatible with existing GATT obligations. In contrast, a number of economic and social indicators supported reclassification and, importantly, within GATT it is self-selection that determines a country's status. For example, in the 1990s both the World Bank and the IMF classified South Africa as a "upper/middle income developing country" (with a per capita GDP figure of US$2,470 p.a.).

Thus the initial step was the responsibility of South Africa and any delay in negotiating a new bilateral structure could not justifiably be blamed on Commission ambivalence. However, what was clear was at these formative stages the Community was not trying to impose a particular format on South Africa: conversely, nor was the EC totally compliant to any South African suggestion. European interests, those of South Africa as well as the regional issues already specified all had to be balanced and given due consideration.

The Community approach to trade preferences created a "pyramid of privilege" for developing countries, each leveling offering more advantageous conditions. In descending order these are the Lomé Convention; Super GSP; bilateral association agreements; and, lastly the normal GSP. Below this there exists the non-preferential MFN status within the GATT framework, the current regime governing South African trade. The following analysis considers all of these options as well as that of "associate" Lomé status and a reciprocal association agreement; the respective merits and problems with each is examined. The discussion eschews detailed economic analysis on a product-by-product basis (for such an approach, see Page and Stevens, 1993; Stevens *et al.*, 1993), in favour of the presentation of the broad implications within a political and a European context. As one South African analysis reported:

> while there are advantages to be gained from pressing the EC hard for special access, they are not as great as they might seem and might well not be worth the trouble fighting for. (*Trade Monitor*, 1993, no.3, p. 10)

South Africa is likely to gain far less from trade preferences than a typical developing country. The composition of its current exports already face comparatively low EC tariffs; perhaps just one fifth of exports would benefit from reform. The most important barriers are sugar quotas, ECSC coal restrictions and limitations on selected fruit products. The South African products that are the most likely beneficiaries of a preferential trade regime are fruit, vegetable and flower products; leather and paper products; and a limited range of engineering and chemical products (Page and Stevens, 1993, *passim*).

Without presenting a definitive position, by early 1994 the Commission in its revised briefing on future trade options advocated that South Africa be treated as a country in transition. However, this assumption did not, necessarily, preclude or advance any of the specific options being considered. The practical implications were that in certain areas South Africa could be treated as a developing country, and in others as a developed economy. Determining exactly what fell into each category was a matter both for negotiation and circumscribed by laws governing international trading regimes. Thus, whenever the bilateral economic relationship demanded a multilateral context (principally GATT), Europe's coherence with its responsibilities in affected global fora took precedence.

The January 1994 Commission paper echoed much of the detail of the 1992 document. In particular it emphasized that the options reviewed should not be considered as mutually exclusive choices: consequently, "some sort of mixed solution, including elements which do not fall within a single heading among those initially considered, could be the one finally retained" (Commission, 1994, p. 1). Innovation rather than a slavish adherence to existing frameworks became the *modus operandi*, at least from the Commission's policy making perspective. Once again, the uniqueness of the South African case demanded experimentation making the predictability of outcomes precarious. The seemingly protracted period before negotiations could commence facilitated, if inadvertently, this open approach to designing bilateral relations. A so-called "off the peg" agreement offered a comparatively quick solution: innovation and creativity in combining approaches to produce the optimum arrangements required an extended period for detailed discussions. Similarly, interim arrangements that were not the preferred longer term solutions could be adopted initially to guide relations through the transition period. It was of greater importance that a limited framework be in place quickly providing at least a legal basis for the development of bilateral cooperation, than wait inordinately long for the ideal partnership to emerge, a process that could take several years. With these considerations in mind, together with the handicap that an assessment of options was dependent, in part, on the objectives and priorities to be emphasized by the still to be elected South African multiparty government, the Commission and the EU were presented with a considerable challenge. While frustrating, the cautious and piecemeal policy making style was unavoidable and contained certain advantages. Interestingly, the Commission document addressed the unequal nature of the bilateral debate commenting on the South African's limited awareness of the range and scope of existing trade and cooperation instruments. Somewhat strangely for bilateral trade negotiations, the Commission defined part of its function to play a descriptive and pedagogic role.

Before examining each option in turn, a clarification of terms is necessary. The Commission eschewed the use of the term "association agreement" which they considered too vague to be of real analytic value. Article 238 of the Treaty of Rome simply states "[T]he Community may conclude with a third State, a union of States or an international organisation agreements establishing an association involving reciprocal rights and obligations, common action and special procedures". Further, the principle of reciprocity was generally avoided throughout the 1994 policy document. The revised series of policy options considered in 1994 was as follows: MFN; GSP; non-preferential agreement; preferential agreement; free trade area agreement; and the two options of full or associated Lomé status.

MFN Option

Although the Commission went to great lengths not to prioritize any specific option, clearly the continuation of the MFN framework was the least likely long-term outcome, despite a number of persuasive attributes. MFN status has the virtue of being the simplest option: it represented the post-sanctions *status quo* and required no change in existing GATT relations, classifying South Africa as a developed country as has been the case since the 1950s. However, the MFN constitutes the lowest level of preference within the GATT system: it operates by guaranteeing that a tariff reduction given to any one country is also offered to all other GATT members. Because of its extensive system of preferential relations, the EU has few countries with whom trade is conducted on an MFN basis (South Africa is grouped with Australia, New Zealand and the USA, for example – see, *Trade Monitor*, 1993, no.3, p. 10). The role of GATT should not be dismissed as peripheral. Third countries, both developing and developed who are direct competitors with South Africa in certain product sectors, may well object to any changes that provide post-apartheid South Africa with preferential treatment. Thus any GATT member could challenge an alteration to the existing MFN regime if it believed its own trading interests were being compromised (Swain, 1992, p. 14). Similar problems could be encountered within the OECD and ACP-Lomé forums. Essentially, the new relationship is not an exclusive bilateral issue, but a multilateral one cross-cutting at least three international regimes.

Maintaining the MFN relationship also had the advantage of acting as an interim position while a new specifically tailored trade relationship was negotiated. The framework existed that was useable and mutually beneficial at least in the short-term. Indeed, as discussed in greater detail below, there are in fact very few South African products that are likely to be granted significantly more beneficial trade preferences under a different regime (with the exception of full Lomé status). However, critics of this approach argue that it would simply reassert the economic *status quo*; do nothing to address South Africa's development needs; fail to stimulate European investment; and continue to hinder the intra-regional production of exports to Europe. Perhaps the only benefit accrued would be the effect of bringing some of South Africa's exports into an MFN framework that were previously excluded by sanctions. Conversely, the Commission identified areas where MFN status could be used to greater advantage. In particular, Article 31 of Protocol 1 of the Lomé Convention provides a mechanism through which South Africa can increase its contribution to manufacturing products in ACP states that then enjoy preferential access to the European market. This could result in both a boost to South Africa's manufacturing export sector as well as increase "opportunities for intra-regional investment, technological transfer and, in general, the development of joint ventures and activities between South Africa and its neighbour countries" (Commission, 1994, p. 3). Derogations on a product-by-product basis could be negotiated. Again, such incremental sensitivity could provide a short-term framework to bridge the immediate post-election trade requirements prior to the implementation of a comprehensive bilateral trading regime.

GSP Option

The effects of changing to a GSP system were difficult to assess, especially as during the mid–1990s the EC was in the process of revising its approach with a view to introducing new elements of graduation and conditionality. The revision reflected the major changes in the international position of certain GSP Third World members since the signing of the last GSP protocol in 1985. For example, the GSP group combined the comparatively competitive countries of Korea, Singapore and Hong Kong with the poorer countries of Central America, China and India. Since the beginning of 1990 the Community had anticipated a reform of the system, but this revision was successively postponed due to delays in the completion of the GATT Uruguay round. Despite the formal conclusion of the round in late December 1993, the final texts were not expected to be finished before the end of 1994 and additional concessions to market access were possible. Consequently, the EC Development Council adopted an interim position with respect to the GSP. The solution was to maintain the existing temporary 1993 regime (regulation no.3917/92) for the first half of 1994, and, if necessary, extend this until 1995 (*Agence Europe*, no.6137, p. 6).

Given the uncertainty, in terms of scope, content and requirements, prior to the South African election it was impossible to calculate whether South Africa would qualify under the new regime, or whether there would be any advantages in the proposed new product coverage. In such an uncertain environment estimating possible advantages was regarded as an extremely hazardous exercise by the Commission. Against this background of uncertainty, one interpretation suggests that essentially, like the MFN, it provides few advantages beyond South Africa's existing position and would be chosen only if other more preferential options proved impossible to negotiate. Further, assessing how South Africa should be treated within a GSP system was clouded by the past distorted and statistically under-reported patterns of South African trade – a consequence of European and international sanctions. As a framework, it too would be subject to international ratification. An alternative and less parsimonious assessment suggests that GSP treatment provides certain non-reciprocal possibilities. It grants preferential access meaning lower although not zero tariffs which are subject to quantitative restrictions.

GSP is a flexible trade regime that has a non-contractual nature; in principle, bilateral negotiations are not needed prior to granting tariff concessions to recognized developing countries under this framework. A decision to grant GSP status is an autonomous European prerogative, making entry into force comparatively easy. Despite the revisions already foreshadowed, an attractiveness of the system was that the Community also had the experience of applying GSP elsewhere. Also, like MFN, it has the appealing virtue that it can offer a temporary method for preferential access to the Community while perhaps more complex bilateral association agreements were being negotiated. Such a strategy has been used for bridging trading relations between the EC and central European countries in lieu of a more comprehensive agreement and, for a fixed period, relations with the Andean Pact countries and Central America. It seemed unlikely that the more advantageous Super GSP that shapes relations with the least developed countries would to be extended to South Africa on economic grounds. Indeed, any extension of GSP to South Africa would be dependent on its reclassification.

In general, however, while GSP could provide South Africa with certain specific advantages, it would not necessarily advance South Africa's integration into the regional economy. Arguably the reverse might occur as the preferences could erode particular competitive margins enjoyed by the SADCC states. To facilitate the regional perspective – which remains a European objective – agreement on origin accumulation under GSP would have to be determined. To achieve this general regional rules of origin will have to be developed and applied to trade within the southern African region, a future prospect perhaps, but not an option that can be implemented in the relative short-term. For example, such a process would require the creation of a regional secretariat: none of the existing structures (SACU, SADC or the PTA) provide the necessary bureaucratic infrastructure to oversee the workings of regional cumulation arrangements. The benefits for the region of GSP status for South Africa, while difficult to quantify, are of some significance. As Lomé beneficiaries, the SADC states are not advantaged by using GSP for their exports to Europe; however, cumulation could provide them with benefits for those items they contribute to South African manufactures that then benefit from GSP preferences in Europe.

Lomé Membership

Much has been speculated about the third possibility, namely full Lomé status for South Africa. Its appeal was as much symbolic politically, as crucial economically. The option was the first to be seriously discussed as early as 1992: however, by mid-1993 it seemed increasingly unlikely that it would be the chosen framework for the new relationship despite specific trade advantages that Lomé potentially offered. The products most advantaged would be coal and the clothing/textile industries. Thus, despite the fact that many products would enter the EC market duty-free because of the GSP arrangements or their zero tariff rating, "the trade differences do make at difference at the margin, particularly the access for some agricultural products . . . and for certain processed tropical products" (Ravenhill, 1993,

p. 55). Compared with the GSP, however, Lomé offered considerably greater security of access. The general belief was that Lomé could offer the greatest trade preferences to the Republic and that South African membership would also assist regional cooperation by placing the Republic on the same economic trading plateau as the SADC states. Equal treatment of all southern African countries would become the operating principle. Thus regional processing of products would be able to meet the "rules of origin" requirements promoting both regional integration and intra-regional trade, key objectives of Europe's broader southern African policy. Further, preferences could also be negotiated to cover a wide range of possible future export products that are currently underdeveloped. Full Lomé status would also allow South African companies to tender for European Development Fund aid contracts (EDF) for the ACP region (Swain, 1992, p. 15). This could even result in South African companies having a competitive edge over EC contractors in certain sectors (with the probable result of those EC interests lobbying against South African membership).

The argument against membership focuses once again on South Africa's imprecise developed/developing classification. South Africa's GDP would put it well above the other Lomé states; the commodities for which trade preferences are available would give South Africa an advantage over other Lomé states as well as possibly meet with resistance from certain member states who produce similar agricultural products as South Africa. At best, South Africa could expect a strict quota system across a variety of sensitive product areas; however, even this implies an increase in the existing overall Lomé quotas rather than a cut in the existing levels for other ACP states to accommodate South African membership. The Sysmin and Stabex Lomé schemes could not financially accommodate South Africa. Further, accession to Lomé would be the longest route to establishing normal bilateral relations. It would involve extensive bi- and multilateral negotiations lasting, perhaps, for several years: the immediate post-election needs of South Africa could not be met. The decision to consider the Lomé alternative came too late for it to be a practical option. Perhaps most crucially of all, to gain accession to the Lomé Convention South Africa requires the consent of several multilateral bodies: GATT, the OECD and the ACP Lomé signatories. These could pose significant hurdles to South Africa.

The conditional agreement of the OECD and of GATT concerning South Africa's developing status is a prerequisite (as it is for several of the other options discussed here). Significantly, accession might well bring into question the entire compatibility of Lomé with the GATT accord and should be avoided for this if no other reason.

Article 363 of the Lomé Convention stipulates:

> Any request for accession . . . submitted by a State whose economic structure and production are comparable with those of the ACP States shall require approval by the Council of Ministers . . .

> Such accession shall not, however, adversely affect the advantages accruing to the ACP States signatory to this Convention under the provisions on development finance cooperation, the stabilization of export earnings and industrial cooperation.

Two issues arise: first, the argument that South Africa's economy can be considered as "comparable" to that any of the existing ACP states requires a reinvention of reality, more reminiscent of Lewis Carroll than orthodox economic analysis. South Africa possesses a large industrial capacity, developed financial and service sectors and a sound infrastructure and communications network – hardly the typical ACP profile. Second, it is hard to sustain the argument that the Republic's putative accession would not adversely affect a number of ACP states and be contrary to the legal provisions of Convention Article 363. Accession to the Convention would need the unanimous assent of all the other 70 signatories as well as the EU's agreement. It is far from certain that all other Lomé countries would be willing to allow South Africa to join. Even if this were achieved, it would only be after lengthy negotiations to protect and safeguard existing individual ACP members' advantages. In addition, within the Union itself there is growing criticism of the entire Lomé framework and a suggestion that its global approach should be abandoned for more regionally specific arrangements separating out the various components of the ACP states. Adding the South African economy into an already under-funded and financially strained framework might precipitate the early death of Lomé.

Lomé was not designed with future South African membership in mind. Consequently, it is hardly surprising that many of the Convention's attributes simply do not match the requirements of contemporary South African needs. Sysmin and Stabex could not accommodate South African participation. However, as already noted, although the Community did confidentially discuss a Commission proposal assessing the various options available and making recommendations on the feasibility of each, the policy process is dependent on South Africa first defining how they see themselves and which of the various Community frameworks best service their needs. To ask Europe whether it wishes to extend Lomé to South Africa improperly inverts the question; it is South Africa that should ask itself whether Lomé membership matches its requirements. In particular, while Lomé did give preferential import access to certain African primary commodities, "it did not encourage manufactures", a sector crucial to South Africa's economic revival (Thompson, 1992, p. 126).

A related concern was expressed by some member states who were resistant to South Africa down-grading its status in GATT. From the South African perspective there were also investment consequences: a developed status suggests, albeit symbolically, a safer and more predictable international investment proposition. In general, throughout 1993 no clear South African consensus emerged on this issue: Keys, the Finance Minister as late as October 1993, called categorically for a special bilateral agreement that acknowledged South Africa's developed status. Conversely, for essentially regional political reasons rather than economic necessity, the ANC initially favoured a position that recognized South Africa's developing status and reflected its regional identity. Hence the exploration of an associated Lomé status and the intermittent ANC comment asserting South Africa's interest in full Lomé membership. Also in October 1993 an ANC economics spokesperson called for the extension of "core market access provisions of Lomé IV including the cumulation provisions of the Lomé rules of origin, to South Africa, for the duration of the Convention" (Hirsh, 1993, p. 2). In general, however, these comments indicated no great policy analysis of the implications of Lomé membership, but rather suggested politically correct wishful thinking. Indeed, many encouraged South Africa to look beyond Lomé, as its continuation beyond the IV Convention date of 1999 seems increasingly doubtful, at least in the current unified ACP form. Rather than waste effort on securing Lomé accession in such a context of uncertainty, South Africa would be better advised to plan regionally in order to take advantage of any new regional preferential schemes introduced to replace Lomé.

Following on from the discussion of the agenda-setting role of the Commission noted in Chapter 5, while technically the Commission is simply the guardian of the Lomé Convention and the negotiating mandate a political prerogative, intra-Commission competition was clearly important. The relative seniority and importance of DGI was a further impediment to the Lomé option being accepted, the responsibility for which would have fallen to the DGVIII. The rejection of the Lomé framework had serious implications for DGVIII influence upon EU-South African relations as the core policy shifted from a development focus to a more traditional foreign and trade policy perspective.

Although ultimately unsuccessful, the discussion concerning Lomé membership served one essential function. It focused debate on the multilateral consequences of a new South African relationship and indicated that a bilateral decision taken in isolation was unworkable.

Associated Lomé Status

Because Lomé offered the greatest economic advantages, yet realizing the scope and nature of the difficulties membership posed, a fourth option floated in both the November 1992 and January 1994 Commission papers was for associated status. No other such example of associated status existed and no explicit legal basis was provided by the Convention other than the general provisions of Article 30 empowering the Council of Ministers "to take any political decision for the attainment of the objectives of this Convention". The specifics of what such a relationship would amount to in terms of trade, or how it might differ from full membership or a bilateral association agreement, were not comprehensively articulated. Theoretically, any such associated status could be as limited, or as expansive, as necessary, and the option was given some serious consideration throughout 1993. The idea evoked a kind of intermediate status under which South Africa could obtain access to certain qualified provisions and advantages within a Lomé framework: these would be selective and chosen not to conflict with sensitive ACP interests in the areas of trade or aid, for example. Elements within Lomé such as rules governing the cumulation of origin, could be used as a bridge between whatever EC–South Africa bilateral arrangement was concluded and the regional ACP Lomé framework.

The option presented a number of difficulties, however. First, the unspecified nature of what exactly such an associated relationship would mean in practice made a valid assessment extremely problematic for the Commission. Second, negotiating an associated status would demand the involvement of the ACP states: this could prolong the exercise excessively and could, depending on the scope of the association, result in additional financial burdens for the EU by way of compensation to adversely effected ACP states. Third, just as for full Lomé status, granting trade preferences involved the risk of reexamining the justification of any Lomé preferences under the GATT and potentially dilute the coherence of the argument. Lastly, there was a potential for fragmentation and unintended policy contradiction: such a unique arrangement could encourage a more general *à la carte* approach to Lomé by its other signatories corrupting the advantages of unicity.

Bilateral Agreements: Preferential and Non-Preferential

Thus we are left with the option of a specific bilateral agreement that offers preferential or, more likely, non-preferential terms.

A non-preferential agreement provides a legal framework for trade and cooperation between signatory states without granting specific trade preferences to a country. This type of relationship has been concluded between Europe and Asian and Latin American developing countries. Such an agreement could be used to provide both technical and financial trade assistance for the promotion of targeted South African exports. For example, the creation of marketing networks, personnel training, trade mission and promotional activities can all be facilitated through this mechanism. This consideration is of significance given the almost monolithic control of the South African economy by just half a dozen major corporate conglomerates. A traditional tariff preference approach tends to advantage such existing large-scale corporations; in contrast, a non-preferential agreement can prvide the possibility for assisting sectors of the population previously disadvantaged and encouraging the development of small scale entrepreneurial activities. In addition, a non-preferential approach appears more regionally sensitive than direct preference concessions which would increase the trade competition between regional national economies. It is also compatible with regional joint ventures and the broader aspects of regional integration.

A form of association agreement, perhaps paralleling those in existence with Brazil, for example, would provide a relationship that was geared specifically to South Africa's needs: the negative side for South Africa might be the requirement to dismantle certain protectionist measures in exchange for market access. DGI argued strongly for such a line in keeping with the Europe's commitment to trade liberalization and competition. Negotiating such an agreement could be time consuming. Yet this approach gained increasing support throughout 1993 as a likely option, particularly as the EU had already negotiated similar agreements with comparable states, most notably Brazil. The implications here are that beyond the existing Special Programme, further development aid would not be forthcoming: the policy emphasis would be on promoting economic cooperation, industrial cooperation and trade and investment promotion. Thus despite the probable negative consequences for regional integration, such an approach seemed likely, despite the greater development and preferential advantages under Lomé.

In determining the content of any bilateral preferential agreement the legality of such an agreement under GATT becomes paramount. For that reason a two-way preferential agreement on specific products that gives exclusive rights to Europe and South Africa conflicts with GATT article XXIV and is, therefore, unlikely to receive approval. A unilateral agreement giving South Africa specific preferences is the less hazardous option, but here again compatibility with GATT demands close attention and much hinges on the acceptance of the designation of South Africa as a developing country. Undoubtedly, any one-way preferences negotiated could offer considerable advantage to South Africa and would naturally provoke vocal opposition from other third countries who considered that their existing preferential advantages were being eroded. The SADC states may well be negatively effected (and regional integration under some circumstances possibly retarded), as might South Africa's direct southern hemisphere export competitors. Consequently, such an agreement would be complex and demand protracted negotiations to accommodate all third country considerations and product sensitivities.

Free Trade Area Agreement

Europe has had substantial experience in signing agreements that establish free trade areas or customs unions with third countries (for example, with Israel, Turkey, Cyprus and the former EFTA organization). Such regimes are internationally acceptable as they corresponded to the conditions set out in Article XXIV of GATT. They are seen as particularly appropriate where the participating partners already enjoy close and competitive trade and economic relations. The institutionalization of this existing pattern was a mechanism for enhancing these ties.

Such an agreement is the most ambitious of those contemplated by the Commission: but the unfettered scope of a free trade option is both its strength and its weakness. The advantage (in compliance to GATT article XXIV requirements) is that it envisages that restrictive regulations on commerce be substantially lifted with a view to their eventual abolition and the creation of a bilateral free trade environment. Such a framework would comply with international law and presents South Africa with maximum access to the European market (with EU exports receiving reciprocal and equivalent advantages in due course). The geographical and development limitations are not insurmountable as proven by the comparable experience of the North American Free Trade Association.

The disadvantage is that such a comprehensive scheme will have a fundamental impact on different production sectors within South Africa an within the Union. South Africa's relatively uncompetetive manufacturing sector and some of Europe's sensitive products could be adversely affected. In addition, membership of the existing South Africa Customs Union (SACU) would mean that any such EC–South African free trade agreement would also apply to the other SACU countries of Botswana, Lesotho, Namibia and Swaziland. For domestic reasons member states may be unwilling to expose their industries unnecessarily, whereas South Africa may baulk at the prospect of liberalizing their existing trade regime. Were such an option accepted a negative regional impact could result unless significant steps were simultaneously taken to create an equivalent integrated southern African economic market that extended beyond the SACU countries. A free trade area is a high risk option; the specific consequences are unpredictable.

It would be wrong to conclude, that Europe was a passive partner in the post-apartheid debate for the future framework for relations between South Africa and the Union. Certainly, the EU did not dictate the terms of the relationship and the onus lay with South Africa to set the agenda for the type of relationship it desired. This should not be construed, however, as implying that the EC would accept any proposal made. The Community treated South Africa in the same way as other third countries wanting a bilateral association; this implied that EU interests as well as those of South Africa would be protected. The legacy of apartheid and European sympathy for the new state will not overrule more pragmatic demands. Various options were considered and it was not the case that the new framework could take only one form.

THE CHOSEN FRAMEWORK

The over-riding criterion for the preferred policy, whatever one was chosen, was the recognition that South Africa is essentially an African country and not some geographically misplaced part of the Western world. The chosen policy had to reflect that reality and acknowledge the SADC component. Trade with the EU was primarily a medium term strategy for South Africa: its future markets lay in the African continent.

It was not until the last quarter of 1993 that the issue of a new bilateral economic framework came to be seriously addressed by either the ANC or the National Party Government. Understandably, domestic political debates had been the major focus of attention during the initial phase of the transition process: a new framework for South Africa's foreign affairs and regional development issues was given, with hindsight, mistakenly low priority. In one sense this was the result of Europe's generally perceived low profile within South Africa, and at least from the Government's perspective, a negative profile. The Community had been associated with funding anti-apartheid groups during the 1980s and with the imposition of sanctions. While the ANC did not share these negative images, their assessment of the potential role of the EU as a major international player within southern Africa was largely ill-defined and undeveloped. Traditional thinking prevailed encouraging a somewhat myopic focus on bilateral ties. While the Special Programme had been a welcome contribution, the low-key approach towards its implementation did little to raise awareness. Rather than herald this as a European initiative, attention was directed through the four channels, particularly the Kagiso Trust: the Community's role was tantamount to a silent partner financing the operation from overseas. The lack of any direct EU presence was obviously a contributing factor to this state of anonymity. The European profile really only entered the political consciousness in South Africa since September 1992 with the first deployment of observers. As Chapter 8 concludes, however, the profile of the EU was far from distinct or widely known even during the election observing process itself.

The full text of the chosen option is given in Appendix Document 7. As expected it contained immediate interim measures as well as a framework for a comprehensive long-term relationship. The option, agreed at the 18 April 1994 General Affairs Council in the context of the joint action, was the basis on which discussions with the new South African Government would focus. It is important to note that these were proposals for consideration by South Africa, not a prescriptive definite ultimatum. It was significant, however, that the Commission did accept the challenge to initiate the bilateral dialogue after the interregnum that had resulted in a policy vacuum since 1992. The earlier criticism of Commission reticence was no longer a valid accusation. Given the draft nature of the Council decision, only broad parameters were defined with the specific implementation of details left to the bilateral dialogue. The Commission interpreted the wording "to conclude an agreement quickly" as its mandate to start negotiations as soon as the multiparty Government was operational (the initial official visit was scheduled for June 1994 with the expectation that the precise nature of the interim package would be finalized by the Autumn).

The simplest aspect of the initial measures was a commitment by the Union to the removal of those international and European sanctions still in place. Within a month this had been achieved.

The actual initial package of measures were presented "without prejudice as to the form of the future more global arrangement", but were also considered to be consistent with, and a legal basis for, the foundations of the longer-term agreement. Consequently, it suggested a simplified structure that contained three broad clauses concerning human rights, a comprehensive cooperation agreement, and provisions for specific bilateral cooperation policies. However, the expansive scope of the elements contained within the joint action demanded that the main features of these initial measures were expansive: trade and economic cooperation; development cooperation; and political dialogue. The dilemma of delimiting areas of administrative competence within such a comprehensive joint action was again a sensitive issue. South Africa merely raised the problem of "contamination" of Commission prerogatives by the intergovernmentalism of the CFSP; the experience did not adequately solve the issue.

Trade and Economic Cooperation

The policy isolated four aspects of this component. First, the Community proposed extending market access by offering GSP privileges to South Africa (although this was made conditional on regional sensitivities and any new principles introduced as part of the overall GSP review (see below). Second, to facilitate regional economic cooperation it was advocated that the conditions for "rules of origin" cumulation be developed and monitored by a new administrative secretariat. Third, European support and funding for investment protection and promotion was suggested, involving EU investment in small and medium-sized companies in South Africa with the possibility of funding through an instrument similar to the European Community Investment Partners scheme. Further, it was proposed that the European Investment Bank should consider extending its area of authority to include South Africa. Fourth, bilateral cooperation across a wide range of areas was encouraged; for example in education and training, industry, commerce, telecommunications, science and technology.

Development Cooperation

This component of the policy outline constituted a continuation of the Special Programme and the objectives of the Development

Council Declaration of 25 May 1993 (see Appendix Document 4) while reflecting the changing development context of a post-election South Africa. Thus longer-term structured development approach and sector specific policies were the priority within the general philosophy that development programmes in the new South Africa should replicate the mechanisms and procedures found elsewhere, ending the *sui generis* procedural character that characterized the first decade of the development relationship. Without guaranteeing a specific level of financing, the Council statement reconfirmed the earlier verbal commitment to maintain EU funding at "a substantial level" of support "during the transitional period".

Political Dialogue

Creating such a bilateral dialogue was symbolic of the final normalization of political relations. Paralleling the EU's other global bilateral relationships, an emphasis was placed upon support for democracy, the rule of law, social justice and the promotion of human rights. The appropriate content, level and form of the dialogue was left for discussion and mutual agreement, although it was the EU's view that this should include ministerial and high official level contacts and incorporate a foreign policy perspective.

Following the announcement of the EU's interim GSP initiative for South Africa, in June 1994 the Commission issued the global GSP revision plan for the next ten year period (1995–2004). Commencing on 1 January 1995, it proposed two major innovations designed to reorientate the system to facilitate LDC (Least Developed Countries) development. First, "special encouragement regimes" that offered further customs reductions would be available to countries that can demonstrate a commitment "to improve their social and environmental practices": and second, a reevaluation of the development needs of GSP beneficiaries was recommended with, where appropriate, the gradual phasing out of certain countries, or sectors of production from GSP advantages (*Agence Europe*, 1994, no.6243, p. 5). These changes were designed to make the GSP instrument consistent with both the post-Uruguay Round GATT agreement and the Treaty on European Union's extended involvement with development policy. However, there were significant implications for South Africa.

First, somewhat perversely, the Republic's proposed inclusion in the GSP framework coincided with a potential weakening of the benefits from a South African perspective. First, the modulation of preferential rights implied that reduction in access for certain products or sectors would no longer be determined by their origin, but according to their overall impact on European production. Second, a procedure was enacted whereby a specified export sector of a country can be provisionally excluded from GSP advantages. This would occur where one country's particular exports were proving more competitive than those of other GSP members; suspension would therefore enhance the trade possibilities for the less competitive countries. At this stage it is impossible to calculate which of South Africa's product sectors would benefit or be disadvantaged by these clauses. The preferences, however, are becoming increasingly circumscribed and the marginal advantages constrained.

Two forms of conditionality were also included in the Commission proposal. First, a suspension clause provided for the Union provisionally to withdraw any benefits from a country that engaged in unacceptable behaviour. Second, incentives in the form of reduction GSP duties were offered to countries attempting to promote social and environmental protection (such as respecting the International Labour Organization Conventions, or maintaining sustainable deforestation programmes), and those that demonstrated a respect for intellectual property rights. Conditionality has become an increasingly typical European external relations instrument. In the case of South Africa these new conditions appear at this stage to offer potential advantages rather than constraints. However, these new GSP conditionalities do place additional limitations on the economic options available to the new multiparty government.

THE IMPORTANCE OF THE EC FOR SOUTH AFRICA

There have been strong historical links between the economy of South Africa and the Community, as well as between various member states and the Republic. However, the relationship has been largely asymmetrical with European trade and direct foreign investment of vital importance to South Africa, but South African trade with the EC of peripheral importance despite a degree of mineral dependency. For example, in the two years prior to the imposition of economic sanctions, EC exports to South Africa represented just 2 per cent (1984) and 1.5 per cent (1985) of the EC's total volume of exports. In contrast, in 1985, 41.2 per cent of South Africa's imports came from the then Ten and the Community took 20.4 per cent of the Republic's exports (Holland, 1988a, p. 54). In some respects Europe appears to have been a beneficiary of South Africa's international isolation. As noted in Chapter 2, European sanctions left the volume of trade largely unaffected: figures for the decade of the 1980s show an increase in trade with South Africa. The percentage of South Africa's imports that originated from the EC was 36.0 per cent in 1980 rising to 43.1 per cent by 1990: the percentage of South Africa's exports destined for the EC were 19.1 per cent in 1980 and 25.6 per cent ten years later (*Agence Europe*, 1993, no,5895, annex). Although the overall pattern was one of an enhanced trading relationship there were sizeable fluctuations in 1986–87 reflecting the modest impact of sanctions; however, as Table 6.1 shows, by the end of the decade both exports and imports had returned to approximately their pre-sanctions levels. Thus imports from South Africa were worth 8,825m ECU in 1984 and 8,211m ECU by 1989. Community exports to South Africa amounted to 5,688m ECU in 1985 and had increased to 6,433 ECU by 1989.

Data after 1986, however, should be read with caution. Unlike those available up until 1986, statistics for the post-sanctions period are considered unreliable by the Commission owing to a lack of transparency of trade flows. The Commission suspects a number of triangular trade patterns existed, involving countries which did not belong to the "sanctions cartel" (Commission, 1991). More reliable statistics can only be provided by the South African Government.

Within the EC perspective, the importance of individual member states as South Africa's trading partner has altered. Traditionally, South Africa relied heavily on the UK market; however, the 1980s has seen this challenged significantly. In the early 1980s Germany replaced the UK as South Africa's major supplier. By the end of the decade Germany dominated a massive 46.0 per cent of the EC's exports to South Africa and was the only Community member state substantially to increase its share of

Table 6.1   EC–South Africa Exports and Imports, 1983–89 (1,000ECUs)

Imports

Year	1983 ECU	%	1984 ECU	%	1985 ECU	%	1986 ECU	%	1987 ECU	%	1988 ECU	%	1989 ECU	%
B/L	1.343.000	20.3	2.337.120	26.5	2.225.777	23.5	2.235.065	27.9	724.357	13.3	1.008.357	8.0	1.159.827*	14.1
DK	154.000	2.3	153.865	1.7	206.795	2.2	102.169	1.2	3.551	0.1	5.917	0.04	230	0.0002
D	1.166.000	17.6	1.284.346	14.6	1.359.066	14.4	1.288.783	16.1	1.026.416	19.0	1.403.689	11.2	1.431.753	17.4
GR	44.000	0.6	37.556	0.4	56.783	0.6	54.486	0.7	50.355	1.0	34.683	0.3	36.265*	0.4
E	160.339	2.4	199.155	2.3	248.307	2.6	262.098	3.3	237.248	4.0	287.004	2.2	397.615	4.8
F	645.000	9.8	853.161	9.6	825.601	8.7	479.746	6.0	485.350	9.1	625.753	4.9	733.313	8.9
IRL	11.000	0.1	14.455	0.2	18.208	0.2	14.060	0.2	6.397	0.1	10.683	0.08	15.004	0.2
I	1.464.000	22.1	2.189.653	24.8	2.424.261	25.6	1.951.223	24.3	1.547.720	29.0	1.834.717	14.6	2.426.605	29.5
NL	116.000	1.7	189.669	2.2	237.620	2.5	219.981	2.7	196.556	3.7	250.169	2.0	263.023	3.2
P	38.290	0.6	39.949	0.5	61.697	0.7	61.486	0.8	62.763	1.2	82.442	0.7	128.162	1.6
UK	1.480.000	22.5	1.526.762	17.2	1.791.909	18.9	1.352.735	16.9	1.041.315	19.5	6.972.305	55.9	1.629.631	19.8
E.C.	6.621.629	100	8.825.691	100	9.456.024	100	8.021.832	100	5.382.028	100	12.515.719	100	8.211.328*	100

* Provisional.

Exports

Year	1983 ECU	%	1984 ECU	%	1985 ECU	%	1986 ECU	%	1987 ECU	%	1988 ECU	%	1989 ECU	%
B/L	249.000	4.2	320.440	4.4	243.522	4.3	218.107	4.7	240.101	4.7	308.642	4.9	330.311*	5.1
DK	74.000	1.2	88.379	1.2	77.394	1.4	53.429	0.3	13.435	0.3	12.547	0.2	8.425	0.1
D	2.194.000	36.8	2.970.560	40.5	2.246.190	39.5	1.970.369	44.0	2.200.201	44.0	2.830.325	44.6	2.962.852	46.0
GR	4.000	0.06	5.843	0.08	2.258	0.03	2.456	0.1	2.540	0.1	2.911	0.04	3.340*	0.05
E	106.321	1.84	163.238	1.84	124.000	2.1	87.324	1.6	80.811	1.6	122.676	2.0	113.858	1.8
F	562.000	9.4	637.300	9.4	510.995	8.9	411.031	8.0	403.708	8.0	554.533	8.5	553.988	8.7
IRL	45.000	0.8	53.340	0.8	41.312	0.7	41.136	1.1	52.654	1.1	73.649	1.2	37.484	0.5
I	534.000	8.9	660.452	9.02	434.092	7.6	357.401	7.9	394.031	7.9	528.812	8.4	576.817	9.0
NL	263.000	4.4	352.053	4.8	279.064	4.9	260.147	5.1	254.229	5.1	291.871	4.4	278.703	4.4
P	33.524	0.6	44.248	0.6	20.000	0.4	15.866	0.3	15.486	0.3	25.547	0.5	35.836	0.5
UK	1.901.000	31.6	2.033.320	27.8	1.709.219	30.0	1.257.481	26.9	1.342.768	26.9	1.603.809	25.2	1.531.559	23.8
E.C.	5.965.755	100	7.326.173	100	5.688.046	100	4.674.747	100	4.999.964	100	6.355.242	100	6.433.273*	100

*Provisional.
Source: Directorate-General I, Commission of the European Community.

exports during this period. In contrast, Britain's percentage share declined the greatest (almost matching the German increase), although the UK was in second place with 23.8 per cent. Between them these two countries were responsible for more than two-thirds of Europe's export trade with South Africa: only France (8.7 per cent) and Italy (9.0) made a significant contribution, leaving the remaining eight EC states contributing collectively just 12.5 per cent of exports (see Table 6.1).

The import of South African goods was somewhat more evenly distributed although in one year, 1988, trade patterns were dramatically and abnormally skewed (the UK took 55.9 per cent of the Community's South African import, a figure almost triple its usual level). In general during the 1980s Italy has been the leading importer into the Community, taking roughly one quarter of South Africa's exports. By 1989 this figured reached an all-time high of 29.5 per cent. The UK was in second position with almost one-fifth, closely followed by Germany. France was in fourth place (as was the case for exports) with a little under one tenth of Community imports from South Africa. Thus the four leading exporters to South Africa were also the four leading importers of South African products. In 1989 these four member states accounted for all but 24.4 per cent of the Community's trade in South African imports.

The most significant economic area where trade was directly effected by sanctions was in iron and steel exports to Europe. The trade in Krugerrands, while effectively halted by the end of 1987, was of minor economic consequence (Holland, 1988b, p. 420). The iron and steel products covered by the ECSC Decision implemented on 27 September 1986 did have an impact, even if the effect was somewhat delayed. As Table 6.2 indicates, 1985 and 1986 were peak years with 479m kg. and 472m kg. of South African products imported; Germany, Britain, Greece and Portugal were the major markets. In 1987 this fell to 367m Kg. with these four countries remaining responsible for approximately two-thirds of the trade. The following year this again fell to 225m Kg. and the provisional figures for 1989 recorded the level at just 167m Kg., one third of the 1985 level. Throughout, Germany remained the biggest buyer and only one member state, Denmark, actually ceased importing all embargoed iron and steel from 1 January 1987 onwards.

Table 6.2   EC imports of South African Iron and Steel 1985–89 (1000 kg)

Year	EC	B/L	DK	D	GR	E	F	IRL	I	NL	P	UK
1985	479	22	*	103	76	71	3	3	20	16	79	85
1986	473	24	*	121	89	58	4	2	16	22	45	90
1987	367	24	*	91	88	23	5	3	17	4	36	76
1988	225	17	0	91	28	25	2	2	5	1	27	27
1989	167	15	0	28	22	26	4	4	7	1	38	21

* = less than 1.
Source: Directorate-General I, Commission of the European Community.

Table 6.3 outlines the official level of trade that existed between South Africa and Europe in 1992. Focusing on member state imports first, the UK took a significant lead with 29.1 per cent (worth R4,524m), followed by Germany at approximately one fifth (R3,007m), The Netherlands 12.3 per cent (R1,928m), Italy 10.6 per cent (R1,656m) and Belgium 10.5 per cent (RI,638). Clearly the easing of sanctions saw South Africa begin to explore new markets within the EC, as well as build on existing trading patterns. In terms of EC exports to South Africa, Germany and the UK continued to outstrip the other member states followed in the distance by France and Italy, as had been the case in the 1980s: 40.7 per cent of exports came from Germany, 25.6 per cent from the UK, with France on 9.8 per cent and Italy 8.8 per cent. In 1992 six Community member states (in descending order Germany, the UK, Italy, The Netherlands, France and Belgium) were ranked in South Africa's top ten trading partners, collectively making the EC South Africa's most important relationship (see Table 6.4 and *Trade Monitor*, 1993, no.3, p. 10). In the same year 38.5 per cent of South Africa's visible trade was with the EC, an increase from 34.0 per cent in 1985, the year when many trade and financial sanctions were expected to become effective. Europe supplied 45 per cent of South Africa's imports and took 34 per cent of her exports. (Gawith, 1993, p. 17). However, South African exports destined for the EC are predominantly composed of gold, coal, and other precious minerals. Overall, mineral products accounted 20.7 per cent of

Table 6.3 South African Imports from and Exports to EC Members States 1992

Imports

R(1000)	Denmark	Ireland	UK	Luxembourg	Belgium	Netherlands	Germany	France	Portugal	Spain	Greece	Italy
Live Animals	4934	18616	22083		30323	23359	33946	50395	2644	2716	72	2175
Vegetable Products	7376	389	75326		38049	31298	63405	75053	977	10344	146	23396
Animal Fats	5	15	9732		610	20129	8792	325	1275	1523	232	903
Prepared Foodstuffs	3062	6561	234599		9092	25300	19230	22942	8327	3287	700	15248
Mineral Products	348	2703	30735		14556	8054	29442	15693	390	3140	833	11719
Chemical Products	43989	81306	1000371	559	323355	371853	1115647	333304	5133	63744	2855	146509
Plastics	2197	5173	297868	11653	124311	90654	421771	128206	1552	26810	592	107786
Hides and Skins	9	6	20489		173	2232	17217	2797	267	987	94	29100
Wood & Wood Products	93	1	9740	21	648	1096	10071	20005	32254	1911	2	4478
Pulps	1084	1290	351531	66	20481	27079	234476	61144	152	15800	468	40413
Textiles	791	2290	166231	3031	43151	50430	252483	45857	24371	15515	5010	102528
Footwear, Headgear. etc	18	13	10422		1190	1472	3440	2817	3953	1211	1035	22767
Stone, plaster, cement	489	2049	90747	873	11326	8272	117169	53273	3933	25074	1578	100036
Precious & semi-precious stones	0.4	17117	61493	2	136097	142	7803	1386	1572	228	3	1967
Base Metals	2719	8011	299327	17558	71307	45960	497079	117069	9063	28167	1544	117422
Machinery & appliances	40017	42078	1800486	8021	240629	400906	3317267	723411	9886	81383	3076	818287
Vehicles & others		53	467216	1267	10755	33895	1906308	299259	405	64086	646	187265
Optical, photographic etc		14002	318550	2507	54910	89409	433311	70957	1908	6941	203	70645
Miscellaneous manufactures		2460	64532		3611	5568	63066	21493	1403	6859	296	36623
Art & Antiques			12214	9	645	2522	288	1381	1	1	6	145
Other classified goods		193	37047		959	2944	33821	5712	131	847	98	3483
TOTAL	107131.4	204326	5380939	45367	1138128	1224815	8554086	2052479	110097	360574	19489	1842895

Exports

R(1000)	Denmark	Ireland	UK	Luxembourg	Belgium	Netherlands	Germany	France	Portugal	Spain	Greece	Italy
Live Animals	188	227	39362	179	16	26018	34748	27174	23324	107321	3038	88085
Vegetable Products	573	679	707158	3138	344	43993	221728	50281	10727	18747	8444	43361
Animal Fats	1269	73	517	3146	742	113	3592					9965
Prepared Foodstuffs	6916	10366	219703	16	36608	100777	208889	34449	26942	60934	2311	
Mineral Products	28125	19460	294259	324314	776377	353311	263990	161944	447122	73600	533325	69865
Chemical Products	291	1957	172537	15	57595	290586	125090	57673	5640	13260	3691	3001
Plastics	228	2390	47179	138	5698	19206	21103	4546	1994	2120	2241	
Hides and Skins	15	28285	3698	919	27910	19651	1460	17013	3600	192567		
Wood & Wood Products	650	929	62888	2	6708	12371	19763	7203	1340	7455	2760	15090
Pulps	17	311	181934	0.7	7043	7405	84438	63583	2438	51853	13642	159302
Textiles	202	2760	302499	199	42642	51619	198753	111280	12894	22495	2648	93655
Footwear, Headgear.	10	9	19070		423	1323	3241	2883	150	409	264	353
Stone, plaster, cement etc	80	1521	22841		9376	5149	20345	10910	1817	11986	3389	26536
Precious & semi-precious stones	163	171022	692270	8	703061	234	57717	6333	32	482	34	2910
Base Metals	435	11608	243619	1751	211836	462533	364831	148653	33932	151353	51306	279175
Machinery & appliances	1746	3958	183518	82	79398	40447	260495	51425	4252	44748	2536	49383
Vehicles & others	829	357	103465	64	137642	35452	459774	29633	11375	32788	2985	28823
Optical, photographic etc	357	1140	21549	1308	3326	33487	7405	456	317	273	1497	
Miscellaneous manufactures	193	709	108278		7065	2458	23105	18683	561	2103	161	2353
Art & Antiques	114	24	5599	10	472	228	733	269	97	650	3	214
Other classified goods	0.5	60231	1047409		3260	47249	485010	88376	5	1	8	33135
TOTAL	41132.5	289658	4524691	5602.7	1638580	1928187	3007817	1007142	303380	993270	176934	1656387

Source: Trade Monitor (1993) no.4, pp. 6–7.

Table 6.4   South Africa's Top Twenty Traders – 1992

Rank SA Exports		SA Exports (R billion)	SA Imports (R billion)	Total Trade	Rank Total Trade
2	USA	4.8	7.1	11.9	1
5	Germany	3.0	8.6	11.6	2
3	U.K.	4.5	5.4	9.9	3
4	Japan	3.7	5.6	9.3	4
1	Swtzerland	5.4	1.2	6.6	5
6	Taiwan	2.1	1.8	3.9	6
9	Italy	1.6	1.8	3.4	7
8	Netherlands	1.9	1.2	3.1	8
13	France	1.0	2.1	3.1	9
7	Belgium	2.0	1.1	3.1	9
10	Zimbabwe	1.6	0.8	2.4	11
11	Hong Kong	1.5	0.8	2.3	12
14	South Korea	0.9	0.7	1.6	13
15	Spain	0.9	0.4	1.3	14
16	Israel	1.0	0.3	1.3	15
12	Zambia	1.1	0.04	1.1	16
17	Malawi	0.7	0.13	0.8	20 +
18	Mozambique	0.7	0.05	0.7	20 +
19	CIS	0.6	0.07	0.7	20 +
20	Norway	0.5	0.03	0.5	20 +

Source: *Trade Monitor* (1993) no. 3, p. 10.

exports; food and agricultural products 16.3 per cent; precious and semi-precious stones 15.2 per cent; and base metals 12.3 per cent (*Trade Monitor*, 1993, no.4, p. 5).

With the exception of coal which had no preferential access, these products did not face significant tariffs under the existing regime. Approximately 60 per cent of the EC's imports from South Africa cannot gain any additional benefits from another-form of preference (*Trade Monitor*, 1993, no.3, p. 10). Consequently, much contemporary analysis has questioned the importance of trade preferences for South Africa. Only a limited range of non-primary South African products would be competitive in the single European market, whereas agricultural exports such as beef, sugar and wine are either excluded from

Europe or disadvantaged through Common Agricultural Policy tariffs. Only within a Lomé framework would there be possible (but not guaranteed) benefits for products such as deciduous fruits and vegetables, paper and leather products and some chemicals (*Trade Monitor*, 1993, no.4, p. 8). Consequently, the proposed 1994 GSP framework reflected a conservative rather than provocative readjustment of Europe's bilateral economic relations with South Africa. Furthermore, quite how this approach could accommodate regional needs and promote regional integration remained problematic and it is this topic that the next chapter now examines.

7 SADC, Regional Integration and the Role of the Union

It would be inappropriate to come to a new agreement with Europe designed to assist the Southern African region without the full engagement of the other countries of Southern Africa in the process. Whether or not the new arrangement is structured within the Lomé Convention or parallel to this Convention, the new framework of cooperation will affect the region, and we feel we should consult with members of the ACP group in the course of the negotiations. (Hirsch, 1993, p. 3)

This statement from an ANC spokesperson provides the context for this chapter and provides a bridge to develop a number of the themes already introduced relating to regional integration outside a Lomé context. As noted in the previous chapter, Lomé was the obvious choice if regional integration was the sole criterion guiding European policy: however, the potentially contradictory, or at best mutually exclusive interests that shaped both the EU and the South African position, overruled this one condition. Consequently, the EU was confronted with a series of difficulties in attaining regional development as a consequence of the rejection of the Lomé option. This chapter addresses the EU's southern African regional policy and examines its coherency *vis-à-vis* the bilateral cooperation agreement with South Africa; second, it examines the difficulties inherent in regional integration around SADC; and third, the Community "model" is discused as an appropriate example for the region.

The 27 April elections did not symbolize the end of the South African issue despite the transition to democratization: rather, from a policy perspective this date marked the beginning, not the end, of a significant phase in EU involvement. The question of regional integration – South Africa within southern Africa – became a priority, if belatedly. Historically, regional development

188

had constituted the second aspect of the Community's "twin track" approach. However, the content of the policy had altered since first being formulated in the 1970s. The purpose of regional integration in southern Africa was no longer to develop the region in order to reduce the economic dependency on South Africa for trade and infrastructures: the revised policy focused on using South Africa's comparative economic strength to foster regional development. From a policy of excluding South Africa, the change was made to incorporating South Africa as the core around which regional integration and development could be sustained.

Since its inception, part of the Community's political ideology has been to encourage globally the creation of equivalent integrated regional groupings. In a general sense this ambition has been remarkably successful, although the role played by the Community was often that of a catalyst as a perceived external threat, rather than as a positive role model. The creation of ASEAN, the Andean Pact, NAFTA for example were, in part, responses to the Community's increasing economic hegemony. In contrast, the EC was prepared to be more explicitly involved in promoting the regional virtues of first SADCC, and latterly SADC, and it was made clear at an early stage of discussions that policy towards the new South Africa would have to be regionally balanced. While the logic of regional integration assumed mutual benefits for the eleven countries involved, there were a number of sensitive issues that made cooperation hesitant, both on the part of the region and South Africa. The challenge is to find a coherent policy for the whole region. Essentially, the main issues of concern were: the imbalance in South Africa's economic strength; the attraction of the "core" (South Africa) at the expense of the periphery; the danger of South African enterprises invading the region and assuming a monopolistic position; the question of "rules of origin" and the overlap with Lomé provisions enjoyed by SADC; the level of integration – monetary union, free movement of peoples, goods, capital, political union, common external affairs, etc.; the complexity and conflicting nature of existing regimes (PTA, Customs Union, etc.); regional security issues (which are particularly sensitive for Zimbabwe); the contrary case of South Africa ignoring the region and becoming preoccupied with its own economic issues; and, the transfer of resources from South Africa to SADC in general.

These last two points are particularly crucial given the domestic demands that will be placed on the new Government of National Unity that assumed office in 1994. South Africa, despite regional sympathies and obligations engendered by the frontline states anti-apartheid role, may not be in an economic or political position to advocate such a transfer of resources. The parallel is with the North–South debate within the Community itself and the role played by the Cohesion Fund whereby the four less developed economies receive assistance. In the southern African context, perhaps eight of the SADC states become the recipients with South Africa (alone or possibly assisted by Botswana and Zimbabwe) assuming the equivalent role played by the richer half dozen or so EU states. The numerical imbalance points to the precarious nature of such a unidimensional form of regional development.

EC POLICY TOWARDS SADCC

A variety of attempts at regional institutional arrangements have been explored in southern Africa during the twentieth century. The choice, and debate, has been between integration or just regional cooperation (Maasdorp, 1992b, p. 124). The earliest example was the Southern African Customs Union (SACU) established in 1910 and most recently renegotiated in 1969. It provides for duty-free trade in goods and services between South Africa and the contiguous states of Botswana, Lesotho, Swaziland and, since its independence, Namibia, as well as a common external tariff. As such it constitutes the region's only existing common market promoting economic integration. The Common Monetary Area (CMA) of 1986 now draws these same countries together to facilitate the free-flow of capital and a common exchange rate (Maasdorp, 1992c, p. 6). Both of these organizations promoted the concept of regional integration, rather than regional cooperation which was the original focus of SADCC. The 1983 Preferential Trade Area (PTA) for Eastern and Southern Africa was conceived with the objective of promoting all forms of economic cooperation and regional trade between its eighteen members. However, such a preferential area constitutes just the first cautious step towards a free trade area and possible future integration. The current date for a PTA-wide free trade zone is the year 2000 (p. 7). There is a degree of overlapping membership: apart from Botswana and Namibia, the SADC states also belong to the PTA; and two SACU members are also components of SADC and the PTA. In the past joint membership of SACU and the PTA has proved conflictual. The unanimous approval of all SACU member states is required for any concessionary trade agreements with third countries, whereas the PTA Treaty demands MFN treatment amongst member countries (p. 19). Consequently, both Lesotho and Swaziland were in the past in breach of their PTA obligations in order to conform to SACU (which constitutes the more important of the two partnerships from their perspective). South African membership of the PTA would extend the application of the MFN principle. This could disadvantage several member states who are unable to compete directly with South African products without some form of protection. This experience suggests a possible parallel for the potential problems of regional compatibility and consistency that the new European cooperation framework with South Africa might encounter. Clearly, the new regional circumstances present the existing structures with a fundamental challenge to their role, and foreshadow the probability of significant alterations in both function and organization after 1994.

Initiated independently in 1979, SADCC was typical both of these broad regional aspirations, as well as of the cross-cutting objectives and competences. Although not devised at the behest of the Community, SADCC provided the EC with the mechanism for focusing its regional foreign policy objective. Without EC and other international support SADCC would certainly have been stillborn. The founding 1980 Lusaka policy declaration specified SADCC's four objectives as: the reduction of regional dependence on the South African economy; the development of structural links to facilitate equitable regional integration; the mobilization of resources to implement national, inter-state and regional policies; and, the coordination of efforts to mobilize international support for the economic liberation of southern Africa (Commission, 1981, p. 14). Coordination rather than competition was the guiding criterion, and the approach was in contradiction to the widely advocated international reliance of market neoliberalism and private foreign direct investment (Stoneman and Thompson, 1992, p. 75). SADCC was concerned with trade, but also with equitable regional industrial development (Thompson, 1992, p. 130). However, these grandiose aspirations lacked both effective inter-regional institutions and the compulsion of a treaty basis: despite the references to regional integration the organization was exclusively intergovernmental and did not formally compromise national sovereignties. Simultaneously, explicit coordination and implicit integration goals were espoused, inspired as much by political determinants as by economic rationale. This paradox was identified by one school of criticism as the explanation for the SADCC's comparatively modest achievements. The combination of its catholic inclusiveness, a confusion between strategies for enhancing regional economic cooperation as opposed to regional economic integration, and an absence of concerted political will to act regionally, conspired to hinder the successful implementation of its agenda (Ching'ambo, 1992, p. 50).

SADCC was an attempt to provide a broad framework for development initially covering policy sectors such as agriculture, energy, mining, and labour resources, with increasing emphasis subsequently given to expanding industrial and service production and intra-SADCC trade. However, for these developments to be realized it was essential to improve transportation and communication links, and these twin objectives became both SADCC's and the EC's top priority for removing regional economic dependency. Without such a reform, the other methods to facilitate intra-SADCC trade would be ineffective. The importance of this linkage was underlined by the South African Government's policy of regional destabilization which targeted transport links. SADCC's efforts were severely impaired by sabotage during the 1980s; five of the seven SADCC railways were routed through Mozambique and it was here, particularly the Beira Corridor line, that South African disruption was the most catastrophic. As one parliamentary study concluded, "if Mozambique's economy can be disrupted – and the routes to Angola's Atlantic ports blocked – then much of the SADCC region can be forced to import and export via South Africa" (AWEPAA, 1987, p. 25). Estimating the real cost of this regional destabilization is precarious; one study put the figure at US$10 billion for 1980–84, tantamount to one third of SADCC's combined export earnings for the period (*The Courier*, no. 95, p. 44); another measured the direct costs as $16–17 million by 1985, but with indirect costs something like ten times this figure (Green and Thompson, 1986, p. 271–3).

Despite destabilization, SADCC made some progress in integrating the region's transport and communication networks; more modest achievements were evident in the energy and water sectors, but almost none in the coordination of industrial investment. However, as one analysis concluded, overall the picture for the 1980s was one of stagnation not development: "[N]ot only did intra-SADCC trade decline over the period but figures suggest some increase in the concentration that the Lusaka Declaration had been so anxious to avoid" (Hawkins, 1992, p. 116). In addition, between 1980–88 manufacturing fell from 13.1 per cent to 12.0 per cent as a share of GDP, and in "the region as a whole, economic expansion failed to match the rate of population growth, and per capita incomes fell 13 per cent" (ibid., p. 107). A consequence of this economic malaise was a virtual doubling of the external debt servicing ratios during the 1980s (ibid., p. 113). Lastly, there was no indication that reliance on South Africa for both imports and exports had declined. Trade with the Republic exceeded intra-SADCC transactions by a ratio of almost three to one (p. 117).

The scale of the problem that faced SADCC in its first decade of operation was formidable. In a 1986 review, 158 separate SADCC transport and communication projects had been identified for assistance, although full international funding was not guaranteed. Between 1980–87 the Community provided US$192 million, a figure that represented 11 per cent of total funding for the period (Stoneman and Thompson, 1992, p. 74). Several Community instruments were employed in this support: under the first Lomé Convention (1976–80) 548.5 million EUA (European Units of Account) were provided; by the time of the signing of Lomé III this had risen to 776 million ECU donated to the nine individual SADCC national indicative programmes. Additional funds of 110 million ECU were provided through the 1986 "Memorandum of Understanding", a unique five year regional resource programme (*The Courier*, no. 96, p. 20). This was subsequently increased to 141 million ECU, the extra money being "devoted chiefly to transport, for projects such as the Lobito Corridor and the Limpopo railway, which are designed to reduce dependence on South African ports for the shipment of goods"

(*EPC Bulletin*, 1989, 89/136). Overall, from 1975–90 the EC contributed 3.2 billion ECU to SADCC, with almost half of that earmarked for 1985–90 under Lomé III (*EPC Bulletin*, 1988, 88/ 459). Lomé IV saw a 30 per cent drop in EC funding: just 121m ECU was exclusively devoted to SADCC, although additional funding of up to 825m ECU was available from the European Investment Bank for venture capital in the private sector (*Agence Europe*, no.5954, 1993, p. 9). Despite an overall trade deficit with the ACP countries of 2.3 billion ECU in 1991 and of 1.0 billion in 1992, the EC has recently had a trade surplus with southern Africa. For example, for the first nine months of 1992 the Community enjoyed a surplus of 90m ECU (*Agence Europe*, no.5935, 1993, p. 16).

Despite being SADCC's most important single financial contributor, there were pressures from within the Community as well as from some SADCC members for increased assistance. In a practical sense, the allocated funds were inadequate for the task and those funds that were dispensed tended to favour transport and communication over all other projects. One critical interpretation of this tendency argued that the EC, like other international donors, was unwilling to support manufacturing and industrial development that would be in direct competition with the Community's own products. Whatever the truth behind the rationale, throughout the 1980s SADCC made only modest progress towards breaking out of its economic dependency on South Africa. Despite this objective being a shared one with the Community, as already noted the regional objectives of the EC were consistently regarded as secondary to the political objectives *vis-à-vis* South Africa. As an earlier study concluded, by the late 1980s the "first objective of Community policy in Southern Africa has yet to be achieved; in the medium to short-term, economic freedom for Southern Africa remains a vision, not a reality" (Holland, 1988a, p. 29). The verdict on how successful the Community's post-apartheid attempts to re-examine the regional economic question have been remains open.

By 1992, SADCC had clearly shifted beyond limited project cooperation towards the direction of regional trade integration (Maasdorp, 1992c, p. 5). In its end of year review "development integration" was advocated stressing the necessity of close political cooperation as a precondition for integration. The selective lowering of trade barriers was to be balanced by a role for state planning in regional industrial projects, in energy coordination, and by creating an investment climate infrastructure. A rejection of zero-sum market economics was still evident, however, in favour of equitable regional relations that facilitated compensatory measures where needed.

[P]ast theories of regional cooperation addressed mainly the market sector. SADCC in practice is saying that infrastructure, production, exchange and distribution of benefits are all equally important in promoting regional cooperation . . .

Further, national plans no longer suffice; regional cooperation is becoming a necessary, if not sufficient, condition for growth. (Thompson, 1992, pp. 143–4).

POLICY TOWARDS SADC

One commentator noted that in practice SADCC was "bound together more by the cement of anti-South African sentiment than economic common interest" (Hawkins, 1992, p. 120). It was not surprising then, that initially the metamorphosis of SADCC into SADC was not indicative of a major change in policy direction, but extended and deepened the existing approach. SADCC's original objectives had been to generate economic cooperation motivated by opposition to South Africa; SADC developed this commitment into support for regional economic integration. The only significant departure in principle was a new preference for a *dirigiste* over *laissez-faire* approach: regional integration was to be driven by a more regimented, interventionist and centrally directed policy approach, although the institutional structures and policy content of this reorientation were not specified. The rationale behind this change was that the past unstructured approach had tended to replicate existing inequalities; deliberate intervention was seen as part of the solution so that "all countries in the region have a fair share of investment, production and employment creation opportunities" (Leistner, 1992b, p. 8).

Like its predecessor, SADC has to be understood within the Lomé context and it was changes in Europe's view of SADCC's role within the Convention that provided the motivation behind SADC's reorientation. Title XII of Lomé IV is specifically devoted to regional cooperation; as Article 156 states:

1. The Community shall support the ACP States' efforts through regional cooperation to promote long-term collective and self-reliant, self-sustained and integrated social, cultural and economic development and greater regional self-sufficiency.
2. Community support shall be given within the framework of the major regional cooperation and integration objectives which the ACP States have set or will set for themselves at regional, inter-regional and international level.

In contrast to earlier Conventions, greater emphasis was placed upon economic integration and functional cooperation with approximately one tenth of the entire budget (1,250m ECU) allocated for such regional initiatives globally during the period 1990–95. SADC states were further advantaged by the special provisions for the Least Developed ACP countries (which covered seven SADC members) and for Landlocked states (six countries). Prior to Lomé IV, SADCC's Programme of Action had been the exclusive avenue for EC funding. However, from 1990 onwards the 121m ECU allocated specifically for southern Africa was also available for PTA projects which traditionally were more dedicated to the principles of free trade and establishing a common market (Leistner, 1992b, p. 8). SADC's decision to move towards deeper and more directed form of economic integration was also a response to this external challenge to the exclusivity of its role.

At the time of its launching in 1992 South African participation was not envisaged. A high level SADC delegation visit to Brussels in December 1992 emphasized its continued opposition to South Africa's inclusion in either SADC or in the Lomé Convention while any vestiges of apartheid and undemocratic rule persisted. At the January 1993 SADC Annual Consultative Conference, Commissioner Marin of DGVIII urged SADC to prepare for South Africa's eventual inclusion into this fledgling organization for regional economic integration, and to adapt its development strategies accordingly. Although short-term difficulties should be expected, areas where economic exchanges would be mutually beneficial included investment, trade and technology transfers, and in energy and water supplies. In the longer-term, solutions to problems such as food security could only be met through regional coordination (*European Report*, no.1831, 1993, p. 12).

By the time of the ACP/EC Joint Assembly session held in Gaborone in April 1993, SADC's position had shifted to anticipating the participation of a democratic South Africa as the eleventh SADC member, paralleling the response already advocated by the Commission (*Agence Europe*, no.5954, 1993, p. 11). To facilitate this a SADC mission based in South Africa was proposed. SADCC's former rejection of the role of free market forces was also set aside. As the experience of assessing and negotiating a bilateral European-South African cooperation agreement suggested, a rapid incorporation of the Republic within SADC should not be anticipated. The issues were complex and politically sensitive. As the following section illustrates in detail, the fear was that rather than SADC incorporating South Africa, the Republic would in effect annex the region economically becoming the dominant economic core surrounded by dependent economic satellites states. Within a SADC context in 1988 South Africa represented 31.6 per cent of the population and 74.5 per cent of the GNP (the per capita GNP equivalent of 235 per cent for the region)(Maasdorp and Whiteside, 1992, p. 3). The comparison with the economic integration of the nascent European Community of the 1950s and 1960s was used to support the argument that economic differences in themselves were not impediments to establishing regional integration. While appealing, the analogy with Germany's role as the economic core of the EC, misrepresents both South Africa's economic capacity and the complex political and economic rationales that promoted European integration (see the final section of this chapter for a fuller analysis of the EC as a model for SADC).

South Africa was faced with three broad choices (not necessarily mutually exclusive options) with respect to regional structure: SACU could be deepened and enlarged; existing functional cooperation in energy and infrastructure could be extended and separate bilateral trade agreements sensitive to specific products could be negotiated with third countries in the region; or, South Africa could accede to SADC and possibly the PTA and approach trade from a multilateral perspective. The current structure of SACU and its limited revenue base makes this an improbable long term strategy (Gawith, 1993, p. 31). The accession of South Africa to SADC (or its membership of some new, but similar, regional grouping) will be determined as much by political as by economic arguments. There is understandable reluctance to embrace South Africa unconditionally and a cautious option for the region might be to design a series of specific bilateral agreements. The danger of "divide and rule", setting regional economies in competition with each other, would of course be exacerbated by this approach.

The record of regional development excluding South Africa suggests that in reality there is no alternative. Arguably, the entire philosophy behind constructing such an economic framework was ill-conceived and has only persisted because of external donor support motivated by political rather than economic considerations. Balanced development

> and reduced dependence have been described as SADCC's two guiding principles. Neither has been achieved. Ten years on, it can legitimately be argued that the whole concept of reduced dependence was misplaced, while development, and not just balanced development, has proved elusive. (Hawkins, 1992, p. 130)

The relationship is mutually dependent and can be mutually beneficial. South Africa's economic future is dependent on its regional market; and, a regional economy requires South African participation. It can even be argued that in the longer term South Africa's dependency will be greater: its industrial growth is preconditioned on functional cooperation, particularly water and electricity supplies from the region, and its manufactures currently remain only competitive and exportable within the region and further into Africa (Thompson, 1992, p. 134).

The question of conditionality for Southern Africa seems destined to be both topical and controversial during the 1990s. If the experience of the ACP states in general, and sub-saharan Africa in particular, is indicative, aid and development will become increasingly and explicitly tied to specific criteria. Lomé IV saw structural adjustment programmes and conditionality introduced for the first time by the Community. The extension of this tendency seems probable during the 1990s through "the linkage of aid provision with political reforms and human rights" (Riddell, 1993, p. 152). The application of human rights conditionality is, however, less obvious than its rhetoric would suggest. Nonetheless, continued European support for SADC and other regional development initiatives will certainly conform to this contemporary Community requirement. Perhaps of more direct economic consequence is the pattern for the EC to link its support to the adoption of market economy domestic policies. Consequently, it has been predicted that "conditionality related to the retreat of the state and support for the nascent private-sector development is likely to become more widespread and probably more specific in nature" (ibid., p. 153). The Commission proposal of April 1994 concerning the future bilateral framework confirmed that economic conditionality was seen as the quid pro quo for the normalization of trading relations with South Africa: the reduction in protectionist policies, the use of exchange control regulations and industrial subsidies were all targeted for reform (see Chapter 4 and this discussion of the Commission's role for further elaboration of this point). Similarly, the earlier May 1993 Development Council Declaration on South Africa referred to the application of the EC's general development conditions and criteria (see Appendix document 4).

THE ANATOMY OF DEPENDENCY

The scale and breadth of the region's historical dependency is profound, covering such sectors as transport, bilateral trade, migrant labour, GDP ratios and the structure of production. As one commentator noted almost a decade after the Community first signalled its support for SADCC, these states were unequivocally economic appendages of South Africa, poor, non-industrialized and deficient in food (Friedland, 1985, p. 288). SADCC was established specifically to change this situation. Its approach was a "pragmatic step-by-step approach to regional cooperation" (Blumenfeld, 1992, p. 138). It was based on a minimal bureaucratic structure without central institutions; the responsibility for fostering cooperation and reducing economic dependency was delegated to the participating states. Through this informal and flexible structure it was hoped that practical proposals would be advanced rather than the grandiose plans typical of other African regional schemes that were invariably unsuccessful. Despite some modifications in SADCC's favour, the overall conclusion form the 1980s holds firm mid-way through the 1990s: while SADCC "has made not inconsiderable progress" the record has been patchy and the fundamental structural constraints have yet to be adequately resolved (ibid., p. 143). The following illustrations give an idea of the scale of the problem that faced SADCC during the 1980s (see, Holland, 1988a for a more detailed account).

Historically, the region's dependency was not based solely on the Republic's obvious economic superiority, but also on its stranglehold over all transportation links. The most efficient trade routes for Botswana, Lesotho, Malawi, Namibia, Swaziland, Zaire and Zimbabwe were via South African airports or harbours: for example, even the comparatively northern state of Zambia still sent approximately half of its mineral exports through South Africa for logistical reasons, as was approximately 90 per cent of Zimbabwean trade. Military destabilization of the region by the South African army (or its surrogates) effectively removed the possibility of seeking alternatives routes. This infrastructural limitation was partially responsible for the distorted bilateral regional trade patterns. In 1979, intra-SADCC trade amounted to less than 3 per cent of SADCC's cumulative total foreign trade; by 1987 this had increased to just 4.4 per cent (Blumenfeld, 1992, p. 142). In contrast, in 1979 20 per cent of overall trade was with South Africa (a figure that rose to 29 per cent for South African imports to the SADCC group) (ibid., p. 136). The most recent estimate suggests that South Africa represents roughly 40 per cent of SADC's total trade (Gawith, 1993, p. 29). Historically, six of the nine SADCC states' bilateral trade links to South Africa have far outweighed any other intra-regional aspects of trade. By way of example, the BLS states (Botswana, Lesotho and Swaziland) were reliant on South Africa for all oil supplies and derived a significant percentage of their revenue from membership of SACU (totalling between two-thirds and three-quarters of all revenue for Lesotho and Swaziland between 1982–86). A remarkable 91 per cent of Lesotho's trade was with South Africa and South Africa provided the bulk of imports for Botswana, Swaziland, Malawi and Zimbabwe (88, 87, 42 and 38 per cent respectively) (Blumenfeld, 1992, p. 136). However, without South Africa as the sub-continent's dominant exporter and importer, the economic plight of the SADCC states would be disastrous unless massive foreign investment were increased.

The regional trade dependency was and is very much a one-way street: for South Africa, trade north of the Limpopo has always been its lowest priority. Taking 1984 as a typical year, South African imports that originated in Africa amounted to a mere 1.9 per cent of the total; South African exports were only marginally more important at 3.5 per cent. However, of South Africa's non-gold exports approximately one-fifth go to SADCC countries (Maasdorp, 1992b, p. 123). From the SADCC perspective, between 1983–86 South Africa provided 24 per cent of all imports, whereas SADCC exports to South Africa represented just 4.5 per cent of their collective trade (Thompson, 1991, p. 61). After 1986 Pretoria halted the publication of trade figures (in an attempt to circumvent the impact of international sanctions); consequently, the reliability of statistics after this date is questionable. One estimate suggested that for 1988 South Africa exported R12 billion in goods to Africa, 85 per cent of which was with SADCC (Maasdorp, p. 123). The latest estimates of South African trade with SADCC confirm the historical pattern. In 1990, South Africa imported goods to the value of R2 billion, over three-quarters of which came from just three countries (Swaziland R681 million, Namibia R495 million and Zimbabwe R441 million). South African exports totalled R11.3 billion with five main markets accounting for more than four-fifths of trade (Botswana R3.3 billion; Namibia R1.9 billion; Lesotho and Swaziland R1.6 billion each; and, Zimbabwe R1.0 billion)(Maasdorp, 1992c, p. 12). Two overall conclusions can be drawn from the most contemporary data. First, South Africa is principally an important export market only for the BLS states, Namibia and Zimbabwe; export trade for the other SADC states is negligible. Second, SACU membership advantages South Africa by providing it with a guaranteed export market for its manufactures (which resulted in a trade balance of around US$1.7 billion in 1990) (Goodison, 1992b, p. 2).

A further sector where dependency was substantial was in the flow of migrant labour into South Africa; here Lesotho's predicament was the most vulnerable with some 150,000 migrants, half the regional total working in South Africa in 1985. On average, 80 per cent of migrant workers were employed in mining; for reasons of mechanization and cost, levels of employment in this sector declined from 336,000 in 1973 to 236,000 in 1986 with migrants from Malawi and Mozambique the greatest affected. Agriculture is the next most significant employer of migrant workers (approximately 4.0 per cent), with manufacturing accounting for less than 3.0 per cent at the end of the 1980s. For both Lesotho and Mozambique, remittances from migrants are vital to their domestic economies. Taking 1986 as a typical year, Lesotho's remittances amounted to five times the value of their commodity exports, and for Mozambique they totalled 63 per cent of export revenue (Goodison, 1992b, pp. 13–14).

In addition, the region's dependency was further highlighted by structural macro-economic constraints: the SADCC states have replicated the pattern typical of much of the developing world – weak or immature manufacturing sectors coupled with a few raw materials for the bulk of export revenues. Only Zimbabwe has a sizeable manufacturing base accounting for roughly one-fifth of its GDP, a figure that represented nearly two-fifths of the combined total SADCC industrial output (Green and Thompson, 1986, p. 265). To end the comparative illustration, South Africa exceeded the GDP per capita ratio of its nearest regional rival by three-fold, had overwhelmingly the largest and most efficient manufacturing and industrial economies, the greatest mineral resources and most productive agricultural sector (Holland, 1988a, pp. 22–5). The task the Community set itself, and SADCC, was considerable: in comparison, ending legislated racial discrimination appeared the easier option.

While acknowledging the force of the dependency thesis outlined above, an alternative regional perspective argues that South Africa is more similar to, than different from, the region's macro-economic pattern. Table 7.1 provides World Bank data on a range of regional economic indicators for the ten SADC states and for South Africa. While the imbalance between the economies is substantial (for example, the combined GNP for SADC is only just over one fifth of that for South Africa), the similarities between them as developing economies should not be overlooked. Thus during the 1985–92 period South Africa, like four SADC states, experienced a negative growth rate and its inflation rate was the fifth highest. Despite being the largest economy, in both a regional and a comparative global context South Africa more closely resembles a developing country than a developed one, and faces many of the same challenges of its neighbouring SADC states. For example, the size of the South African economy disguises a structural weakness that is shared throughout the region: dependence on export revenues from the mineral sector. In South Africa's case this is extreme, but the pattern is regionally familiar: in 1990, 61.5 per cent of South Africa's exports were derived from the mining sector (half of which came from gold),

Table 7.1 Southern African Regional Economic Indicators

	GNP	GDP per capita		Inflation	GDP		
	$m	$	Real growth rate %	% average	% share agriculture	% share exports	% share investments
SADC States	(1992)	(1992)	(1985–92)	(1985–92)	(1992)	(1992)	(1992)
Angola	*	*	*	−0.8	*	43	12
Botswana	3797	2790	8.1	12.9	5	*	*
Lesotho	1090	590	0.8	13.5	11	19	78
Malawi	1896	210	−0.3	17.6	28	24	19
Mozambique	1034	60	−1.3	48.1	64	29	47
Namibia	2502	1610	1.1	10.2	10	58	14
Swaziland	930	1080	6.4	12.7	15	77	20
Tanzania	2561	110	1.4	25.2	62	17	19
Zambia	2580	290	−2.1	69.1	9	26	28
Zimbabwe	5896	570	−0.6	17.6	20	35	22
South Africa	106019	2670	−1.3	14.4	5	25	16

* = not known.

Source: *The World Bank Atlas 1994* reprinted in *Agence Europe*, 1994, no. 6150, supplement.

33.2 per cent from manufacturing and the remainder from agriculture, fishing and forestry (South Africa Foundation, 1994, p. 49). In contrast to the global trend towards export diversity, South Africa's reliance on minerals actually intensified rising from 29 per cent to 55 per cent of export revenues between 1960 and 1987 (Goodison, 1992, p. 5). Under the apartheid regime South Africa was rated by the World Bank as a middle income country, a classification shared by twenty one ACP Lomé nations. However, a recent increasing rate of decline in black per capita living standards has lead to estimates that "by the twenty-first century the per capita income of the average black South African is likely to be lower than that currently prevailing in neighbouring Zambia" (ibid., p. 1).

Successful development and integration requires balanced trading relations, a basic objective of SADC. While a potential for complementarities within the region exists, as suggested above, such forms of economic cooperation remained largely untested and undefined. Arguably, the SADCC region had never really constituted an effective regional grouping: for example, between 1981–86 intra-SADCC trade represented less than 5.0 per cent of their total trade (Thompson, 1991, p. 62). The question then arises that given South Africa's unquestioned dominance within the southern African region, does it possess the capacity – or desire – to act as the economic engine of regional integration?

One perspective argues that there would be a "spillover" effect from the South African centre that would be of general benefit to the region; conversely, the alternative interpretation describes the relationship in core–periphery terms with the regional periphery increasingly marginalized. While intuitive expectations and a good deal of wishful thinking encouraged this first view in the 1980s, more recent analyses have concluded that this putative role is extremely unlikely, at least not before the twenty-first century. For example, in 1993 DGVIII argued that South Africa was unlikely to become the driving force for development in southern Africa. South Africa depended heavily on the primary sector and relied on protection and subsidies to maintain an otherwise uncompetetive manufacturing and limited agricultural sector. Blumenfeld (1992) has challenged the entire notion that southern Africa is a candidate for economic integration. Others cite dissimilar levels of economic development, uncompetetive economies, imbalanced industrial concentration and the unequal distribution of rewards as evidence that as a regional economy "the region rates poorly in terms of conventional yardsticks" (Maasdorp, 1992a, p. 139). However, despite contemporary evidence, the expectation, or hope, persists that South Africa will constitute the regional economic motor for development. As such, parallels with the regional integration in post-war Europe have been drawn. It is an assessment of the veracity of these claims that this chapter now turns.

A MISPLACED ANALOGY? THE EC MODEL AND SADC

At one level, an embryonic southern African community already exists that is comparable in its level of economic integration to that of the pre-1992 European Community. All that is required for the five countries that compose SACU and CMA to achieve "a common market is for the member countries to agree on the free mobility of labour": the other theoretical attributes of a common market already exist (Maasdorp, 1992b, p. 124). Faced with its own unacceptably high level of unemployment, the mobility of labour within any putative new arrangement is set to be a crucial issue for South Africa. However, the uncertainty about the future regional frameworks suggests that the current level of integration is not, necessarily, inviolate. A down-grading to a more classical free-trade area (either within or distinct from the PTA) rather than up-grading to a common market is equally as likely. Rather than follow the model of one-speed integration, southern Africa may be better suited to an *à la carte* approach that recognized the requirement of what is described as "variable geometry" in the European context. A multi-tiered structure could be envisaged not dissimilar from the distinction that is made between full membership of the EU and that of the European Economic Area of seventeen states (the EU plus five former EFTA countries). Thus different levels or stages of regional integration and cooperation might be combined creating a *sui generis* and indigenous response to southern African circumstances. As one economic analyst has suggested:

At the core could be a common market (or perhaps even an economic and political union) between South Africa and

Lesotho. A second layer could represent the SACU and CMA consisting of South Africa, Lesotho and Swaziland. A third layer could be a customs union of South Africa, Lesotho, Swaziland, Botswana and Namibia. A further layer could be the PTA which may or not include any of the SACU members . . . The outer layer could consist of bilateral or multilateral sectoral or project agreements perhaps on SADCC . . . lines. (Maasdorp, 1992b, p. 125)

Other analyses have pointed to the ineffectual nature of all existing regional arrangements and their tendency to create an inequitable distribution of rewards. The evidence pertaining to SACU is conflicting, however: a critical interpretation suggests that it has only benefitted South Africa, not the other partners (Thompson, 1992, p. 131). Conversely, a traditional conclusion opines, somewhat complacently, that in general for Botswana, Lesotho and Swaziland "membership is advantageous . . . otherwise they would have withdrawn at some stage since becoming independent in the late 1960s" (Maasdorp, 1992c, p. 20). Consequently, an undifferentiated application of the neoliberal Community model has been challenged, presenting Southern Africa with the opportunity to both learn from, and be critical of, the theory of regional economic cooperation inherited from Europe. Thus,

[I]n developing their own forms of regional coordination, Southern Africans are questioning what specific elements of the European Community . . . are relevant to addressing their poverty and their economic dependence on South Africa as well as their colonial rulers. This legacy requires a restructuring of economic relations, a process that is much more complex than a simple lowering of trade barriers. (Maasdorp, 1992b, p. 125)

From such a perspective the absolute reliance on free trade ignores conditions specific to southern Africa, paralleling the mistaken indiscriminate imposition of Structural Adjustment Programmes in the 1980s. Because of the economic dissimilarities between Africa in the 1990s and Europe of the 1950s, the ubiquitous neoliberalsim that has driven the EC into a single market and towards monetary union is not, necessarily, the appropriate model for southern Africa (p. 130). As noted above, this analysis was at the heart of the original decision to launch SADCC.

And yet, the abandonment of the existing limited coordination and integration structures would seriously affect South Africa's closest regional partners. Without SACU, the member states would have to devise new tariff and customs systems, or establish a free trade area to replace the customs union. Although less directly affected initially, South Africa's longer term regional interests would be constrained and the basis for its growing regional manufacturing exports jeopardized. As noted above, the elements of SACU and CMA provide an existing framework that is tantamount to a common market in southern Africa (the restrictions on the free movement of labour and capital that currently exist, notwithstanding). The extension of the economic freedoms associated with a full common market would benefit Lesotho greatest given its dependency on the migrant labour system in existence. Conversely, the challenge of the free movement of labour presents South Africa with probably its greatest economic disadvantage. Given the current and possibly structural level of unemployment in South Africa, the magnet of its economy could result in significant additional influx of labour for which employment prospects would be marginal. The economic strain could be excessive and politically unacceptable to a multiracial post-apartheid South Africa. On balance, Maasdorp concluded that with relatively minor additions (namely, common monetary and fiscal policies) SACU could be transformed into an economic union (1992c, p. 24). Ironically, some would suggest that the prospects for a single currency, a common central bank and common interest rate are closer at hand in southern African than they are in the post-EMS European Union of Maastricht. Such a development, following the European logic, could provide a catalyst for expanding SACU to include regional neighbours such as Mozambique, Malawi or Zambia. Thus the shape and content of future possible forms of regional organization remain fluid. SADC may prevail, but it is far from the only possible choice. Consequently, the cooperation framework negotiations that took place between the Commission and the TEC during early 1994 were confronted with the impossibility of addressing the bilateral relationship within the future regional context. No one at that stage could realistically predict quite how southern Africa would look in terms of regional arrangements by even 1995. At best educated assumptions were used to make policy decisions, a process very much akin to squaring the circle.

Since the 1980s the European Community has been frequently canvassed as model for integrating South Africa within the southern African region. Obviously, under the former apartheid regime such ambitions were a practical impossibility, despite the launching of initiatives such as P. W. Botha's putative "Constellation of States" (Holland, 1983, p. 137). The political tranformation of the 1990s has seen a renewed interest in learning from Europe's post-war experience, causing one leading commentator to suggest that regional integration be "pursued with vigour": both economically and politically "[H]anging together may just be preferable to hanging separately!" (Spence, 1993, p. 95). Under the new democratic non-racial conditions of 1994 is the European analogy applicable, appropriate and perceptive?

What exactly is the European experience? With respect to southern Africa there are at least eight aspects that suggest comparative insights. First, above all else the formative experience of the European experiment was an attempt to reconcile a divided society. Twice within two decades Europeans had slaughtered each other: the ECSC and the resultant EEC were essentially peace movements to negate the dangerous and divisive issues of nationalism and sovereignty. By linking key areas of their economies (the symbolism of coal and steel was pronounced – these were the basic elements of war), cooperation rather than competition became the new imperative. The similarity to the southern African context is important. While open and direct conflict was less dramatic, the reconciliation of the frontline states and South Africa is an important political and security regional issue. The fledgling Community and the current southern African region share a "profound desire to bury past antagonisms" (Spence, 1993, p. 88).

Second, the European idea sought to contain a potential regional hegemony – the resurgent West Germany (Spence, 1993, p. 89). The strategy was to incorporate Germany within a structure that harnessed both its economic strength and constrained its political aspirations. Indeed, some argued (most notably Thatcher, the then British Prime Minister) a similar logic in 1990 after the reunification of Germany: it was essential to promote a European Germany, and not a German Europe. The Community's institutional structures and basic principles that protected the interests of the smaller states from dominance by the major members created a new system that curbed the potential for hegemonic behaviour. As addressed already in this chapter, South Africa constitutes the region's economic Leviathan. Binding ties that utilize this capacity for the benefit of the region and not exclusively for South Africa, is an insight that the European experience forcefully demonstrates.

Third, the Community model was a means through which the redistribution of economic benefits could occur, if belatedly, via the mechanism of a single market well as direct subsidies and grants. Certainly, whether through SADC, SACU or some other framework, the advantages of a common market have already made themselves evident in southern Africa. The extension of this to the direct transfer of resources from richer to poorer regional states is more debatable. However, the comparison with the EC is insightful. Such ambitious plans took decades to come to fruition and the major mechanism for this, the European Cohesion Fund, only came into being thirty years after the signing of the Treaty of Rome. Consequently, expectations of immediate resource reallocation are unjustified; in the medium term such benefits can only be provided through the opportunities created by a single market.

Fourth, the European idea was a response to the international situation of the early 1950s. The relative peace of Western Europe for the past half century obscures the fact that one of motivations behind the ECSC was the perceived external threat of Soviet policy. A third war on European soil was widely believed to be probable at the time. Thus the EEC was about strengthening the economic base of Europe's democratic countries as an important aspect of the Cold War. Some have even gone as far as to argue that with the recent demise of the Soviet Union and normalization of East–West relations, the very *raison d'être* of the Community was undermined and has lead to the dissipation of the European dynamic. Clearly, a precondition for the success of the original Community was the support of the USA and the international community in general. Without the financial backing of the Marshall Fund, or America's political blessing, the challenges of European integration would have been insurmountable. Conversely, South Africa has been a beneficiary of the collapse of communism as it provided the international context that facilitated the abandonment of apartheid. The so-called "Total Onslaught" by communist inspired regional states could no longer be used as the alibi for maintaining apartheid. At present no comparable political threat exists that can act as the necessary external catalyst encouraging regional integration. However, the economic threat does exist, and its motivation can be equally as powerful. The globalization of trade within and between trading blocs presents a formidable rationale for a similar approach being adopted in southern Africa, if not on a pan-African level. While bilateral trade within a GATT framework persists, increasingly international economics are being conducted on a group-to-group basis. One of the founding objectives of the EC was to encourage the development of similar economic blocs worldwide: its legacy continues to be of relevance to southern Africa. What is missing, however, is the level of international funding that was available in the post-1945 world. The demands of the newly democratizing East European states have become a European and global priority. Consequently, the level of interest and available funding for peripheral issues such as southern Africa's economic integration has declined, although perhaps not quite to the marginal level that was ominously predicted at the start of the 1990s (see Coker, 1991).

Fifth, a supranational commitment was fundamental. Both the ECSC and EC were not intergovernmental associations but explicitly demanded an allegiance that went beyond narrow self-interest and incorporated a sense of collective action. Nationalism was to be effectively contained and blended with supranationalism. To provide substance to this commitment the role of institutions with effective powers of implementation were stressed, particularly by Monnet (Holland, 1993, p. 26). Thus the original Community emphasized the function of the Commission as the guardian of supranationalism, bolstered by the Council of Ministers that possessed supranational decision-making authority, and overseen by the Court of Justice who presided over the legal application of supranationalism. Without a comparable institutional structure, the best of intentions for regional integration in southern Africa will remain vacuous. Intergovernmentalism, even in a highly competitive form, cannot substitute for supranationalism as the foundation stone of integration.

Sixth, an often cited prerequisite for economic integration along the European model is that member countries require broadly similar levels of industrial development, competitive sectors and possess the potential to develop product complementarity (Maasdorp, 1992c, p. 11). Clearly, this involves a degree of accommodation as witnessed by the comparative strengths of the Italian versus the French or German economies of the late 1950s. As the figures used by way of illustration in this chapter have indicated, it is difficult to sustain such a proposition in a southern African context. South Africa's GDP triples that of the combined SADC GDP and constitutes almost 60 per cent of the larger PTA grouping. Manufacturing and industrial development is profoundly skewed by South Africa's capacity to dominate a wide range of consumer, producer and capital goods. Consequently, South Africa exports roughly six times the amount of goods to the SADC-PTA region as it imports. Additionally, not only should there be reasonable economic parity between member states, political differences should be manageable and containable (ibid., p. 11). This condition reflected the formative experience of the Community. As the 1990s have progressed, signs of an increased political consensus at least within the SADC states, including South Africa, have become apparent – with the exception of Angola.

A penultimate lesson that can be drawn from the European model is that secure regional integration cannot be achieved quickly. Indeed the popular disquiet voiced in many European electorates over the Maastricht Treaty reforms underlined the danger of political elites moving ahead too fast and without the popular backing of the population. While various forms of regional cooperation have been in existence since at least the 1970s in southern Africa, the fundamental step towards economic integration may not occur this century. Advantage should, however, be taken of the regional building blocks that already exist and have proved to function. Just as the EC was spawned by the ECSC, gestation taking five years, SACU, the CMA as well as SADC provide, with necessary adaptation, the basis on which further regional integration might become based. What is missing from all these associations, however, is the commitment to supranational authority as outlined above, the essential hallmark of the European experience. Finally, but crucially, the "idea" of Europe required political and bureaucratic leadership that possessed a vision and the capacity to redesign the political realities of nation-state sovereignty. The concept of functional spillover was never a candidate for popular propaganda; consequently, the creation of Europe was unavoidably elite driven – a characteristic that carries with it other long term costs. Yet it was Europe's good fortune to have the talents of Monnet, Schuman, Spaak and Spinnelli in the formative years, and subsequently those of Delors, Mitterrand, Heath, Schmidt and Tindemans to continue the integration momentum. However, as Spence ruefully has commented, "[t]he South African equivalent of a Jacques Delors has yet to emerge!" (1993, p. 90). As long as regional politicians and bureaucrats continue to exhibit a national myopia, integration will remain an academic and not a practical pursuit.

There are also several negative lessons that the European analogy presents that are instructive for southern Africa. First, an issue that has been touched upon already, is the long term difficulties that have developed because of the absence of popular support. The elite technocratic impetus of the EC failed to take on board the democratic consent of the member state electorates. As the close debacle of Maastricht reminded the Community, Europe has to be more than a series of functional organizations for economic well-being and explicit popular approval and support is a minimum prerequisite for enduring integration. No matter how tempting it is to orchestrate the democratic process, any southern African community that denies a full debate on the content and implications of supranational integration will find itself constructed on sand, not the solid rock of popular legitimacy.

Second, for balanced integration there needs to be a basic symmetry in the respective levels of economic and political integration. The Community failed to achieve this initially when the European Defence Community and European Political Community were abandoned in the mid-1950s. Despite the attempts of Maastricht to promote economic and political union, the current European Union continues to exhibit a decidedly uneven shape; a bulky and expanding economic body coupled with a diminutive and limited political head. Balanced integration is a necessary prerequisite for successful integration.

Third, a decision-making style that was based on consensus and permitted national vetoes was often tantamount to stagnation and detrimental to supranationalism. While a crude majoritarianism is equally as unsuitable, once a commitment to integration in principle has been agreed by consensus, decision-making should not be based on unanimity. The original Treaty of Rome made provision for qualified majority decisions as the typical procedure for the EC, an objective that was eradicated for two decades by the intergovernmental inspired 1966 Luxembourg Compromise. Progress by the slowest common denominator is detrimental to integration, whether in Europe or southern Africa.

Thus, in contrast to the various insights drawn from the European analogy, there are certain features that council caution. The analogy is an imperfect one suggesting that a fervent and unqualified application of the European experience to southern Africa is ill-advised. Furthermore, there are striking differences, perhaps incompatibilities, between the European and southern African experiences. In summary, first, the original power structure in the EC was bi-polar and more recently at least tri-polar. This balanced power ratio is an essential attribute and one clearly missing in the SADC region at present. Second, and related, a degree of economic parity was fundamental: SADC fails to deliver this other than at a minimal level. Third, all post-war member states espoused a common understanding of, and commitment to, democratic ideals. Despite the narrowing of the political spectrum within southern Africa during the 1990s, no comparable fundamental political consensus exists. Fourth, the rejuvenation of the European economy was a precondition for creating a common market. The post-war recovery was preconditioned largely on the externally funded Marshall Aid programme. There is no equivalent external assistance available for southern Africa: the European Special Programme is very modest in comparison. Fifth, the elite leadership is missing. Europe was only built because of deep commitment at the highest political and bureaucratic level. Despite rhetoric invoking the idea of a southern African region, none of the SADC leaders have ever contemplated replacing individual national interest by joint supranationalism.

So, how useful is the analogy? In balance, it does illuminate the potential for the region, but a simple reading of the parallel serves more to obfuscate. The historical epochs are essentially dissimilar and a replication, in the short term, is improbable. That is not to deny a different form of regional grouping emerging based on pragmatic trade concerns. A formalized, institutional and supranational endeavour requires time and history to emerge: currently, the political heritage of southern Africa is too immature to accommodate a presumed diminution of national sovereignty through integration.

SQUARING THE CIRCLE: EC BILATERAL AND REGIONAL POLICIES

While the April 1994 Commission proposal on bilateral EC-South African trade alluded to regional compatibility, quite how this will be translated and how effectively implemented in practice, remain important questions for the future of regional development in southern Africa. The potential for policy inconsistencies that discriminate between SADC and South Africa was not resolved in the document. Indeed, all that was proposed "to encourage intra-regional trade in southern Africa" was an unspecified form of cumulation of origin rules (see Appendix Document 7). As demonstrated elsewhere, the indeterminate form of the post-election economic arrangements within southern Africa complicated the definition of a bilateral EC-South African policy that was also regionally sensitive. At best it became a matter of intelligent guesswork; at worst a basis for prediction as reliable as an astrological horoscope. The negotiators were faced with the dilemma of constructing a new framework that was either compatible with existing conditions, or one that attempted to address regional developments that were still in their formative stages. The consequences were important. A bilateral framework that was broadly consistent with SADC, for example, might well be less accommodating if a new SACU or PTA arrangement were to be adopted. Thus the issue of consistency went far beyond the associated issues of Lomé compatibility.

At a theoretical level inconsistencies between EU bilateral regional economic policies and its multilateral approach (that is between the EU and South Africa versus the EU and SADC), can only be overcome by adopting an explicit regional unit of analysis. This approach suggests that such a regional unit of analysis would:

> emphasize region-to-region relations, providing an alternative to the "bilateralism" strongly preferred by the economic powers . . .

> Employing a regional unit of analysis does not imply that the region will be unitary, but rather emphasizes that the region as a unit should be considered in the discussion of the development of Southern Africa. It does assume that countries are not isolated entities or discrete categories. (Thompson, 1992, p. 139)

By adopting this theoretical condition contradictions and inconsistencies between and within the EC's variety of southern African policies can at least be identified and possibly avoided. What is good for one country is not necessarily good for the region, as the past experience of European integration has shown *ad nauseam*. The difficulty faced by the EU was, as illustrated already, that such an integrated regional policy perspective did not correspond to the bureaucratic structure of policy making. The division between DGI's external economic responsibilities for South Africa and the development concerns handled by DGVIII discouraged any such "regional unit of analysis" approach. Coordination was not impossible, but the policy infra-structure mitigated against consistency.

The rejection of the Lomé option presented a major concern for inter-regional joint production schemes. Within Lomé, there are no difficulties pertaining to "rules of origin"; products could be assembled and manufactured in more than one Lomé state without infringing the right of preferential access to the Community. However, where a partnership with a non-Lomé state, such as South Africa, exceeded the 50 per cent rule the product was denied access under Lomé conditions. In the past this restriction has been a major disadvantage to a number of both Zimbabwean and Botswanan manufactures which failed to qualify because of the "value-added" component contributed in South Africa was deemed too high. The potential discrimination extends to the procurement of goods and services within any Lomé country for European funded projects and programmes. (Stoneman and Thompson, 1992, p. 76).

Thus a paradox is apparent. The EC looks to South Africa to act as the focal point for the economic development of the region, but by denying it access to Lomé it may prohibit, or at best dissuade, joint enterprises emerging at a regional level. The inconsistency between Europe's South African policy and its SADC Lomé policy was profound and potentially contradictory. It remains to be seen whether this issue will be resolved by the new "cooperation framework" negotiated during 1994. The solution lies in the effective coordination of development and external economic relations objectives between DGI and DGVIII and in South Africa's choice between pursuing explicitly favourable bilateral agreements and regionally favourable multilateral frameworks.

8 Foreign Policy and South Africa: Lessons of Wider Importance

In this concluding chapter the broader lessons of the South African case are drawn out. First, its importance as a component of the development of EPC is discussed. Second, its influence in shaping the practice of CFSP joint actions is examined. Third, a theme introduced in chapter 3 is reexamined in the light of the overall policy analysis presented: simply, has the change from EPC to a joint action under the CFSP been significant? How, if at all, did policy towards South Africa change? And did those possible changes enhance Europe's foreign policy capacity or, paradoxically, weaken it?

EPC: THE WIDER LESSONS

The academic study of past Community foreign policy has traditionally been skeptical, or at best cautious, in its analysis of the capacity, capability and effectiveness of the EC as an international actor. In the seminal work of the early 1980s, William Wallace (1983b) characterized EPC as "an alibi for inaction" and a policy determined "by the lowest common denominator", caricatures which set the tone for EPC until after the ratification of the SEA in 1987. Even after the legitimization of EPC through its incorporation into a Treaty format, commentaries continued to be more notable for their criticisms than praise of the procedures for producing joint collective action. Traditional critiques described EPC as more a way of managing foreign policy differences than a procedure for action; as such it was conjectured that EPC was to the detriment of solving problems in that it excelled at achieving common positions *not* to do anything (as in the former Yugoslavia). It was argued that EPC combined inflated goals with inadequate means, or expressed more prosaically EPC was about trying to buy grand results on the cheap! In consequence, EPC was dismissed as being almost purely reactive in nature because of the multitude of actors involved in determining a common position. This made it difficult, if not impossible, for any one body or actor to actually shape an agenda. Leader driven EPC was an illusory chimera.

None of these criticisms are without substance, though taken cumulatively they present an unduly negative impression of the scope, ability and record of success of EPC over its 24 year record. The case of EPC and South Africa offers an empirical opportunity to evaluate these conclusions and provide a balanced assessment of the wider implications and general conduct of EPC and its capabilities. South Africa was one of the EC's earliest foreign policy issues; it is the most enduring foreign policy issue; and, as is demonstrated, one of its more notable achievements, albeit it a qualified one.

While it is important to distinguish between the original inter-governmental nature of EPC and its formal Treaty definition, of greater significance is the informal practice and patterns of diplomatic behaviour that have developed since The Hague conference of 1969. The *modus operandi* has been variously described as evolving through practice and shared experiences; EPC was not intended "as a legalistic exercise", but as "a pragmatic enterprise to establish common positions and common actions" (de Schoutheete, 1985, p. 41) which lacked the institutional structure and formal obligations normally associated with Community policies. Informally EPC became the normal diplomatic response for member states, not necessarily replacing bilateral relations, but complementing them. Both the SEA and Maastricht gave legal recognition to this practice and introduced important procedural advances (such as the potential for majority voting and the imposition of sanctions by a qualified majority under Article 228A). However, the importance of EPC was in its attitudinal and behavioural effect rather than purely legal impact. The initial response amongst the Twelve became to consult, coordinate and wherever possible to adopt a common position, a radical transformation in the historical behaviour of international actors. There are many cases where the dynamic of EPC to stay together resulted in one or more member states modifying what was their preferred bilateral foreign policy position in order to maintain a consensus. The case of South Africa bears witness to this.

The case study of EC policy towards South Africa presents an ideal, perhaps unique, opportunity for demonstrating four attributes of EPC. Thus South Africa can be evaluated as an example of: EPC "success"; the limitations of EPC; the use of Treaty-based competences; and, the EC's capacity to be more than a reactive foreign policy actor and to engage in the process of foreign policy transition (a rare, perhaps unique example within the framework of EPC).

THE FOUR CONJECTURES: SOUTH AFRICA AS AN EXAMPLE OF

... Success

In what sense can EPC and South Africa be regarded as a "success" – a much needed antidote to the presumed failure of EPC over the ex-Yugoslavia? The first question to address is "success" in what terms and for whom? The traditional measure of foreign policy success is the realization of objectives. The EC's South African objective has always had a dual focus: the abolition of apartheid and the creation of a democratic society; and, the reduction of South Africa's hegemonic economic role in the SADC region. Admittedly, the abolition of racial discrimination has been a drawn-out process and the EC cannot take exclusive credit for the removal of apartheid legislation, nonetheless, this objective was finally achieved after almost two decades. With respect to the regional objective, modest progress has been made although the 1994 policy initiative does little to clarify this goal. Overall, the foreign policy actions have been broadly consistent with EPC objectives, though caution is necessary when claiming cause and effect.

An alternative criterion for measuring success is the impact on the third country. Community sanctions were, on their own, of marginal importance: taken within the context of the wider international community, EC sanctions and divestment procedures were instrumental in bringing about the economic conditions that were a precondition for political change. Again, the process was extended over several years, but from the point of view of the disenfranchised majority, EC foreign policy was a contributing factor. The EC was and remains South Africa's largest economic market, supplier and investor.

Another technique is to evaluate EPC in terms of its proactive versus reactive characteristics; theoretically proactive policy is considered of greater utility than simple policy reactions to events. Prior to 1990 EPC on South Africa was almost exclusively reactive (even the Code was the response to a crisis, not a policy initiative *per se*). However, during the 1990s the Community has become vigorously proactive and introduced a series of policy initiatives that have helped to define the nature of EC-South African relations. The EC has become the leading international external actor involved in South Africa.

The success of EPC also has an internal dynamic. It is well established that the processes of political and economic integration are linked; there needs to be a rough balance, if not symmetry, between the two. Historically, political integration has lagged behind economic integration with EPC appearing to be a significantly less developed form of Community activity than the CAP, Single Market, or even Monetary Union, for example. It is important, therefore, for the overall integration process that EPC was seen to work, that consensus based collective foreign policy could be established and maintained. This important theoretical point is what Weiler has referred to as the reflexive content of EPC. He argues that irrespective of the actual policy content, a prime motivation behind EPC is the "actual formation of a common policy as an integrative value *per se*", an activity unique to EPC (1985, p. 21). The South African record in this respect provides a measure of success. It was only in 1991 that a member state broke consensus and adopted a bilateral policy that was in conflict with the collective position (and consensus was belatedly restored by the end of the year). More importantly, during the 1985–6 period when sanctions were adopted, the internal need to maintain consensus led three member states to abandon their preferred bilateral opposition to sanctions in favour of a collective response to impose sanctions. In a narrow sense, it was deemed more important to retain the behaviour and appearance of acting collectively than sacrificing this over specific policy details. The behavioural norm of acting together dominated diplomatic and political behaviour, a change of not inconsiderable significance.

In this respect, it is interesting to note that both the EC's major policy decisions relating to South Africa coincided with the two periods of treaty revisions. The 1985–6 decision on sanctions was taken against the background of the SEA and Title III; whereas the 1991–93 period of policy transition has been at the time of the Maastricht and the Title V debate on a Common Foreign and Security Policy. This coincidence was perhaps fortuitous as it made a common position on South Africa even more directly related to the wider integration process within the Community.

To conclude this assessment of success, familiarity should not breed complacency. It was remarkable that the EC could operate a collective foreign policy *vis-à-vis* South Africa for two decades. The national bilateral policies of the Twelve were not initially consistent or complementary. The scale of member state interests and their traditional historical and cultural ties varied substantially. However, the process of consultation and coordination made consensus possible, if at times this was only achieved with difficulty and somewhat precariously. In one sense, simply staying together is a sufficient measure of success.

. . . the Limitations of EPC

In the opening chapter a series of general dilemmas and limitations on a common foreign policy were outlined. While a "success", the South African case also specifically demonstrates the inherent limitations of past EPC procedure. First, the intergovernmental nature of EPC removes foreign policy making from the normal discipline of *communautaire* decision-making. The only form of coercion is effective argument, not legal obligations.

Second, and related, is the requirement to act by consensus. While the Twelve may share broad foreign policy outlooks, there can be significant differences on how to achieve shared goals, as was clearly the case in South Africa in the 1980s. While consensus policy has the guaranteed support of all member states, as a procedure it allows a minority, even of one, to cause policy stalemate and stagnation. Consensus can imply policy inertia; however, whether a South African foreign policy that is not consensual is a better basis for joint action remains untested and contentious.

A third limitation is the tendency for EPC to reflect the lowest common denominator. The maintenance of unity can take precedence over policy content resulting in a common position that lacks effective substance. This limitation is the counter argument to Weiler's notion of reflexive foreign policy. There is some evidence of this in the South African case. The early adoption of the Code seemed to reflect a lowest common denominator process; however, this cannot really be extended to the imposition of sanctions which if not the highest common denominator, reflected a middle ground: the lowest common denominator would have been no sanctions at all.

A fourth limitation that is more clearly illustrated by the South African case is the Community's scope of foreign policy instruments. One perspective argues that the Community's civilian power basis restricts its foreign policy tools to economic instruments; a more radical view suggests that through its intergovernmental nature the Community has, by extension, use of all the member state foreign policy instruments. Prior to the 1990s in South Africa a varied range of instruments were used: the Code of Conduct; diplomatic démarches; aid and development policies; economic sanctions (imports and exports); military, security and technology sanctions; and, sporting and cultural sanctions. After 1991, the instruments used were designed to normalize relations such as establishing a bilateral economic framework for trade and development assistance. Clearly, the EC did not possess or need a military capacity and both the strengths and weaknesses of economic sanctions were illustrated against South Africa. The clear trend has been for the Community to extend the range and scope of foreign policy instruments actually used; the instruments available for the Community's foreign policy options are not that dissimilar to those of other international actors, with the exception of the USA.

Finally, until the 1990s the South African case illustrated the reactive stance of EPC; it responded to each crisis as it occurred rather than operated according to any set principles to contribute to policy innovations. Consequently, EPC became a fairly laborious procedure with decisions taking several months to be accepted let alone implemented. For example, it took over a year of debate before the Community agreed to adopt sanctions, a further few months before this political decision was given legal competence, and even longer before the policy had any measurable effects. In summary, while a success, EPC and South Africa was not immune from the typical constraints of the procedure found in other case studies.

... the Use of Treaty Competences

The adoption of sanctions against South Africa was a watershed in EPC behaviour in that the former reluctance to use Treaty based competences in achieving foreign policy goals was breached (Nuttall, 1992, p. 327). Thereafter the EC had no objections in principle to the use of the Treaty of Rome to facilitate political cooperation (see later examples such as sanctions against Iraq). However, despite this pioneering initiative, the Community's use of treaty competences was mixed. The sanctions enacted were not all given the same legal authority. This varied between the use of regulations, decisions and statements. Only one sanction was applied at the level of regulation (the ban on the import of Krugerrands); the ban on the import of certain iron and steel products was enacted through an ECSC decision; whereas the cessation of new EC investments in South Africa was adopted in the form of a Council decision. The other sanctions (on oil exports, nuclear collaboration, security technology, military cooperation, cultural, scientific and sports agreements, for example) were all adopted under the non-legal framework of EPC statements. Obviously, the choice of mechanism for enacting policy is a significant determinant of its successful application. Thus, the regulation effectively halted the minor trade in Kruger-rands, as did the ECSC decision, albeit more slowly. However, the Council decision on new investments highlighted the inadequacies of this form of legal implementation in South Africa. Decisions are directly binding but not necessarily directly effective. Further, where they are phrased in general rather than precise language their legal vagueness can undermine their applicability. This was very much the case in South Africa: the language of the new investments decision was so indulgent that it was little more effective than a non-binding recommendation. In reality, the decision was open to national interpretation and application especially as Article 1 of the decision stated that the provisions for the suspension of new investments "may be complied with by the issue of guidance to natural and legal persons". It is not surprising that member states opposed to this policy in principle found it comparatively easy to enact in practice. Its effect was rendered insignificant (Holland, 1988, pp. 110–11). Despite numerous accusations on the part of some MEPs, no breaches of any Community sanction were notified by the Commission. This is hardly surprising given the mixed Commission and member state responsibilities for enactment and monitoring. It was simply like asking the poacher also to act as game-keeper.

Finally, the other side of the sanctions coin is worth repeating. Just as sanctions against South Africa had to be by consensus, the removal of sanctions also required unanimity. This process showed the Community severely embarrassed as an EPC decision taken to lift the remaining 1985–6 sanctions was blocked by the Danish parliament. It was not until almost a year later that the Danish position changed and unanimity on removing these embargoes was agreed upon and implemented universally. Further, with the establishment of the Single Market the opportunity for any member state to take additional bilateral sanctions is effectively redundant. Increasingly, sanctions have become an exclusive Community foreign instrument though, paradoxically, exclusively Community level competences are lacking.

. . . Policy Transition

The previous chapters and description of EPC and South Africa have, *inter alia*, provided evidence of the dynamic nature of Community policy. Within a decade the Community had moved from a reactive policy of sanctions that mimicked belatedly other international actors, to a position of leading the international community by setting an active policy framework to meet the demands of the developing situation. The policy adapted to the changing foreign policy demands showing that EPC did not have to be a static reactive policy, but could be dynamic and capable of change. It is even capable of agenda-setting and facilitation. Europe may have appeared disappointing in ex-Yugoslavia, but it has demonstrated real foreign policy actor capacity in South Africa – a foreign policy issue with strikingly similar problems of a segmented society.

The ability to execute foreign policy transition is a sign of the maturity and overall cohesiveness of EPC/CFSP (divisions between the multiple players not withstanding). Perhaps the longevity of foreign policy towards South Africa makes this case atypical. Nonetheless, the Community was able to enter into distinct phases of policy transition – as an EPC actor from the modesty of the Code to sanctions, to development assistance, cooperation framework and dialogue. As such it is perhaps a model against which Europe's current and future foreign policies can be judged.

The history of EPC and South Africa provides an empirical rebuttal of many of the typically dismissive obituaries of EPC. While it is unsound to generalize from one case, the attributes contained within the case study suggests a less pessimistic interpretation would be appropriate. There is empirical evidence that EPC moved beyond being a procedure for managing differences into a procedure leading to foreign policy action, if over an extended time-frame. With respect to South Africa it is hard to conclude that EPC was to the detriment of finding a solution, or agreed upon a common decision not to do anything, at least after 1985. The general criticism that EPC had inflated goals coupled with inadequate means was true prior to the adoption of sanctions, but harder to justify since then, particularly in the post-1991 phase of development policy. And lastly, the reactive nature of EPC was largely overcome and the absence of a single actor setting the Community foreign policy agenda was not necessarily tantamount to inertia.

The South African case showed that the Community's foreign policy could be effective provided that expectations were realistic and the civilian nature of the Community was appropriate for specific problem-solving. The informal political and diplomatic behavioural changes that the process of collegiality and cooperation bred over the past decades was of greater significance in understanding and evaluating the success of EPC than any formal reading of Treaty provisions.

CFSP: THE WIDER LESSONS

Moving beyond the past lessons for EPC, what lessons of a general nature can be drawn from the South African case for the Union's new CFSP and the adoption of common policies?

First, the case-study has shown quite categorically that continuity was the hallmark of the transition from EPC to CFSP common action. As shown, all of the common actions unveiled after 1 November 1993 had been developed in the previous twelve months and were, therefore, technically the product of EPC discussions. While it is reasonable to assume that the Community had begun to work in a post-Maastricht way prior to eventual

Treaty ratification, the designation of South Africa as a common policy was hardly the euphemistic Big Bang. The binding nature of Title V Article J had little impact on what was already a very cohesive and consensus-based approach. In that sense South Africa was an obvious choice as it already exhibited all the necessary characteristics for a common foreign policy.

Second, it has exposed the dimension of Commission involvement in foreign policy making. The Commission's shared right of initiative was not seen as an impediment to its influence: the Commission was an equal and very active partner in shaping the policy framework and subsequently the Union's common action. The emerging role of DGIA requires more detailed study.

Third, but related, is the bureaucratic competition between the different Commission DGs, principally DGIA, DGI and DGVIII. While the development aspect may not be common to all foreign policy issues, the general conclusion holds for the Union. Intra-Commission competition has become a new aspect of foreign policy making. The Commission, while presenting joint reports to the Council should not necessarily be seen as a unified actor, in very much the same way as the Council should not be seen as unified: member state differences prevail just as DG differences exist. Policy debate can of course be a healthy attribute; its danger is that it will dilute the coherence of policy proposals emanating from the Commission, potentially significantly reducing its contribution. Consistency across Community and Union policies is a responsibility of the Commission under Title V: it remains to be seen how efficiently this can be maintained.

Fourth, the incorporation of the EPC Secretariat and enhanced stature of the enlarged Council Secretariat presents the policy making role of the Commission with a further challenge. While at the time of writing this development was at a rudimentary stage, the possibility clearly exists for the Council Secretariat to develop far beyond the restricted and confined role played by its predecessor and to become an alternative source of policy input.

Fifth, the definition of the scope of any joint action is important: is it to be limited, well-defined with set objectives and a timescale (as suggested by TEU Article J.3.1), or will practice prove to be too vague to evaluate success? The sensitivity of the Union to achieve successes suggests that they will follow the conservative route in general, specifying specific actions as joint actions rather than a more broader approach of defining what is covered by the common policy. The South African case confirms this self-imposed modesty. The paradox was that despite a seemingly inclusive joint action, the practice was that CFSP joint action on South Africa was extremely limited in its scope, arguably no less restrictive than the former EPC policy! Indications are that the South African example may constitute the typical approach to common action, rather than an aberration.

Sixth, the frameworks under which joint actions are to be taken need clarifying. The application of a "single institutional framework" seems difficult to realize because of the variety of competences and activities engaged in by the Union and the Community in external relations and foreign affairs. Is a particular aspect of a joint action governed by the Treaty of Rome (where say, external economic relations are concerned), or by the CFSP procedures of Maastricht? The role of the Commission, right of initiative and policy supervision as well as decision-making styles are all effected by the choice of decision-making framework. Foreign policy making under the European Union remains a fragmented procedure because of the pillarization of competences.

Seventh, and more pessimistically, the South African case exposes the inappropriateness of autonomously splitting external political relations from external economic relations. The history of integration has been about linking, in a Monnet sense, these two activities, regarding them as mutually dependent and reinforcing. DGIA may prove a temporary aberration with both portfolios coming together under one DG, albeit with different divisions, in a future Commission. The first year of DGIA existence is crucial to its longevity. If there are policy advantages from separation then its future looks healthy; if there are problems of coordination, then this experiment may expire with that of the tenure of the last Delors Commission.

Eighth, the wider lesson is that CFSP joint actions will proceed with caution and in an incremental fashion. South Africa, like the other four actions, is part of an experiment to define CFSP potentialities. It may be some time before the mechanism and *modus operandi* are adequately determined; indeed, this may not happen before the next 1996 planned intergovernmental conference to reform the CFSP.

At the working group level, consistency is being approximated through the merger of groups in an attempt to bridge the difficulties of operating under different frameworks discussed above.

Again, this has been approached incrementally rather than adopted as a comprehensive approach for all CFSP matters. The related question of bureaucratic linkages has also been highlighted since November 1993. The relationships between the Political Committee, COREPER and the Council Secretariat remain problematic and fluid. The South African case has emphasized that greater clarity is needed and a clear authoritive decision centre is required for the effective execution of joint action. This is necessary for both internal as well as external reasons. Third countries need to have a definite perspective on the Union's core foreign policy authority below the level of the Council.

As discussed in Chapter 3, the South African case has underlined the limited potential for majority decisions. The disagreement over the scope of the joint action did not result in an immediate move to a majority decision, quite the opposite. The response was to delay a decision while a consensus could be formed. This "consensus by persuasion" is likely to dominate the general execution of CFSP joint actions. The threat of a majority decision is a more powerful incentive than its actual imposition given the still fragile nature of the CFSP procedures. All that can be said is that the emphasis on unanimity bred through decades of EPC continues to be a strong motivational factor. Majority voting, as in the Treaty of Rome and SEA, is best applied through abstinence rather than indulgence.

Lastly, the case-study has called into question the planning role of the CFSP. Which institution is responsible for this function? Is it an intergovernmental or Community responsibility? Despite the creation of a planning directorate in DGIA and the enhanced role of the Council Secretariat, initial signs were that forward planning was to rely more on the existing member state foreign offices than on any Union institution. The absence of any European contingency plan for South Africa bore witness to this intergovernmental reliance. The development of a Union planning function is one of the key areas for future CFSP reform.

INSTITUTIONAL ISSUES ARISING FROM THE JOINT ACTION

Externally, the transition from EPC to CFSP seems to have been remarkably tranquil and emphasized policy consistency over change. Was the concern about Maastricht's powers simply a figment of British media imagination, or are there important differences in behaviour, institutions and competences? Certainly from the intra-Community perspective the transition has been more revolutionary than reformist in nature. Four institutional developments are of importance.

First, the TEU reconfirmed the Commission's role within foreign policy as the thirteenth actor. While extolling the intergovernmental nature of CFSP, it accommodated a degree of *communautairization* by providing the Commission with a shared right of policy initiation (Article J.8.3). Over South Africa the Commission has fully utilized its power of initiative and was a leading player in structuring the Union's contemporary response. This emerging role for the Commission is of particular significance to both the South African joint action and to the conduct of CFSP in general.

To support this changing role the Commission adopted certain institutional reforms. One innovation of the two-year Commission that came into office in 1993 was the reorganization of portfolios. For the first time responsibilities for External Relations were split, reflecting in part the CFSP changes of Maastricht, but also in part a response to the appointment of new Commissioners. However, as the South African case illustrates defining the competences of each DG, their inter-relationships and scope of action, is contentious. In particular, the line distinguishing "political" from "economic" aspects of policy *vis-à-vis* South Africa is far from clear-cut. To facilitate efficiency and decision-making, there has been a merger on an *ad hoc* basis of the different Commission and Council groups at the working group level.

The Commission, like all bureaucracies, is not a monolithic actor: within it there exists bureaucratic competition between DGs for influence, prestige and defined areas of competence. The creation of DGIA can only heighten this natural form of bureaucratic behaviour. The bureaucratic context is further complicated as DGVIII (Development) has, in the past, had exclusive responsibility for the conduct of the Special Programme. Bureaucratic competition between at least these three sections of the Commission is a novel and increasingly important aspect of the CFSP and expression of joint actions. It remains to be seen whether DGIA will mature into the dominant foreign policy actor within the Commission (a form of *primus inter pares*), or whether a system of equal partners will emerge with different DGs assuming leadership according to the specifics of each foreign policy issue that arises. The key to this lies with the ambitions of the various Commissioners, the quality of the staff seconded to DGIA from the other DGs, and in the longevity of both Maastricht's CFSP pillar and the internal DGI–IA division. However, it is South Africa's good fortune – or ill luck – that it has become one of the first cases for testing these new arrangements and for defining the demarcation of competences.

A second consequential CFSP institutional development is the incorporation of what was the EPC Secretariat into the Council Secretariat. This enlarged group of twenty four (drawn equally from the member states and the existing Secretariat personnel) can play a significant role as a foreign policy advisory body dedicated to the presidency. As such, the Commission may find itself increasingly competing with the Council Secretariat in terms of policy advice. The question of the decision-making focus for CFSP remains to be resolved.

Third, the concessions given to the European Parliament by the TEU with respect to foreign policy were thought to be fairly modest at the time. Effectively, all that is required is that the views of the European Parliament are "duly taken into consideration" (Article J.7). The Parliament has typically sought to extend or at least give a maximalist interpretation to all such imprecise and seemingly innocuous concessions. In contrast to the 1980s when the Parliament issued a series of reports on EC-South African policy and questions about South Africa often dominated Question Time, during the 1990s the Parliament had not been so preoccupied with South Africa. However, Parliament's exclusion from the debate on bilateral relations should not be anticipated. As noted in Chapter 4, within the first month of the Union, the European Parliament complained to the Council that its views had not, indeed could not have, been taken into consideration concerning the joint action over Russia. Parliament can reinforce its constitutional position and play a more active foreign policy role. This, coupled with condition that its approval for third country agreements is required under the Single Act, indicates that Parliament's role in influencing relations with South Africa cannot be dismissed.

The final institutional issue is the one of who pays for CFSP joint action? As was discussed in Chapter 1, adequate funding constitutes a minimum prerequisite for effective implementation. While the funding of the South African exercise was agreed to on an *ad hoc* basis, a parallel debate was being conducted during the initial six months of the CFSP existence to determine standard guidelines for the funding of future joint actions. The issues at stake went beyond the simple budgetary aspect and challenged budgetary unity. Threats were in the form of intergovernmental funding and management of joint actions; the evolution of the Council budget into a CFSP operational budget; the appropriateness of the Commission budget line for CFSP; and the question of the European Parliament's control over expenditure and its power to make budgetary decisions.

As far as was possible, the General Affairs Council interim agreement of 7 March 1994 established general guidelines for the financing of CFSP. This stipulated three broad principles. i) CFSP actions were part of the EU's external action as a whole and comprise of aspects connected with diplomacy, security, economy, trade and development policies. However, where CFSP measures are bolstered by Community measures, a clear distinction is to be maintained to prevent "contamination" of the Community pillar by the intergovernmental pillar. ii) Whatever the eventual funding framework, it was to guarantee the rapid mobilization of necessary resources. iii) All joint actions agreed to by the Council must state the financial means through which an action will be implemented (*Agence Europe*, 1994, no.6185, p. 9). However, the core political question remained unresolved: the choice between financing from the Community budget or through member state contributions. Or put another way, the choice between the further *communautairization* of CFSP, versus the continuation of explicit intergovernmental control. While the experience of the South African joint action did not definitively resolve the funding issue, it did serve to underline the fundamental importance of the debate. Consequently, funding remains an important institutional priority on the CFSP agenda.

POLICY ISSUES ARISING FROM THE JOINT ACTION

The commencement of the bilateral dialogue within the context of the joint action gave the impression that Union policy was structured, detailed and organized. Despite the Commission guidelines, initially the joint action was in many ways comparatively undeveloped. The process for assisting the election process was clear, but several of the subsequent policy issues remained poorly defined. Some of the problems, limitations and consequences of alternative policy choices are discussed below.

As noted already, the question of the scope of the joint action was initially left unspecified. The underlying reason was disagreement between the Twelve dividing the member states between those who viewed the common approach as limited to just election involvement, and those who argued that all European-South African relations should be the topic of joint action. This dispute had the disadvantage of further delaying the detailed construction of policy, detracting from the Union's proactive ability. Consequently, the impression created was more reminiscent of protracted EPC deliberations than indicative of any significant procedural improvement. If joint actions are to be significant old patterns of behaviour have to change.

One area of the joint action where the scope of involvement was specified was in the Union's election role. However, even here criticism can also be leveled at the policy's inadequacy. The conduct of the election posed substantial problems. With approximately 9,000 voting booths in operation the Union's contribution of 307 monitors to the international effort seemed grossly inadequate. Observers were deployed largely in the areas of unrest, leaving vast tracks of rural areas to local election monitors. As experience has shown in other African elections, success is dependent on comprehensive coverage by the international community. Custom and tradition in rural areas, particularly with respect to the rights of women, have the potential to distort the fairness of the process.

A related problem was the absence of any contingency plan if the democratization process became derailed. The continuing level of political violence, right-wing extremism and the inherent volatility of the South African situation made such a prospect a possibility. While the trigger mechanisms of the three-phased policy could be suspended at any point if need be, given the Union's desire to be a proactive international actor, it seemed remarkable that no policy options were explicitly canvassed. Consequently, the Union exposed itself to the possibility of reactive policy making under such circumstances, a procedure that would again be dependent on forging a consensus.

Perhaps the central policy question that emerged as a consequence of the joint action was the compatibility between policy towards South Africa and that for the southern African region. The mutual dependence of these has been a constant theme since 1977: however, the record is more one of rhetoric rather than effective policy, and the danger is that this tendency will carry over into the application of the joint action. As noted above, the approach that can best address regional objectives is the incorporation of South Africa within the Lomé and SADC frameworks. Although the bilateral relationship is still under negotiation, Lomé is no longer a viable option. Similarly, while SADC has endorsed the principle of South African membership there are no details as to how this arrangement could be constructed. The 1994 negotiations are therefore of crucial importance to both the region and to South Africa. It is imperative that these compatible though potentially conflicting concerns are discussed in the correct bureaucratic framework that links the expertise of DGI and DGVIII. An *ad hoc* taskforce that unifies these and other sections of the Commission involved with South and southern African may prove a policy necessity.

CONCLUSION: PLUS ÇA CHANGE . . .? THE EUROPEAN UNION "JOINT ACTION" AND SOUTH AFRICA

Would policy towards South Africa be any different if it had not been framed within the context of a joint action of the Union? As has been demonstrated, the content of the joint action was largely created under the EPC framework: no policy initiatives can be directly related to these new enhanced level of cooperation. It is in the way the decisions are being made and in the expectations of behaviour that the substantive differences are likely to be found. As described in Chapter 3, once the consensus decision to adopt South Africa as a joint action was taken it assumed the status of a binding commitment, albeit for behavioural rather than legal reasons. A greater discipline and collective responsibility is required. Although at the time of writing those topics where majority voting could be applied had not been defined and the principle not tested, this procedural refinement is expected to have an impact, largely an indirect one, on decision-making style. Whereas EPC was described as decision-making in the shadow of the veto, CFSP is tantamount to decision-making in the shadow of majority voting. As such, the general conduct of CFSP will continue to be based on the search for consensus: the power of majority voting is best exercised through restraint. The danger is that an overly-eager application of majority voting will lead to the collapse of this still fragile intergovernmental process. An effective CFSP requires the full-hearted support of all member states. In an institutional sense, it has been demonstrated that CFSP does matter. The reorganization of the Commission, Council Secretariat and working groups will continue to influence how policy towards South Africa is perceived and defined. The management of the political agenda whereby policy options can either be promoted or excluded remains a central policy variable in the execution of foreign policy. The European Parliament's renewed involvement also appears, at least initially, to be a direct consequence of CFSP obligations.

Joint actions under CFSP also contain at least the promise of a proactive Union foreign policy. Perhaps for the first time in the sixteen year history of relations with South Africa, the 1994 framework resembles a proactive stance in contrast with the essentially reactive characteristic of the former EPC policy of sanctions. In contrast, the joint action also suggests the possibility of unintended policy contradictions developing between regional and bilateral goals, reminding us of the dilemma of consistency within the mixed coordination process of EPC.

While the South African case obviously presents certain unique features, it also provides a good example against which other joint actions can be measured. In that sense it is a typical joint action and its success, or failure, will have repercussions on how the Union employs the CFSP on subsequent occasions. For that reason alone, the Union proceeded cautiously *vis-à-vis* South Africa and on the other four joint actions agreed to at the Brussels European Council meeting. Thus the South African joint action is important for two compelling reasons. First, the shape of South Africa's relations with Europe are intrinsically interwoven with, and dependent upon, the experimental nature of CFSP. Second, this early test of the effective application of the principles and procedures of Title V of the Treaty on European Union will help determine the success of the CFSP and of the Union itself. It remains to be seen whether novelty and timing will prove to be to South Africa's advantage or detriment.

Postscript: The Reality of EU Election Observation

By the end of April 1994 one aspect of the joint action – the election observation – had been completed. This postscript examines the extent to which the EU's CFSP objectives and expectations matched the actual practice of election observation in South Africa. The following comments are from the perspective of the author as a practitioner (see Holland, 1994, for further discussion).

First, the selection of observers underlined the intergovernmental and problematic nature of the joint action. Each member state set its own selection criteria; while on the one hand, such a procedure could enhance the range of skills and abilities available to the observation team, on the other hand the possibility for inappropriate criteria being adopted was created. No central criteria were employed, or any central body (such as the Commission) empowered to oversee selection. Consequently, several observers lacked the basic language skills needed in South Africa, a number had no former South African or equivalent developing world experience, and a few even lacked any direct electoral experience or knowledge. The intergovernmental basis for selection detracted from the potential effectiveness of the EU team.

Second, the EU missed an invaluable opportunity to publicize its international role. Although the EU contribution was significant this was not publicly apparent. The operation was too low-key and the role of the Head of Delegation underplayed considerably. A distinct and distinctive EU identify was not effectively created. It was the UN, not the EU, that symbolized the international presence for the elections (despite the EU's more effective qualitative involvement beyond simply the election days themselves, the principle focus of the UN's activity). The decision to coordinate EU activity under the UN umbrella, while understandable logistically, further exacerbated this problem. To some extent the EU performed the work of the UN (for example, EU observers covered roughly one quarter of all polling booths), but gained little credit for doing so.

Third, the EU mandate was too restricting. A neutral observer role that precluded any form of involvement proved to be both unrealistic and in reality inoperative. The very nature of the South African situation meant that independent observers were valued for advice and non-partisan direct involvement in the pragmatic and practical issues that confronted all political parties and state organizations. In contrast, the observation mandate operated by the UN was more proactive and lent itself to a constructive involvement without necessitating any form of interference.

Lastly, while accepting many of the constraints imposed by time and infrastructural limitations, the organizational structure of the EU Observer delegation was far from perfect. Information was a one-way street with observers on the ground unaware of comparative issues outside their own narrow area. Promised resources were not comprehensively available. For example, the basic requirements of first aid kits, EU logos to identify vehicles, let alone the supply of body armour were not issued to all observers.

Despite these, and other problems the EU observers did perform effectively. However, the success of the observation was as much dependent on individual initiative and dedication than on clear lines of command and organization. For future EU joint actions concerning election observation the following recommendations are suggested to enhance performance.

Recommendations

1. Common selection criteria must be applied to the choice of observers. While member states should continue to nominate individuals, the collective criteria (agreed to within the framework of the joint action) should be overseen and implemented by a single central authority, ideally DGIA. EU joint action demands common criteria.

2. For this task, DGIA should be instructed to create a common data-base composed of individuals with the necessary attributes and those with existing EU experience. This list would then provide the basis for observer selection in future joint actions.

3. A re-think of the observer mandate is required so that the EU can perform the role of facilitator where a political dialogue between parties and groups is sensitive. In this way the EU can act as a confidence-building agency as well as a neutral and impartial observer. The current mandate limits a more useful contribution too severely.

4. The post-election role of the EU needs clarification. In the South African case no debriefing was organized and while observers were deployed from the country according to a set timetable, once again communication from the centre to the periphery was poor. Individual observers left for their own country without knowing what the overall EU observation conclusions were. Although the election count delay was unforeseen, as a general rule all EU observers should remain until the completion of the count (this would be in contrast to the existing UN procedure that sees most of its observers withdrawn prior to any count for security reasons).

5. Lastly, while the shortness of time and personnel limitations were major impediments, the exclusion of the Commission Delegation in Pretoria from any meaningful participation in the EU joint action was unfortunate. In future, where such Delegations exist they should form the basis around which a joint action is designed and not remain detached from the exercise because of intergovernmental sensitivities.

In conclusion, the EU observation exercise emphasized a qualitative as opposed to a quantitative approach. Criticism can be mounted against the scale of the EU operation which sent some 307 observers to cover an election of 23 million voters disbursed between some 9,000 polling booths. But the extended period spent in South Africa by the major of EU observers made their observation and participation of a higher quality than the more numerous UN observers, the bulk of whom spent less than one week in the field. Indeed, rather than counting actual observers (the EU's 307 compared with the UN's more than 1800), measuring actual observer days is a more realistic calculation. In this equation the EU's qualitative approach clearly outstrips the UN's quantitative one. The EU presence did provide transparency and enhanced the general confidence in the electoral process.

Nonetheless, the overall conclusion must be that of a qualified success – a job well done, but one that could have been done much better. The novelty of the exercise was a major challenge and the lessons learnt, if well learnt, should provide the EU with a firm basis on which to undertake future observation roles. The greatest disappointment was in the EU's low profile; great energies and expenses were employed yet the EU's impact as an international actor in South Africa was not sufficiently enhanced. Given the existing concerns over funding joint actions, member states will undoubtedly require more effective publicity of the EU's involvement if CFSP is to prosper. In that sense, intergovermentalism remains both a strength and a central weakness of joint actions.

Appendix

DOCUMENT 1: PRESIDENCY CONCLUSIONS, EUROPEAN COUNCIL, BRUSSELS, 29 OCTOBER 1993

2. Common Foreign and Security Policy

Common foreign and security policy is the framework which must enable the Union to fulfil the hopes born at the end of the cold war and the new challenges generated by the upheavals on the international scene, with the resultant instability in areas bordering the Union. The aim of the common foreign and security policy is to enable the Union to speak with a single voice and to act effectively in the service of its interests and those of the international community in general.

Foreign and security policy covers all aspects of security. European security will, in particular, be directed at reducing risks and uncertainties which might endanger the territorial integrity and political independence of the Union and its Member States, their democratic character, their economic stability and the stability of neighbouring regions. In this context the Western European Union will shortly implement the various provisions embodied in the Treaty and the statement on the WEU. The CFSP will be developed gradually and pragmatically according to the importance of the interests common to all Member States; the European Council asks the Council, as a matter of priority, to define the conditions and procedures for joint action to be undertaken in the following areas:

South Africa
    Support for the transition towards multi-racial democracy in South Africa through a co-ordinated programme of assistance in preparing for the elections and monitoring them, and through the creation of an appropriate co-operation framework to consolidate the economic and social foundations of this transition.

DOCUMENT 2: COMMUNICATION FROM THE COMMISSION TO THE COUNCIL COM(93) 460 BRUSSELS 29 SEPTEMBER 1993.

South Africa and the European Community: Guidelines for a Policy to Support the Transition to Democracy

Introduction

1. The European Community and its Member States have remained, over the years, committed to the total abolishment of the system of apartheid, by peaceful means, and to its replacement by a democratic, united and non-racial system of government in which all South Africans can participate in peace and harmony, regardless of colour and race.
    To this end, the European Community developed a two-track approach to South Africa: mounting pressure on the South African government, through sanctions and by other political means linked to a programme of positive support to the victims of apartheid through non-governmental organisations. The progress achieved in the constitutional negotiations has opened-up the possibility of developing a more integrated EC policy targeted on the creation and strengthening of democratic structures; on the encouragement of sustainable economic policies; on the progressive integration of South Africa into the world economy; and on the continuing support to the development of historically marginalised communities.

2. Following the repeal of statutory apartheid, the agreement on a date for the first fully democratic election, and the approval of the necessary transitional legislation by the South African Parliament,

South Africa will have removed the legal and constitutional obstacles to the creation of a democratic society. The rationale for maintaining sanctions, therefore, has largely disappeared and the Community, along with its partners, can move ahead on the progressive normalisation of relations.

The Community and its Members States have set out the political framework for the progressive normalisation and strengthening of relations between the Community and South Africa (1).

3. The Commission is ready to prepare the necessary steps for the normalisation of the European Community relations with a democratic South Africa, which is the subject of this communication.

The Transitional Executive Council

4. A decisive step in South Africa's transition to democracy is the establishment of the Transitional Executive Council (TEC), on which agreement was reached at the Multi-Party Negotiating Forum on 7 September 1993.

The enacting legislation following the decision taken by the South African Parliament on 23.9.93 for the TEC and other transitional structures (such as the Independent Electoral Commission, the Independent Broadcasting Authority, etc.) will not, however, become operational until agreement has been reached on the Transitional Constitution.

5. The TEC, which will provide for representation from all parties involved in the negotiations (and others which commit themselves to the objectives of the TEC), will be responsible for preparing for the elections and will ensure that no government or administration exercises any of its powers in such a way so as to disadvantage or prejudice any political party. The TEC as such will not have executive powers and the existing Government will remain in office, but the latter's political freedom of action will be significantly circumscribed.

6. How, precisely, the TEC will exercise these responsibilities, and the extent of its involvement into broader policy issues beyond those directly related to the democratisation process, will only be fully clarified as the TEC itself seeks to assert its influence. Furthermore, assuming that the current timetable is adhered to, the TEC will only have a life-span of six months: from November 1993 to the election on 27 April 1994.

In addition to that, pending the resolution of complex constitutional and regional issues still under negotiation, the envisaged participation in the TEC does not yet include prominent political parties (such as Inkatha and the Conservative Party) and other participants to the Negotiating Forum (the "independent" homelands of Bophutatswana and Ciskei).

7. The establishment of the TEC will, however, for the first time, provide a broadly representative interlocutor through which the European Community can consult with the South African state on a variety of issues leading up to a future full-fledged relationship at governmental level. The nature of the European Community's engagement will, to a significant extent, depend on how the TEC operates in practice. The Community should, though, signal its willingness to enter into a dialogue encompassing the whole of South African territory and society.

Programme of Action

8. The process of normalising and deepening relations with South Africa should take place in response to the acceleration of the democratisation process itself. Some initiatives can be taken as soon as the legislation for the TEC has been passed by the South African Parliament; other actions should only be considered once the TEC is actually in place and operational; yet others must await the elections and the establishment of an interim Government of National Unity.

9. *The Commission proposes that the phasing of such actions should take place as follows:*
   * **Actions to be taken following the enactment of legislation to establish the TEC**
   + *Lifting of economic Sanctions*
   The Community has already lifted trade and economic restrictions applied to South Africa. It should now, furthermore, support the complete lifting of trade, financial and investment sanctions by the international community, in order to facilitate the country's full integration into the world economy.
   The Commission believes the Community and its Member States should now also actively seek, through diplomatic action, the lifting of remaining restrictions on South Africa's participation in World Bank and IMF programmes, as well as the latter's early engagement in support of economic stabilisation of the country.
   + *Developing actions under the Special Programme*

a) *Support for Democratisation and Peace.* The first fully democratic selection in South Africa's history will take place on 27th April 1994: that is, only seven months from now. The success of this undertaking is of crucial importance not only for South Africa but also in consolidating democracy in the region as a whole.

The European Community has a major interest in ensuring that the election is successfully conducted and has an important role to play in this process.

The Community, which has already provided MECU 5.2 for voters education, will if called upon enhance its support for these activities.

The Commission, inter alia through the Special Programme, also stands ready to provide support to the monitoring of the election. Once the Independent Electoral Commission (IEC) is in place, a dialogue will thus be established to determine what further assistance can be provided for the election process itself.

In relation to the peace process, the Commission will continue its financial and personnel participation in the European Community Observer Mission in South Africa (ECOMSA) and will continue to enhance its support for the national peace structures (including the Goldstone Commission).

b) *Development Cooperation.* The present extreme social and economic inequality in South Africa combined with heightened expectations will place considerable pressure on a future new government to increase spending on education, health, housing social services and rural development. The financial implications of improving the quality and coverage of such services are staggering and – in view of South Africa's present economic situation and its future prospects beyond the means of the country alone. Foreign Assistance will therefore be necessary to help stabilise the next political dispensation.

The European Community is South Africa's largest external donor: the EC Special programme and the bilateral efforts of the Member States amount to more than 50% of all external development assistance coming into the country.

The role of the organisations (mainly Kagiso Trust, SACC, SACBC) which have traditionally worked as partners in the administration of the Special Programme will continue to evolve in response to the democratisation of South African society. The Commission will continue to broaden the range of organisations involved in and benefiting from these resources.

The Commission, in implementing the Declaration of the Development Council of 25 May 1993, will give particular emphasis on democratisation, the rule of law, human rights, good governance, popular participation and institution building

In this perspective, the scale of resources to support the Special Programme should be maintained at a substantial level, and certainly should not be decreased, during the whole period of political transition.

* Actions to be taken once the TEC is in Place and Operational

+ *Discarding of remaining Sanctions of the European Community and its Member States*

A review of the EPC sanctions still in force is already foreseen, starting with restrictions on military attachés and cooperation in the field of security.

Following discussion within the EPC, the present reporting requirements relating to the Code of Conduct for EC companies operating in South Africa will be discontinued.

+ *Opening of Commission delegation*

The establishment of a Commission delegation will, inter alia, signal the normalisation of diplomatic relations between the Community and its Member States and South Africa.

+ *Preparation of longer term relations*

a) *Global political relations.* The emergence of a representative political establishment in South Africa will allow for the opening of *new lines of communications in the political field* with a view to fostering closer links once a democratic government is in place. Over time, a democratic South Africa will become a major political interlocutor for the European Community. Similarly, during this phase, trade and economic cooperation can be explored.

b) *Trade and economic relations.* South Africa, has the potential to significantly increase its *trade and economic* interaction with the European Community. It can also play a crucial positive role in the development of trade and economic cooperation in the southern African region.

The EC is conscious, however, of the difficulties and the challenges South Africa will have to face in the course of its transition. As a country whose export performance has traditionally been a valuable asset, South Africa must be left in no doubt that, in order to restore much needed trade and inward investment, and in order to provide a firm foundation for growth and the further development of its market economy, it needs to send a clear confidence building message to the business community worldwide. There is no better way of doing this than for South Africa to intensify its efforts to dismantle, as a matter of priority, such trade barriers as export subsidies, import surcharges, formula duties, high level and low number of tariff bindings and to commit itself to a market economy that welcomes foreign investments. It must be borne in mind that any possible type of trade agreement with South Africa will have to be compatible with both South Africa's and the Community's obligations under GATT. Furthermore, it must also be compatible with EC obligations with other trading partners, especially in the region.

> *The Commission is willing to enter into a dialogue with TEC on those issues: and, to this end, is refining its analysis in preparation for such a dialogue. It is now for the South African side to develop a common national position on these issues.*

c) *Development cooperation.* The Commission is also willing to enter into a dialogue with the TEC on *development cooperation*, with a view to preparing the eventual normalisation of relations in this field.

The development prospects of South Africa, and indeed the whole of southern Africa, hinge crucially on the establishment of closer economic ties within the region.

Special attention should be paid in this respect to promoting regional projects which would benefit from regional funds made available to the southern African ACP countries under the Lomé Convention as well as from funds from the Special Programme for South Africa.(2)

One concrete and immediate possibility would be that, at the request of the ACP States concerned, South African economic operators could be allowed to participate in tenders open to these countries within the framework of Lomé financed Import Support Programmes being implemented in the SADC countries.(3)

* Actions to be Taken following a Democratic Election and the effective establishment of a democratic government
Once a Government issued from democratic elections is in place, and depending on the outcome of the exploratory talks, the Commission would be in a position to seek negotiating directives from the Council in order to prepare a comprehensive long-term agreement, encompassing the whole of bilateral relations.

Conclusion

10. The Council is requested to take note and where appropriate approve the above general policy guidelines.

(1) – Informal meeting of EC/UFA in Alden-Blesen, 10–12 September 1993
 – Conclusion of the Copenhagen European Council, 21–22 June 1993
 – Declaration of the Development Council, 25 May 1993
 – Statement by the Presidency following the Foreign Affairs Council, 8 June 1993
 (see the texts in annex)

(2) as allowed by article 251 of the Lomé Convention
(3) Under the derogation possibilities forseen in article 296 of the Lomé Convention.

DOCUMENT 3: 1669TH GENERAL AFFAIRS COUNCIL – EPC STATEMENT, LUXEMBOURG, 8 JUNE 1983

South Africa

The Council heard a report from its President on his recent journey to South Africa and the evolution of the situation in that country.

In his presentation to the press, the President stressed the following points: The Community and its Member States deem it important to be ready to adjust their policy towards South Africa concurrently with developments in that country towards majority rule and democracy.

The Community and its Member States see the establishment of the Transitional Executive Council as one of the most important steps towards majority rule. For the first time in the history of South Africa a kind of government forum with representatives of the majority of the population will come into being.

The Community and its Member States will take the following steps once the TEC is in place:

– a new development initiative will be launched and there will be a dialogue with the TEC on development co-operation. The Council (Development) has already adopted the major outline of the new programme, with more emphasis on democratization and support for institution building;

– Member States will, where appropriate, likewise be ready to enter into a dialogue with the TEC on future economic relations between the Community and South Africa;

– the Community and its Member States will strive to promote a decision within the World Bank, IMF and other relevant international organizations for a normalization of relations with South Africa;

– reporting under the Code of Conduct for European enterprises in South Africa will be discontinued. Heads of Mission will report annually on developments in the area of labour conditions, in particular concerning equality of opportunities;

– the Commission's office in South Africa will be upgraded to a normal delegation;

– the ban on military attachés accredited to South Africa and on granting of accreditation to military attachés from South Africa will be lifted, solely with a view to promoting the democratization and integration process in the security field;

– likewise the freezing of official contacts and international agreements in the security field will be discontinued.

DOCUMENT 4: DEVELOPMENT COOPERATION COUNCIL DECLARATION – FUTURE DEVELOPMENT CO-OPERATION WITH SOUTH AFRICA, 25 MAY 1993

– The Council and the representatives of governments of Member States meeting in the Council agree on the following:

Policy Guidelines

The Community and its Member States reaffirm the importance they attach to the process towards a democratic and non-racial South Africa. They are the biggest single donor in this country in particular through the special programme of positive measures established in the framework of EPC in 1985 and modified since then by the Council.

They recall their commitment to the complete abolition of the unacceptable system of apartheid by peaceful means and its replacement by a democratic, united and non-racial society in which all South Africans can participate in peace and harmony, regardless of colour and race. They reaffirm their readiness to continue and strengthen their support for the ongoing peace process in South Africa.

Concerned by the level of violence which still remains one of the most serious threats to democratisation and economic development in South Africa, they renew their call to all parties to sign the National Peace Accord and to participate in the peace structures. The Community and its Member States welcome the resumption of multiparty negotiations and urge all parties who have not yet done so to commit themselves to a speedy and peaceful transition to a democratic, non racial and united South Africa.

They reaffirm that the respect, promotion and safeguarding of human rights and the furtherance of democratic principles are among the cornerstones of European cooperation policy as well as of relations with other countries.

The deepening and normalisation of economic, trade and development relations between the Community and the Member States on one hand and South Africa on the other will have a profound impact on the future prospects of a democratic administration.

The Community and its Member States will therefore signal to the negotiating partners in South Africa their desire to intensify their relations as soon as a Transitional Executive Council (TEC) is in place.

Member States welcome the way in which the Commission has implemented the special programme of positive measures since its inception in 1986.

Framework for Action

The Community's programme of assistance should be based on the established development priorities and policies of the Community and in particular in relation to the elements of democratisation rule of law, human rights, good governance and popular participation.

The programme should remain flexible. Its content and implementation would vary over a period of time taking into account the changing circumstances in South Africa in particular the pace of democratisation of South African society and in this context, the future government policies in favour of the poorest sectors of the society and the level and development of the South African economy.

It is considered that the political developments in South Africa require as a first step an assessment of how the special programme could be further refined to contribute more effectively to meeting the basic and immediate needs of the people of South Africa and improving the living standards of the population, in particular the poorest sections of it, with a view to making assistance supportive of the emerging democracy in this country.

Objectives

In line with the elements set out above under "framework for action", the main objectives of the EC programme would be
– to support peace structures and initiatives;
– to support the transition to a democratic government, including support for voter education and other preparations for elections;
– to support institution and capacity building, notably in the focal sectors mentioned below, and policy formulation, thus promoting consensus on development issues between the parties involved and to strengthen capacity in order to allow the implementation of social programmes as soon as possible:
while continuing actions of the kind undertaken in the framework of the positive measures to implement activities of longer term nature within a number of local sectors of special importance for the economic and social development of the vulnerable groups of the population.

Modalities

The implementation of the programme would have to take into account the developments towards the establishment of a democratic administration in South Africa and should
– focus on a limited number of sectors and be programme oriented whilst maintaining flexibility notably through decentralised management;
– encompass cooperation with and through NGOs (which play a particularly valuable role in civic society) including community-based

organisations (CBOs) and, where appropriate through organs of the interim/transitional arrangements.

Consideration should be given to the future procedures for allocation and implementation of the programme along the lines which apply to other EC development programmes.

DOCUMENT 5: EUROPEAN UNION COUNCIL BRUSSELS, 7 DECEMBER 1993

COUNCIL DECISION (10503/93) on a joint action adopted by the Council on the basis of Article J.3 of the Treaty on European Union concerning support for the transition towards a democratic and multiracial South Africa

THE COUNCIL OF THE EUROPEAN UNION, Having regard to the Treaty on European Union, and in particular Article J.3 thereof,

Having regard to the general guidelines issued by the European Council on 29 October 1993 which take up as an area for joint action support for the transition towards multiracial democracy in South Africa through a co-ordinated programme of assistance in preparing for the elections and monitoring them, and through the creation of an appropriate co-operation framework to consolidate the economic and social foundations of this transition.

HAS DECIDED AS FOLLOWS:

Article 1

The European Union shall implement a co-ordinated programme of assistance in preparing for the elections taking place in South Africa on 27 April 1994 and monitoring them, on the basis of the following factors:
1) assistance in preparing for the elections will cover the provision of advice, technical assistance and training, continued support for non-partisan voter education, and the provision of a substantial number of European observers as part of an overall international effort co-ordinated by the United Nations;
2) the establishment at this stage of a "European Electoral Unit" in South Africa in accordance with the procedures set out in the Annex.

Article 2

The operational expenditure incurred in implementing the co-ordinated programme referred to in Article 1 shall be charged to the Community budget (Special Programme).

However the salaries and travel expenses to and from South Africa of those monitoring the elections shall be charged to the Member States which send them.

Article 3

The Council will set in motion an internal debate on setting up an appropriate co-operation framework to consolidate the economic and social foundations of the democratic and multiracial transition and will examine any proposals that the Commission may make to that end both for the immediate period of transition and for the longer term.

Article 4

This Decision shall take effect on the day of its publication in the Official Journal of the European Communities.

Done at Brussels, For the Council, The President

Annex Composition, Objectives and Operation of the European Electoral Unit

1. The Electoral Unit will further identify and co-ordinate the support of the European Union for the forthcoming election, as well as its involvement in the monitoring process.
2. The purpose of the Electoral Unit will be:

    (i)   to consult with the Independent Electoral Commission (IEC) on the nature and scale of the European Union's support for the election process; and, in particular, what direct involvement, if any, the European Union should have in the IEC itself or on the International Advisory Committee; and to consult with the IEC on the proposed guidelines and Code of Conduct for observers;

    (ii) to make available to the IEC advice and, where requested, technical assistance in the planning and running of the electoral process – such assistance might include the support for training of IEC personnel and election officials;

    (iii) to consult with the United Nations and the other multilateral organizations on the co-ordination of the international election observer presence in the country;

    (iv) to advise on the number and co-ordinate the deployment of European Union election observers, through the joint operations room;

    (v)   to provide assistance, under the authority of the United Nations, for the establishment of a national and regional joint operations room to manage the deployment of international observers;

(vi) to provide support to the associative structures to mobilize and co-ordinate local non-governmental organizations;

(vii) to advise and, where requested, to provide support for the monitoring of the security forces responsible for the elections process;

(viii) to advise and, where requested, to provide support for the monitoring of the media.

3. The Electoral Unit will be headed by a high-ranking individual with a high political profile, experienced in electoral matters and with a thorough knowledge of South Africa.

4. In addition to the head of the Electoral Unit, the initial staff complement will comprise:

(i) a Deputy: with good understanding of the political situation in South Africa and first-hand knowledge of the main players:

(ii) a Head of Administration: a skilled administrator who can manage the day-to-day running of the Unit;

(iii) experts in the following fields:
    (a) Elections Adviser;
    (b) Legal Adviser;
    (c) Voter Education Adviser;
    (d) Media Adviser;
    (e) Training Adviser;
    (f) Conflict Resolution Adviser;
    (g) Security Adviser;
    (h) Logistics Adviser;

(iv) support staff.

5. The Head of the Electoral Unit and the other staff should be available throughout the anticipated period of existence of the Unit.

    The Council requests the Commission to select this staff on the basis of proposals from the Member States.

6. The lifetime of the Electoral Unit will end one month after the date of elections.

7. The Electoral Unit will have access to a fund to recruit short-term technical assistance personnel to support training and to provide emergency assistance.

8. When setting up the Electoral Unit the largest possible use will be made of the infrastructure of ECOMSA and of its experience. When operational the Electoral Unit will co-operate closely with ECOMSA and will continue to draw on its expertise. ECOMSA

should provide support where and whenever this serves the Electoral Unit's tasks.

9. The Head of the Electoral Unit will be invited to participate in CFSP meetings of the Heads of Mission in South Africa in a manner to be decided by them.

10. The Electoral Unit will enjoy operational independence, based on a delegation of powers, under the control of a contact unit of the Steering Committee type, set up in South Africa. The Electoral Unit will report to the contact unit which will be made up of the Troika and the Commission.

11. Another contact unit will be established in Brussels, made up mainly of the Troika and the Commission, but open to the Member States which wish to take part in its proceedings. This contact unit will deal principally with the matters which its opposite number in South Africa is unable to resolve. It will first examine the applications of persons seeking employment (paragraph 3 and paragraph 4(i), (ii) and (iii) within the framework of the Electoral Unit.

DOCUMENT 6: SOUTH AFRICA'S 1994 NATIONAL AND PROVINCIAL ELECTIONS STATEMENT BY PROFESSOR JACOB DE RUITER, HEAD, EUROPEAN UNION ELECTIONS UNIT, 2 MAY 1994

Introduction

The European Union, together with the UN, the Commonwealth and the Organisation of African Unity (OAU), was invited by the Transitional Executive Council (TEC) to observe South Africa's first fully democratic elections (Resolution of the TEC, 7 December 1993).

The Basis for our Assessment

In response to this appeal, the European Union decided that its observation would cover the electoral campaign as a whole, not just the voting process. To coordinate this task, the European Union Election Unit was established.

It was also given a mandate to provide, where requested, advice and assistance to the Independent Electoral Commission (IEC).

The European Union deployed 307 people to observe the election. We also provided 112 police officers, electoral experts and advisers to the IEC and the IMC. Furthermore, the European Union made available more than R40 million for voter education and to top-up the IEC's Electoral Fund. Details are annexed.

Our observer teams were based in all nine provinces. They visited voting stations in the urban and the rural areas, the townships and informal settlements, the hostels, the prisons, and the hospitals and homes for the aged. Under the overall coordination of the United Nations, the European Union observers visited 2,233 voting stations during polling.

Our Assessment

On the 26–29 April 1994 millions of South Africans voted for the first time for a democratic government. They did so with evident joy and enthusiasm; but also, given the difficulties experienced, with determination and not a little stoicism.

The election campaign was generally free and fair but the voting process less satisfactory. 24% of our voting station reports indicated insufficiencies in supply of materials including ballot papers, ballot boxes, invisible ink, etc. In 10% of voting stations visited, the official procedures were not entirely satisfactory while in 4% unauthorised persons were found in the stations. In some 90% of voting stations the procedures were impeccable. Any final judgment on the election must, however, await confirmation that the counting has been completed satisfactorily. We are following this process carefully.

Our observers throughout the country report that, even given the logistical and administrative difficulties in some places, the election was generally orderly and disciplined. The problems mentioned below, were not in our view serious enough to compromise the overall integrity of the electoral process.

Except for the Conservative Party (CP) and the Azanian People's Organisation (AZAPO), all the main political forces participated. Voter education programmes, although patchy in their coverage, greatly contributed to preparing the people to participate responsibly in the electoral process. They put special stress on the secrecy of the ballot, which is the most potent antidote to intimidation.

The parties campaigned robustly and presented their programmes to the electorate with considerable professionalism. Thanks to the media, advertising campaigns, and public meetings, a lively public debate took place on the choices facing the electorate. There is no evidence that intimidation, although a major issue throughout the campaign, will materially affect the election result. We are confident that the electoral process, even with its manifest imperfections, will reflect the wishes of the people of South Africa.

Given the successful completion of the electoral process, the new government will therefore be able to command the loyalty and support of the population as a whole. South Africans will, at last, have a Government with unqualified legitimacy and the necessary authority to address the urgent social, economic and development problems confronting the country.

The elections, we believe, will transform South Africa from a society based on narrow racial privilege to a truly non-racial democracy. A firm foundation is laid for a mature and sustainable democracy.

An Imperfect Process

Nevertheless, the election was far from perfect. Major problems included:

* Violence and Intimidation

In large areas the campaign took place in relative calm and tranquillity – a remarkable fact given the culture of political intolerance over many years.

KwaZulu Natal and parts of the Witwatersrand did however experience appalling violence, particularly before the Inkatha Freedom Party's welcome decision to participate in the election. The Declaration of the State of Emergency in Natal, given the restrictions this put on normal political activity and the inevitable curtailment of human rights guarantees, can only be seen as a sad defeat for South Africa's political leaders. Although imposed with the broad popular support, it was a chilling reminder of the future confronting the country if politicians did not achieve an inclusive settlement. Fortunately, the State of Emergency was implemented in a responsible manner, even given the limited resort to detention without trial. Although initially at least the killings continued, it did help significantly to reduce violence and intimidation in some areas.

Intimidation, or the threat of intimidation, played some part in the election campaign throughout the country. None of the main parties can claim a monopoly of injury. In particular, some supporters of the ANC, the NP and the IFP sought in various ways to exert undue influence on the electorate. ANC militants in townships with a history of conflict have refused to allow other parties to hold political meetings. The party did, however, make real efforts to discipline wayward supporters.

Similarly, the ANC found if difficult if not impossible to campaign effectively in Bophutathswana and Ciskei before their affective reincorporation in South Africa; and among farm and other workers in many parts of the country.

The impact of intimidation was significantly mitigated by the fact that South Africa is a highly mobile society. Political debate, and voter education, is much influenced by the interaction among rural and urban communities. Another positive major factor was the influence of the media throughout the country, particularly broadcasting.

The mediation and adjudication systems set-up by the IEC helped to defuse conflicts and to encourage the political parties to discipline their followers.

Acts of sabotage and terrorism, probably undertaken by white right-wing groups, caused some disruption but did not undermine confidence in the electoral process. Particularly horrific was the spate of bombings in the week of the election which claimed 21 lives and injured hundreds.

The experience or the fear of intimidation did blemish the election. We do not, however, believe that violence and intimidation during the election campaign materially effected the result.

* Electoral Administration

The Independent Electoral Commission (IEC) did a commendable job in organising the election in such a short time.

It had to create from scratch an organisation capable of running an election for some 20 million people. To be credible to South African society as a whole, the IEC tried to ensure that all communities felt a sense of ownership of the electoral process. The Commissioners therefore sought to fashion the IEC into an instrument which truly reflected the diversity of South Africa. One result of this policy was that a large number of the staff had little or no management or electoral experience.

Uniquely, the Commission also had to monitor its own performance – another massive logistical enterprise. Ambiguities and inconsistencies between the various pieces of legislation, and between the functions of the IEC Directorates, made the task more difficult.

Furthermore, its work was complicated both by security concerns, especially in relation to the siting of polling stations, and by politically driven changes to electoral arrangements which continued right up to the election itself.

Although the IFP decision to participate in the election was warmly welcomed by all parties, it greatly added to the practical and logistical problems facing the IEC.

As a result of all these factors, the administration of the election left much to be desired. The siting and suitability of polling stations, the issuing of identity documentation, the coverage and impact of voter education programmes, and critically the procurement and distribution of the election materials, all proved problematic. Claims of sabotage have been made and must be carefully examined.

At the national level these problems will not have materially effected the outcome of the election but a careful evaluation of the problems experienced will be needed to ensure that future elections conform to the standard of democratic practice to which the IEC itself aspires. Planning should start now for South Africa's next elections.

Before the election campaign, concerns were expressed about bias in the media, especially the state controlled radio and television, and about the role of the security forces. In our view, these concerns proved generally unfounded:

* Media

    The Independent Media Commission (IMC), established to ensure that all political parties contesting the election had equitable access to the media, provided an able watchdog and regulator. Official and independent monitoring of the state controlled media shows that all parties received reasonable treatment during the campaign.

* Security Forces

    The SAP, which was responsible for providing security for the election, has played on the whole a positive and constructive role. Although in the pre-election period, they were sometimes inflexible in their assessment of the number of polling stations that could be successfully protected, they facilitated a secure and tranquil environment which gave people the confidence to vote. On election day, the policing was of a good standard. It was unobtrusive and did not in any way hamper the election process. In 29% of all voting stations observed, no arms check took place. We believe this can be considered as an indication of the peaceful atmosphere around the election.

Conclusion

Overall, the election was a remarkable achievement.

Nearly 200,000 South African citizens of all race, colours, classes and political persuasions worked together under the IEC to place South Africa irreversibly on the path to a democratic future. Millions of ordinary citizens, formally excluded from the political process, were allowed to become active agents of political change.

Party militants, whose former political experience was often restricted to mass action, had to learn the new language of parliamentary democracy. The election, which maintained a peculiarly South African character, will in retrospect be seen as a massive national learning experience in the theory and practice of democracy.

The difficulties and the mistakes will provide raw material for improvements. The experience will pay dividends for the future.

Given South Africa's history of racial discrimination and oppression, its massive problems of poverty and unemployment, and the tragically high levels of violence, the success of the election is little less than miraculous. Only democracy offers the prospect of exorcising the anger and despair that inevitably builds up in oppressive societies.

Without this process, South Africa faced a violent transformation which would have plunged the country into anarchy and chaos. Instead, it will now be possible to build a better future for all South Africans.

Finally, we want to applaud the people of South Africa and their political leaders for the manner in which the election was conducted. The European Union Observers are deeply honoured to have been able to play a small but we hope constructive role in the birth of democracy in South Africa.

Annex

South Africa's 1994 national and provincial elections: involvement of the European Union
European Union involvement in the electoral process falls into three distinct areas: the coordination of its election related activities; the observing of the electoral campaign and the voting; and the provision of advice and assistance to the IEC and the IMC.

Coordination
The European Union Election Unit, which was responsible for the coordination of the observation exercise and for the provision of advice and assistance, was established on 24 January 1994. The Unit is headed by Professor Jacob de Ruiter, a former Minister from the Government of the Netherlands. His Deputy is Ambassador Jacques Warin, from the French Foreign Service. The Unit has a dozen European advisors who specialise in all aspects of the electoral process.

Advice
The Advisers attached to the European Union Elections Unit sought to maintain a close dialogue with the Independent Electoral Commission (IEC) and the Independent Media Commission (IMC) and, where requested, to provide advice.

Observing the election
The European Union deployed 307 observers in all nine South African provinces. These observers were recruited by the twelve EU member

states and by the European Commission. In addition, the European Parliament fielded a team of 14 observers who were integrated into the overall deployment. There were also large numbers of observers from Europe under the umbrella of the UN, the Commonwealth, AWEPAA, EMPSA, national parliamentary delegations, and NGOs.

Technical assistance
The European Union seconded experts to the IEC and the IMC in these fields:

Monitoring Directorate of the IEC

* Security

The European Union, at the request of the Chairman of the IEC, provided a team of 82 European police officers – drawn from Germany, Ireland, Portugal and the United Kingdom – to help observe the implementation of the election security plan. These European Union Police Observers, under the command of Deputy Police Commissioner Keith Biddle from Britain, were responsible to and reported to the IEC.

* Mediation

The European Union made available to the IEC Mr Eduardo Marin, a mediation expert from South America, to work with the Monitoring Directorate of the Commission. Mr Marino was appointed by the IEC to act as the International Observer of the State of Emergency in the Province of Natal.

* Investigations Unit

The European Union has made available the services of 12 senior police officers, with experience investigative work, to assist the Investigations Unit of the Monitoring Directorate of the IEC.

* Analysis

The European Union has made available the services of Mr Paul McKee, a senior information consultant from Europe with wide electoral experience, to work with the Analysis department of the Monitoring Directorate of the IEC.

* Logistics

The European Union has made available the services of Colonel Michael Wright, a serving officer from the Irish Army, to assist the logistics department of the Monitoring Directorate of the IEC.

Election Administration

The European Union financed the secondment of 12 experts from Europe and Africa to work as training officers with the Election Administration Directorate of the IEC. They were deployed across the country.

Independent Media Commission

European Union has made available the services of Mr John Grist, the former supervisor of Parliamentary Broadcasting from the United Kingdom, as an adviser to the IMC. The European Union also made available the services of William Miller, Professor of Politics from the University of Glasgow, to advise on media monitoring.

Financial Assistance

* Voter Education

The European Union has provided a grant of R10,500,000 to the IEC to support voter education programmes. The European Union also seconded an expert, Mr Francois Dronnet, to assist in the implementation of this programme. This is in addition to an earlier grant of R20,000,000 to IFFEE.

* Electoral Fund

The European Union has provided a grant of R10,000,000 to the IEC for the Electoral Fund. This fund provides financial assistance to political parties contesting the election.

Conclusion
The European Union has some 450 people in South Africa for the election. In addition, we have provided R40,500,000 to support voter education programmes and the Election Fund.

DOCUMENT 7: GENERAL AFFAIRES COUNCIL *ITEM 15: SOUTH AFRICA* (19 APRIL 1994)

1. The Council has adopted a package of immediate period's measures to be presented and discussed with the future South African govern-

ment emerging from the democratic and multiracial elections the 26 to 28 April 1994. These decisions are to be seen in the context of the framework of the joint action decided last December following the European Council's guidelines of the 29 October 1993. In so doing, the Union intends to send a strong political signal to the incoming government and to the South African population. Thus proving its firm determination to support the transition towards democracy and its willingness to contribute to the reconstruction and economic development of South Africa after the elections.

2. The establishment of the future relations between the EU and SA for the immediate and mid-term period falls into two phases:
   a) a package of initial measures to be presented to the incoming South African government following the election of 26–28 April.
      The initial measures, aiming at addressing the immediate needs and aspirations of SA, without prejudice as to the form of the future more global arrangement between the two parties (EU/SA), should be autonomous in nature and should help create the foundation upon which a long-term relationship could be built.
      Included as part of the initial package of measures should be the announcement of the EU's intention to work for the earliest possible lifting of remaining UN sanctions and to concurrently withdraw related EU measures.
This package should also include an offer to conclude an agreement quickly;

   – this agreement should have a simplified structure and contain measures that can be quickly put into effect. The practical purpose of this agreement would be to provide the legal basis for the development of future cooperation with the new SA government and the allocation, as appropriate, of the corresponding funds from the Community budget. It should have only a few articles including:
   – a strong *human rights clause*, making the respect of democracy and human rights an essential element of the new relationship between the EU and South Africa;
   – a comprehensive *cooperation clause*, which could be drafted flexibly to include future development, covering all areas of cooperation which are within the limits of the respective powers of the Parties;
   – *provisions* wherever necessary to enable the EU (or SA, as may be the case) to engage in specific cooperation activities or the further development of certain policies.

Provisions should be laid down, in parallel, in order to provide access to the appropriate budget lines for the funding of activities under this Agreement and

b) an offer to negotiate a comprehensive and long-term relationship with South Africa, should the new government so request.

3. The main features of the initial measures will be trade and market aspects, development cooperation and elements for a future political dialogue.

a) *Trade and economic cooperation*
   i) *Market access*
      Being a contracting party of GATT, South Africa already has MFN status.
      The Community expresses its readiness to consider rapidly the granting of the benefit of GSP to South Africa taking into account the specific characteristics of SA, the interests of the other countries in the region as well as those of the Member States and any new principles soon to be agreed in the review of the existing GSP.
      The EU will also offer technical assistance, in order to facilitate the opening-up of the South African market and the gradual integration of SA in the international economy.
   ii) *External economic cooperation*
      – *Regional economic cooperation*
        In order to encourage intra-regional trade in Southern Africa and with countries in the Indian Ocean, it could be useful to explore, with the regional partners concerned, the possibilities and conditions for origin cumulation within the region in conformity with the agreements concluded between the Community and the countries in the region. Recalling that origin cumulation in this context should serve development purposes, the Community will take into account its possible impact on the neighbouring ACP countries. Proper administrative procedures and a regional secretariat linked to SADC (Southern African Development Community) or SACU (Southern African Customs Union) could be put in place in order to monitor any cumulation arrangement.
        The EU could provide technical assistance for the process of regional economic cooperation.

– *Investment protection and promotion*

To encourage EU investments in small and medium-sized companies in SA, advantages equivalent to the ECIP (European Community Investment Partners) or its follow-up instrument could be granted to SA. Specific financing of this instrument would be provided.

It would also be advisable to extend the BC-Net to SA, since the information channelled through the BC-Net system will be useful for the identification of parties with specific interests in industrial cooperation.

The conclusion of bilateral investment protection and promotion agreements between SA and the EU Member States should be encouraged.

Finally, the EIB will be consulted whether and under what conditions it could consider expanding its activities to SA, in accordance with its regulations. The EIB would have to be fully associated, at an early stage, with the preparation of any initiative concerning SA within the Bank's area of authority.

– *Preparation for other areas of cooperation*

In a number of areas, including – inter alia – education and training, industry, commerce, telecommunications and science and technology, cooperation between the EU and SA should be developed. Cooperation in the fields of education and training would go beyond the measures undertaken in the context of the Special Programme and includes for instance institutional relationships between universities. Exploratory missions will immediately be sent to SA, in order to define the most effective approach to future policy action in these areas.

b) *Development cooperation (Special Programme)*

The European Union's development cooperation should – in both content and implementation – take account of the changing circumstances in SA, in particular the pace of democratisation of SA society and the future government's expected priorities in favour of the poorest sectors of society. Such an approach will be in line with the declaration adopted by the "Development" Council on 25 May 1993, which calls for the implementation of activities of a longer-term nature focused on a limited number of sectors of special importance for improving the living standards of the population, in particular the poorest sections of it, with a view to making assistance supportive of the merging democracy in SA.

The election of the new SA government will for the first time enable a dialogue on development assistance to be undertaken. This dialogue, which should aim at a structured development approach, will include both the areas of assistance as well as the channels for implementation.

Consideration should be given to the future procedures for allocation and implementation of the programme along the lines which apply to other EC development programmes.

The EU should continue to support actions aiming at peaceful and democratic transition in SA. During the transitional period, the scale of resources necessary to support the Special Programme should be maintained at a substantial level.

c) *Political dialogue*

- the establishment of a political dialogue, both on the bilateral and regional level, on matters of mutual interest should be part of any initial measures. In this context the European Union will recall its initiative to organise in Berlin on 6/7 September 1994 a conference with all countries of the region;

- this dialogue should be developed so as to encourage the support by the new South African government for democracy and the rule of law, respect of human rights and promotion of social justice, creation of acceptable conditions to eliminate poverty and all forms of racial, political, religious and cultural discrimination;

- the precise provisions as to content, level and form of the dialogue will evolve, but the initial EU position should include provision for meetings at ministerial and senior official level, as appropriate, and should allow for an exchange of views on foreign policy issues.

References

ALLEN, D. and P. BYRNE, (1985) "Multilateral decision-making and implementation: the case of the European Community" in S. Smith and M. Clarke (eds) *Foreign Policy Implementation* George Allen and Unwin, London, pp. 123–41.

ALLEN, D. and M. SMITH (1991) "Western Europe's presence in the contemporary international arena" in M. Holland (ed.) *The Future of European Political Cooperation*, pp. 95–120.

AWEPAA (1987) *Southern Africa's future: Europe's role*, background paper for a European Parliament seminar on support for SADCC, 13–15 May, The Hague.

BARBER, J. (1983) *The uneasy relationship: Britain and South Africa* Heinemann/RIIA, London.

BLUMENFELD, J. (1992) *Economic interdependence in southern Africa: from conflict to co-operation*, Oxford University Press/RIIA, Cape Town.

BOT, B. (1984) "Cooperation between the diplomatic missions of the Ten in third countries and international organizations", *Legal Issues in European Integration*, 10, pp. 149–69.

BRITTAN, SIR LEON (1993) "South Africa: working from a stable business climate" address to the Forum Europe conference – South Africa: forging new links, 28–29 June, Brussels.

BULMER, S. (1983) "Domestic politics and European Community policy-making" *Journal of Common Market Studies*, 21, pp. 349–63.

CHING'AMBO, L. (1992) "Economic integration in southern Africa: whither SADCC?" *Southern Africa*, 5, pp. 50–2.

COKER, C. (1991) "Experiencing southern Africa in the twenty-first century", *International Affairs*, 61, pp. 281–92.

COMMISSION OF THE EUROPEAN COMMUNITY (1981) *The European Community in southern Africa*, European Information DE32, Brussels.

COMMISSION OF THE EUROPEAN COMMUNITY (1991) private correspondence with the author.

COMMISSION OF THE EUROPEAN COMMUNITY (1993a) *The European Community's Special Programme on South Africa: report and sector papers 1–5*, European Community, Brussels.

COMMISSION OF THE EUROPEAN COMMUNITY (1993b) *Communication from the Commission to the Council. South Africa and the European Community: guidelines for a policy to support the transition to Democracy* COM (93) 460, 29 September, European Community, Luxembourg.

COMMISSION OF THE EUROPEAN COMMUNITY (1994) DGI confidential document.

COUNCIL OF MINISTERS (1986a) *Decision concerning the suspension of new direct investments in the Republic of South Africa, 86/517*, 27 October, European Community, Luxembourg.

COUNCIL OF MINISTERS (1986b) *Council regulation no. 3302/86 suspending imports of gold coins from the Republic of South Africa*, 27 October, European Community, Luxembourg.

COUNCIL OF THE EUROPEAN COAL AND STEEL COMMUNITY (1986) *Decision suspending imports of certain iron and steel products originating in South Africa, (86/459/ECSC)*, 16 September, ECSC, Brussels.

COUNCIL OF THE EUROPEAN UNION (1993) *Council decision of a joint action adopted by the Council on the basis of Article J.3 of the Treaty on European Union concerning support for the transition towards a democratic and multiracial South Africa*, 10503/93, European Union, Brussels.

DE SCHOUTHEETE, P. (1985) *The external relations of European Political Cooperation and the future of EPC* (with E. Regelsberger, S. Nuttall and G. Edwards) Florence, EUI Working Paper no.172.

DEPARTMENT OF TRADE (1978) *Code of Conduct for companies with interests in South Africa* HMSO, Cmnd 7233, London.

DEPARTMENT OF TRADE AND INDUSTRY (1986) *Code of Conduct for companies with interests in South Africa* HMSO, Cmnd 9860, London.

DEPARTMENT OF TRADE AND INDUSTRY (1993) *Code of Conduct for companies with interests in South Africa: analysis and summary of companies' reports submitted under Cmnd 9860 for the period 1 July 1991 to 30 June 1992* HMSO, London.

DEVELOPMENT COUNCIL OF MINISTERS (1993) *Future development cooperation with South Africa – Council declaration*, 25 May, 1663rd. EC Development Council meeting, Brussels.

DIRECTORATE-GENERAL VIII (1986) "Guidelines for the implementation of the Community's Special Programme for victims of apartheid" (Budget article 953), Commission of the European Community, Brussels.

DIRECTORATE-GENERAL VIII (1992) "The European Community's Special Programme on South Africa", 10 December, Commission of the European Community, Brussels.

DUCHÊNE, F. (1990) "More or less than European? European integration in retrospect" in C. Crouch and D. Marquand (eds) *The Politics of 1992: beyond the Single European Market, The Political Quarterly*, Basil Blackwell, Oxford, pp. 9–22.

EUNELSA (1994) *Statement by Head of European Election Unit: South Africa's 1994 national and provincial elections*, EUNELSA, Johannesburg.

EUROPEAN COUNCIL (1986) *Thirty-fourth European Council meeting: statement on South Africa*, 27 June, European Community, The Hague.

EUROPEAN COUNCIL (1993) *Presidency conclusions*, 30 October, European Community, Brussels.

EUROPEAN PARLIAMENT (1990a) *Opinion of the Committee on Development and Cooperation for the Political Affairs Committee*, Document EN/RR/101712, 17 October 1990.

EUROPEAN PARLIAMENT (1990b) *Report of the Political Affairs Committee on the political situation in southern Africa*, Rapporteur Antonio Capucho, session document PE 141.405, 20 December 1990.

EUROPEAN PARLIAMENT (1993) *Report of the Committee on Development and Cooperation on the development prospects in South Africa and Southern Africa*, Rapporteur Ursula Braun Moser, session document PE 205.701, 29 November, European Parliament, Luxembourg.

EPC BULLETIN (1988–1990) vols. 4–6, European Policy Unit, European University Institute, Florence/ Institut für Europäische Politik, Bonn.

FOREIGN MINISTERS OF THE EUROPEAN COMMUNITY (1976) *Statement on the situation in southern Africa*, 23 February, European Community, Luxembourg.

FOREIGN MINISTERS OF THE EUROPEAN COMMUNITY (1985a) *Press release*, 19 November, European Community, Brussels.

FOREIGN MINISTERS OF THE EUROPEAN COMMUNITY (1985b) *Declaration of the Ten – South Africa*, 1 August, European Community, Helsinki.

FOREIGN MINISTERS OF THE EUROPEAN COMMUNITY (1986) *Decision: European Political Cooperation*, 28 February, European Community, Brussels.

FOREIGN MINISTERS OF THE EUROPEAN COMMUNITY (1990) *Statement by the Twelve on South Africa*, 9 June, European Community, Brussels.

FOREIGN MINISTERS OF THE EUROPEAN COMMUNITY (1992) *Statement on South Africa*, 27 October, European Community, Brussels.

FOREIGN MINISTERS OF THE EUROPEAN COMMUNITY (1993) *Statement on South Africa*, 30 March, European Community, Brussels.

FORUM EUROPE (1993a) *South Africa and the European Community: forging new links: background report*, Forum Europe, Brussels.

FORUM EUROPE (1993b) *South Africa and the European Community: forging new links: summary of debates*, Forum Europe, Brussels.

FRIEDLAND, E. A. (1985) "The Southern African Development Coordination Conference and the West: co-operation or conflict?" *Journal of Modern African Studies*, 23, pp. 287–314.

GAWITH, P. (1993) *South Africa and the European Community: forging new links*, background conference briefing, Forum Europe, June 28–9, Brussels.

GENERAL AFFAIRS COUNCIL (1991a) *EPC press release*, 4 February, 1471st General Affairs Council meeting, Brussels.

GENERAL AFFAIRS COUNCIL (1991b) *Press release*, 15 April, 1482nd General Affairs Council meeting, Luxembourg.

GENERAL AFFAIRS COUNCIL (1992a) *EPC statement*, 10 January, General Affairs Council, Brussels.

GENERAL AFFAIRS COUNCIL (1992b) *EPC – declaration on South Africa*, 6 April, General Affairs Council, Brussels.

General Affairs Council (1993) *EPC statement*, 7–9 June, 1669th General Affairs Council meeting, Luxembourg.

GEORGE, S. (1991) "European Political Cooperation: a world system's perspective" in M. Holland (ed.) *The Future of European Political Cooperation*, pp. 52–69.

GINSBERG, R. (1989) *Foreign policy actions of the European Community: the politics of scale*, Lynne Reinner, Boulder.

GOODISON, P. (1992a) "South Africa as a developing country", paper no. 2, The Africa European Institute conference, 23 November, London.

GOODISON, P. (1992b) "Ties that bind: SADCC and South Africa" paper no. 7, The Africa European Institute conference, 23 November, London.

GREEN, R. H. and C. B. THOMPSON (1986) "Political economies in conflict: SADCC, South Africa and sanctions" in P. Johnson and D. Martin (eds) *Destructive engagement: southern Africa at war*, Harare, Zimbabwe Publishing House, Southern African Research and Documentation Centre, pp. 245–80.

HAGUE CONFERENCE (1969) "Final communiqué of the conference" *Bulletin of the European Communities*, 6.

HAWKINS, A. (1992) "Economic development in the SADCC countries" in G. Maasdorp and A. Whiteside (eds) *Towards a post-apartheid future*, pp. 105–32.

HIRSCH, A. (1993) "A democratic South Africa and the EC: towards a new relationship", conference paper – Future Cooperation between the European Community and Southern Africa, Club de Bruxelles, 14–15 October Brussels.

HOLLAND, M, (1983) "The European Community and regional integration in southern Africa: a misplaced analogy", *Politikon*, 10, pp. 139–54.

HOLLAND, M. (1987) "Three approaches for understanding European Political Cooperation: a case-study of EC–South African policy" *Journal of Common Market Studies*, 25, pp. 295–314.

HOLLAND, M. (1988a) *The European Community and South Africa: EPC under strain*, Pinter, London.

HOLLAND, M. (1988b) "The European Community and South Africa: in search of a policy for the 1990s" *International Affairs*, 64, pp. 415–30.

HOLLAND, M. (1988c) "The other side of sanctions: positive initiatives for southern Africa" *The Journal of Modern African Studies*, 26, pp. 303–18.

HOLLAND, M. (1989) "Disinvestment, sanctions and the European Community's Code of Conduct in South Africa" *African Affairs*, 88, no. 352, pp. 529–47.

HOLLAND, M. (ed) (1991) *The future of European Political Cooperation: essays on theory and practice*, Macmillan, London.

HOLLAND, M. (1993) *European Community integration*, Pinter, London.

HOLLAND, M. (1994) "Plus ça change . . .? The European Union 'joint action' and South Africa" *CEPS Paper Series*, no.57, Centre for European Policy Studies, Brussels.

HOUTMAN, J. (1992) "The European Community and southern Africa" *Journal für Entwicklungspolitik*, 8–4, pp. 419–23.

IFESTOS, P. (1987) *European Political Cooperation: towards a framework of supranational diplomacy*, Avebury, Aldershot.

KEESING'S RECORD OF WORLD EVENTS (1988) Longman, Harlow.

LEISTNER, E. (1992a) *South Africa's options for future relations with southern Africa and the European Community*, SACOB discussion document, Africa Institute of South Africa, Pretoria.

LEISTNER, E. (1992b) "SADCC into SADC – what does it mean?" *South African Foundation Review*, 18–11, p. 8.

LODGE, J. (1986) "The European Community: compromise under domestic and international pressure" *The World Today*, 42, pp. 192–5.

LUDLOW, P. (1993) "Implementing the CFSP", Working Group background paper, 30 September, Centre for European Policy Studies, Brussels.

LUXEMBOURG REPORT (1970) "Report by the Foreign Ministers of the Members States on the problems of Political Unification" *Bulletin of the European Communities*, 6–11.

MAASDORP, G. (1992a) "Trade relations in southern Africa – changes ahead?" in G. Maasdorp and A. Whiteside (eds) *Towards a post-apartheid future*, pp. 133–52.

MAASDORP, G. (1992b) "Economic prospects for South Africa in southern Africa" *South Africa International*, 22, pp. 121–7.

MAASDORP, G. (1992c) *Economic cooperation in southern Africa: prospects for regional integration*, Conflict Studies Paper 253.

MAASDORP, G. and A. WHITESIDE (eds) (1992) *Towards a post-apartheid future*, Macmillan, London.

NUTTALL, S. (1992) *European Political Cooperation*, Clarendon Press, Oxford.

NUTTALL, S. (1993) "Changing conceptions of the Commission's role in EPC/CFSP", conference paper – The Community, the Member-States and Foreign Policy: coming together or drifting apart? – European University Institute, 1–3 July, Florence.

PAGE, S. and C. STEVENS (1993) *Trading with South Africa: the policy options for the EC*, ODI Special Report, Overseas Development Institute, London.

PIJPERS, A. (1984) "European Political Cooperation and the CSCE process" *Legal Issues of European Integration*, 10, pp. 135–48.

PIJPERS, A. (1991) "EPC and the realist paradigm" in M. Holland (ed.) *The Future of European Political Cooperation*, pp. 8–35.

POOLEY, P. (1992) "South Africa and the Lomé Convention", AWEPAA conference, 23 November, London.

PRESIDENCY OF THE EUROPEAN COMMUNITY (1986) *Sixth synthesis report on the application of the Code of Conduct by Community companies with subsidiaries, branches or representation in South Africa : 1 July 1984 – 30 June 1985* European Community, Brussels.

PRESIDENCY OF THE EUROPEAN COMMUNITY (1990) *Ninth synthesis report on the application of the Code of Conduct by Community companies with subsidiaries, branches or representation in South Africa : 1 July 1987–30 June 1988* European Community, Brussels.

PRESIDENCY OF THE EUROPEAN COMMUNITY (1992) *Eleventh synthesis report on the application of the Code of Conduct by Community companies with subsidiaries, branches or representation in South Africa : 1 July 1989–30 June 1990* European Community, Brussels.

PRESIDENCY OF THE EUROPEAN COMMUNITY (1993) *Presidency report: implementation of the Treaty on European Union*, General Affairs Council, 9252/93 CAB 8, 21 October, Brussels.

RAVENHILL, J. (1993) "When weakness is strength: the Lomé IV negotiations" in W. I. Zartman (ed.) *Europe and Africa: the new phase*, Lynne Rienner, Boulder, pp. 41–57.

RIDDELL, R. (1993) "Aid performance and prospects" in W. I. Zartman (ed) *Europe and Africa: the new phase*, Lynne Rienner, Boulder, pp. 143–55.

SECRETARIAT GENERAL (1993) *Implementing the Treaty on European Union*, Commission of the European Communities, SEC(93) 1655/5, Brussels.

SPENCE, J. (1993) "A post-apartheid South Africa and the international community" *The Journal of Commonwealth and Comparative Politics*, 31, pp. 84–95.

SOUTH AFRICA FOUNDATION (1993) *South Africa 1993*, South African Foundation, Johannesburg.

SOUTH AFRICA FOUNDATION (1994) *South Africa 1994*, South Africa Foundation, Johannesburg.

STEVENS, C., J. KENNAN and R. KETLEY, (1993) "European Community trade preferences and a post-apartheid South Africa" *International Affairs*, 69, pp. 89–108.

STONEMAN, C. and C. THOMPSON (1992) "SADCC – the realistic hope for southern Africa" *The Courier* no.134, Brussels, Commission of the European Communities, pp. 74–6.

STRINGER, J. and J.J. RICHARDSON (1980) "Managing the political agenda: problem definition and policy making in Britain" *Parliamentary Affairs*, 23, pp. 23–39.

SURVEY OF CURRENT AFFAIRS (1992) vol. 22, Foreign and Commonwealth Office/ HMSO London.

SWAIN, R. (1992) "The European Communities and South Africa – new threats, new opportunities" *South Africa International*, 23, pp. 11–17.

THE COURIER (1986) nos. 95/96, Commission of the European Communities Brussels.

THOMPSON, C. (1992) "African initiatives for development: the practice of regional economic cooperation in southern Africa" *Journal of International Affairs*, 46, pp. 125–44.

THOMPSON, L. (1992) "Of myths, monsters and money: regime conceptualisation and theory in the southern African context", *Journal of Contemporary African Studies*, 14, pp. 57–83.

TOMKYS, R. (1987) "European Political Cooperation and the Middle East: a personal perspective" *International Affairs*, 63, pp. 425–37.

VAN DEN BROEK, H. (1993) "South Africa and the European Community", address to the Forum Europe conference – South Africa and the European Community: forging new links, 28–29 June Brussels.

TRADE MONITOR (1993) numbers 3 and 4, Trade Policy Monitoring Project, University of Cape Town.

VAN PRAG, N. (1982) "European Political Cooperation and southern Africa" in D. Allen, R. Rummel, and W. Wessels (eds) *European Political Cooperation: toward a foreign policy for Western Europe*, Butterworth's European Studies, London, pp. 134–46.

WALLACE, W. (1983a) "Political Cooperation: integration through intergovernmentalism" in H. Wallace, W. Wallace and C. Webb (eds) *Policy-making in the European Communities*, John Wiley, London, pp. 373–402.

WALLACE, W. (1983b) "Introduction: cooperation and convergence in European foreign policy" in C. Hill (ed.) *National foreign policies and European Political Cooperation* George Allen and Unwin/RIIA, London, pp. 1–8.

WEILER, J.J. (1985) *The evolution of the mechanisms and institutions for a European foreign policy*, EUI Working Paper no. 202 Florence.

WESSELS, W. (1992) "EC–Europe: an actor sui generis in the international system" in B. Nelson, D. Roberts, and W. Veit (eds) *The European Community in the 1990s: economics, politics, defence*, Berg, Oxford, pp. 161–73.

Index